The Turks of Central Asia
in History and at the Present Day

An Ethnological Inquiry into the Pan-Turanian
Problem, and Bibliographical Material relating
to the Early Turks and the present Turks of
Central Asia

By

M. A. CZAPLICKA

Mary Ewart Lecturer in Ethnology in the School of Anthropology,
University of Oxford; sometime holder of the Mary Ewart
Travelling Scholarship, Somerville College, Oxford;
Author of ' Aboriginal Siberia ',
' My Siberian Year', &c.

LONDON : CURZON PRESS
NEW YORK : BARNES & NOBLE BOOKS

First published 1918

New impression 1973

Published by
Curzon Press Ltd · London and Dublin
and
Harper & Row Publishers Inc · New York
Barnes & Noble Import Division

UK 7007 0033 1
US 06 491352 X

Printed in Great Britain by
Biddles Ltd · Guildford · Surrey

TO

R. R. MARETT

PREFATORY NOTE

I WOULD gratefully acknowledge my debt to the Trustees of the Mary Ewart Trust, as also to the Principal and Council of Lady Margaret Hall, for enabling me to carry on at Oxford the research of which the present work is a by-product. It is also my pleasant duty to thank Mr. Henry Balfour, Curator of the Pitt-Rivers Museum, Oxford, and Sir E. Denison Ross, Director of the School of Oriental Studies, London, for the kind interest with which they read this work in manuscript, and gave me their valuable suggestions. To Mr. Arthur Thomson, Professor of Human Anatomy in the University of Oxford, I owe all the facilities which his Department afforded me.

Mr. Henry Balfour was also kind enough to read the work in proof.

Miss B. M. Blackwood, of Somerville College, has rendered me most useful assistance in preparing the manuscript for the press.

CONTENTS

THE TURKS OF CENTRAL ASIA:

IN HISTORY AND AT THE PRESENT DAY[1]

AN ETHNOLOGICAL INQUIRY INTO THE
PAN-TURANIAN PROBLEM

The Pan-Turanian Movement.

THE Pan-Turkic or Pan-Turanian movement, supported by the most aggressive portion of Turkish and
German public opinion, is a diplomatic activity, the object
of which is to subjugate to the Osmanly Turks directly,
and to the Germans indirectly, all those countries in
which various Turkic languages are spoken. Although
its purpose is probably strategical and economic—
the acquisition of the cotton of Turkestan, the gold of
the Altai, and Central Asian riches in general[2]—this is
hidden beneath the cloak of fostering the supposititious
desire of various peoples between Thrace and Mongolia
for racial and national unity. Only a close study of
the peoples whose tongues belong to the Turkic
linguistic family can throw light on the moral side of
this activity, and show whether the Pan-Turanian programme involves merely a desire for aggrandizement
or whether it covers any other relationship, more

[1] The present work is an enlargement of a lecture delivered in
the School of Oriental Studies in London on October 24, 1917.
[2] See Appendix A.

essential than the linguistic one, uniting Central Asia with Constantinople.[1]

A brief review of the Pan-Turanian programme will be necessary before approaching the main object of this essay, i. e. the study of the Eastern or Central Asiatic Turks. The term Central Asia, in accordance with Humboldt's definition, embraces the area lying between the Himalayas and the Altai Mountains, the Caspian Sea and Khingan Range. As far as the Western or Osmanly Turks are concerned, they are dealt with in several recent publications, namely, Sir William Ramsay's *The Intermixture of Races in Asia Minor* (Oxford University Press, 1916), Professor H. A. Gibbon's *The Foundation of the Ottoman Empire* (Oxford University Press, 1916), Lord Eversley's *The Turkish Empire: its Growth and Decay* (Fisher Unwin, 1917), and *Le Problème Turc*, by Count Léon Ostroróg.[2] Though not dealing primarily with the racial question, these books give a vivid picture of the variety of races living under Osmanly (Ottoman) government, and of the artificiality of the ties that unite them. Sir William Ramsay further tells us how the Osmanly government has tried to develop feelings of unity and patriotism among its subjects on the ground of the common participation in the Islamic religion. But Pan-Islamism—Islam not being exclusively the property of the Turks—would in itself hardly serve to strengthen the position of the Turkic elements of the empire against Arabian and

[1] Since these pages were written the British advance in Asiatic Turkey, together with the situation produced by the Russian Revolution, has led the German-Osmanly diplomatists to revise some 'details' of their programme. See Appendix B.

[2] An English version of this work, entitled *The Turkish Enigma*, in Winifred Stephens's translation, has just been announced by Messrs. Chatto & Windus.

other alien Mahometans. To give prominence to the Turkic element was not so simple, considering that five centuries of residence in Europe have influenced the ruling classes of the Osmanly in such a way that they have completely lost contact with the Turkic masses subject to their rule ; while these, again, by mixture and contact with the races of Asia Minor and south-eastern Europe, have lost the Asiatic character that they once possessed. Yet the upper classes of the Osmanly did not become thoroughly Europeanized, as the Hungarians did under similar conditions, and hence their chances of assimilating the lands and peoples that they conquered in Europe were almost non-existent even before the Balkan War. After that war, there was nothing left to the Osmanly but to turn to Asia, upon which they look as a land of expansion and of compensation for what they have lost in Europe. Hence, a justification for this change of policy was necessary, and this was easily found in the so-called principle of the self-determination of nationalities. The Osmanly thereupon proclaimed themselves to be of one nationality with the people of the far Asiatic lands of Turkestan, Jungaria, and the Siberian steppes.

It may be argued that there is something in the political atmosphere of our century which makes people revert, as it were, to past ages. All who have affinities with both Europe and Asia seem to be ready now to claim their Asiatic blood, as we see that the Bulgarians, the Hungarians, and the Siberian Russians are doing.

But in the case of the Osmanly the sincerity of such a movement becomes doubtful, when we consider that the Osmanly *intelligentsia* have so far never felt themselves at one even with their own Osmanly common people. Thus they have never passed, as have the

educated classes of the European countries, through
a stage of 'folklorization' and 'nationalization' due to
contact with the masses, who through their backward-
ness preserve more of their national traditions.   Even
the Revolution of the 'Young Turks' did not bring
about the breakdown of the caste distinction, and it
was, in fact, like all other events in the political history
of the Osmanly, a mere imitation of the Western nations,
rather than a spontaneous outbreak of national feeling
against imperialistic government.   There is no doubt
that such a truly national movement did begin when
some years before the Balkan War a literary attempt
led by Ziya Bey, Ahmed Shinassy Bey, and Namyk
Kemal Bey, was made to purify the Osmanly language
from its Arabian and Persian admixture.   It is noteworthy that two of those leaders, Ziya Bey (later
Pasha) and Kemal Bey, when exiled from Turkey
by Sultan Abd-ul-Aziz for their political ideas, found
refuge in London.   But, before their brilliant writings
brought about any literary revival or social revolution,
the movement was checked by the subsequent political
action of the 'Young Turks', or strictly speaking
by the Committee of Union and Progress (Ittikhad),
after they successfully abolished the influence of the
more sound rival group, the Committee of Unity
and Freedom (Ittilaf).   The Pan-Islamic propaganda—
bound up as it is with the Arabic language and culture—when carried on by that party in non-Turkic
Islamic countries, ran contrary to the attempts of the
literary reformers to free themselves from foreign
culture.   Meanwhile, the political and economic dependence on Germany imposed by the ruling classes
on the Osmanly country did not favour the further
development of linguistic and other internal reforms.

And so it happened that before Turkey had succeeded in emancipating herself from her obligations to Europe, Persia, and Arabia, she fell a victim to ambitions [1] the extent of which nothing but the outcome of the war and the fate of the peace settlement will decide.

When, after the Young Turks' Revolution, various European institutions arose in the Ottoman State, there was set up the Academy of Turkish Science ('Turk Bilji Dernayi'), which utilizes the researches of English, French, German, Russian, and other European scientists to further the political plans of the Osmanly. Thus all attempts at finding what the culture of the Turks was like in their original home and in pre-Mahometan times, and what survivals of that culture and of the old race exist, are being interpreted by the Young Turks in such a way as to support the hypothesis of the racial identity of the Osmanly with the Eastern Turks. It seems almost cruel that the process of nationalization started among the educated classes of the Osmanly should be checked by a new 'revival', which, through its very artificiality, is disturbing the natural development of the Osmanly. Just as the first movement led to the substitution of the name 'Turk' for that of 'Osmanly', so now, with the rise of political dreams concentrated on Central Asia, the name 'Turk' is being abandoned in its turn for a name with a more Asiatic sound, viz. 'Turanian'. By using this word, the Osmanly intend to emphasize their claim to descent in the direct line

[1] Tekin Alp, *The Turkish and Pan-Turkish Ideal*, English translation, London, 1916; M. Hartmann, *Unpolitische Briefe aus der Türkei*, Leipzig, 1910; J. Germanus, *Turk Darnay*, K. S., 1909, X, Budapest; V. A. Gordlewski, 'Note on the "Turk Darnay" in Constantinople' (Russ.), *Eastern Antiquities*, Trans. E. Sect. I. R. Arch. S., IV, 1913; A. Tyrkova, *Old Turkey and the Young Turks* (Russ.), Petrograd, 1916; H. M. A. Sarron, *La Jeune-Turquie et la revolution*, Paris, 1912.

from the people who left behind the old archaeological remains in Turan (Central Asia).

In many instances this propaganda assumes naïve form. Half-legendary kings and leaders of the Turks in Asia have been set up by the propagandists before the Turkish soldiers as hero-ancestors—to say nothing of such historical personages as Attila and Timur! Then again, a legend found by European investigators among many Asiatic Turks, to the effect that they originated from a she-wolf, has now provided an occasion for the abandonment on Turkish standards of the Mahometan crescent in favour of the pre-Mahometan Turkish wolf. The legend, of which there are several versions current among the Turks and Mongols of Central Asia, relates that a white she-wolf—or perhaps a woman with the name Zena (sometimes Bura), which means 'she-wolf'—found and reared an abandoned man-child, who became the ancestor of the Turks (or in the Mongol version—of the Mongols). This explains the appearance of that animal on the war standards of the early Central Asiatic Turks, particularly the Tu-kiu branch, a design imitated by the Osmanly during the present war. Though the Osmanly took up this legend as having been originally Asiatic, the latest researches seem to support the theory of de Guignes that it had a European origin, and was imported into Asia by the Huns. Assuming that the Huns were of Turkic stock, de Guignes thinks that when they were defeated in Europe and retired by way of the Volga, the Urals, and the Altai into Turan, they brought with them the Roman legend of Romulus and Remus, and gave it a Turkic setting by associating it with local Turkic traditions, so that subsequently it was accepted as if it had been of local origin.[1]

Such is the story of one of the 'historic heritages' claimed by the Osmanly. But, as a matter of fact, the more current version of the origin of the Turks is that which derives their tribes from Ogus-Khan, son of Kara-Khan, grandson of Dik-Bakui, great-grandson of Abuldji-Khan, who was a direct descendant of Noah. Such at least is the version given in one of the first attempts at recording the Turkic myths relating to their origin.[2]

If from the realm of mythology we turn to the physical or racial side, we are in perplexity as to why the drafters of the Pan-Turanian propaganda entirely disregard the fact that the Osmanly have now more Albanian, Slavonic, Thracian, and Circassian blood in their veins than they have Turkic; that their culture is more Persian, Arabian, and European than Central Asiatic; and that even in language there are divergences no less wide than are to be found among the languages of the Germanic family. All differences are disregarded, and linguistic similarity is magnified into linguistic identity.

Had the Turks and their allies, the Central Powers, been successful in their military plans, their intentions as regards Central Asia were as follows: ' *Thirty to forty millions of Turks will become independent, and together with the ten millions of Ottoman Turks, will form a nation of fifty millions, which may perhaps be compared with that of Germany in that it will have the strength and*

[1] J. de Guignes, *Histoire générale des Huns*, vol. I, pt. ii, Book I, pp. 371-3.

[2] Recorded by Rashid al-Din, quoted by Radloff, *Concerning the Uigur*, p. 1.

energy to rise even higher.' [1]   It should be noted that the
total number of the Turks is here exaggerated by some
twenty million, and that the term 'nation' is used
somewhat vaguely.

It is pretty certain that the several Turkic nations
which the author has had the opportunity of meeting
in Asia would be surprised if any one proposed to
unite them in one local group on the ground of some
remote tradition.   Thus they would not understand
any reason for a voluntary union, even with the Turks
of European Russia, not to speak of still less known
people.   One cannot disregard the local national awaken-
ing of some of these groups, as for instance that of the
progressive 'Young Sarts', or retrogressive Usbegs of
Bokhara, or even the Kaizak solidarity which may
develop into national feeling, but there is now no moral
link which would unite these groups in opposition to
a Democratic Russia.   Apart from conquest, the only
thing that would effectively bring them together would
be identity of religion, language, and education, and
some economic organization under which they would
retain their lands, and be encouraged to a more progressive mode of life—not too rapidly introduced.
Identity of religion does not exist at present, for within
the Mahometan world—to say nothing of others—
there are as many distinctions as among the Christians;
nor do they know any common language except the
Russian.

Since the Chinese and Russian Revolutions the con-
fiscation of lands belonging to these Turkic natives is
less likely to occur on the part of Russia [2] and China.

[1] Tekin Alp, *op. cit.*, Foreword, p. 5.
[2] On June 25, 1916 (old style), there appeared a Ukaz from the

On the other hand, the Russian collapse has left the way open to the activity of the Pan-Turanian propagandists, who seem to have been successfully checked by the Revolution at its *first* stage—warmly greeted as it was in Siberia and Central Asia. The Second Revolution, with its Marxian spirit foreign to Asiatic people, had in this region adherents almost entirely composed of Russian colonists. It would seem that

Tsar calling all the male natives of the Caucasus, Turkestan, the Caspian Steppe country, Siberia, and the Astrakhan and Stavropol steppes, for service connected with the war, a proceeding contrary to the fundamental law relating to the native population, under which these natives were definitely exempt from any form of military service. This order came at a time when the natives were all occupied with the cotton-fields of Turkestan, the wheat-fields of Siberia, or with reindeer-breeding in the mountains. The President of the Mussulman Party of the Duma, K. B. Tevkeleff, made a vigorous protest to the then Prime Minister, M. Stürmer, against the coercive measures employed in calling up the natives. In spite of this, the ruthless behaviour and corrupt methods of the local administration of some parts of Turkestan brought about a rising of the population, especially of the Kara-Kirghis and the Sart. The most terrible conflicts occurred at Djizak in the Samarkand district, and in other parts of Semirechie, as a result of which the local administration confiscated all the land and property of the natives, took away forcibly all men of military age, and sent what remained of the population (about 20,000), chiefly women, to die of starvation in the bare mountain region. General Kuropatkin, then Governor-General of the country, decided that the shores of Lake Issyk-kul, the valley of the River Tekes and of the River Keben, and the eastern part of the River Chuya, were to be cleared of the Kara-Kirghis and colonized only by Russians. See the official publications, *Turkestan News*, No. 185, 1916, and *Semirechie District News*, Nos. 201–15, 1916. The question was brought before the Duma, and the Investigation Committee, guided by M. Kerensky, was sent to Semirechie and Samarkand. But it was only after the First Revolution, and by order of the Provisional Government, that the natives were allowed to return to their country.

the prolongation of the Russian chaos would encourage
the congregation of the Turkic elements, if the dis-
association from the other people of the once Russian
Empire was their aim. But so far neither the 'All-
Russian Mahometan Congress' nor 'Mahometan Re-
gional Councils' separate themselves from the general
problems of Russia, even though they express interest
in the Mahometans abroad, and the majority favour
some kind of federal form of government. The
Turkic population of Russia is not more uniform in
political opinion than the Slavonic or Finnic branches;
and so, the reactionary portion of them guided by
Mullahs, and on the whole less affected by the Russian
and more by the Central Asian culture, form an
opposition to the Mahometan federalists.

The term Turanian.

The term 'Turan', from which Turanian is derived,
is so Asiatic that we do not find it in the Greek authors,
though the fact that it occurs in the *Avesta* in the form
Tura points to its ancient origin.

It is said in the *Avesta* that Thraetona had three
sons, Airya (Arya), who received as his portion Iran;
Sairima, who received the western lands; and Tura,
to whom fell the oriental lands. Again, Tuirya (Turya)
is used in the *Avesta* as an epithet applied to the
countries now called Turanian.[1] The people of Tuirya
are spoken of as enemies of the people of Airya. Another
reference is found in the epic of the Persian poet
Firdusi, the Shâh Naméh dating from the tenth century

[1] E. Blochet, 'Le Nom de Turc dans l'Avesta', *J. R. A. S.*, 1915,
pp. 305-9.

A. D.; a prominent figure in this work, the Turkic Khan Afrâsiyâb, is said to have reigned over Tura in the sixth century B.C., and to have been the great foe of Iran.[1] In this poem Turan is placed in the north of Iran.

The name Turan is very often given to the region otherwise called Tartary. Neither of these names is known to the Asiatic Turks, but curiously enough Turan occurs as a clan-name among the Turkic tribe of Sagai, the tribe least mixed with Finnic and Samoyedic people of all the so-called 'Tatars' of Siberia. The Turkic state of Siberia, conquered by the Khan Kuchum in the sixteenth century, is often called also the Turan state, but this name is derived from the name of the River Turu, on the banks of which the town Chingi-Tura (now Tiumien) was erected by the Beg Chingi in the fourteenth century.[2]

Like the term Aryan, 'Turanian' is used chiefly as a linguistic term, equivalent to 'Ural-Altaic' linguistic group.[3] The use of this linguistic term for the designation of a racial group is no more satisfactory than the use of the linguistic term 'Aryan' in the same sense. But still more unscientific is it to apply this adjective to things Turkish, for the Tungusic and the Mongolic languages have just as much right to be called Turanian as the Turkic. However, 'Turanian', not unlike

[1] Skrine and Ross, *The Heart of Asia*, p. 115.

[2] P. M. Golovacheff, *Siberia*, Moscow, 1914, p. 35.

[3] Although the term Turanian is now generally applied to the Ural-Altaic languages (Turkic, Tungusic, Mongolic, Samoyedic, and Finnic), it will be remembered that some linguists, for instance Max Müller, give to the Ural-Altaic group the name of North Turanian as against the South Turanian group (Tamulic, Gangetic, Lohitic, Taic, and Malayic) (Max Müller, *Lectures on the Science of Language*, London, 1861, p. 322).

another vague term, 'Tatar', has become so deeply rooted in European books on Asia, that there seems to be no hope of either of them ever being abandoned for the names by which the tribes of Central Asia call themselves.[1]

Division of the Turkic-speaking peoples.

The ethnological evidence must now be examined, and to make what follows intelligible, it is necessary to preface some explanation of the broad division into Western and Eastern Turks which is here proposed.

By the term *Western Turks* is understood all the Turks—or people speaking Turkic languages, most of them subject to the Ottoman Empire—as far east as Persia and Afghanistan. Their number is 8–9 millions.

The term *Eastern Turks* is used to embrace the people of Turkestan and Central Asia as far as Mongolia and China. Their number is about 10 millions.

There are also Turks in European Russia, viz. in the Crimea, in the Caucasus, and along the Volga, especially round Kazan and Astrakhan. These number $3\frac{1}{2}$–4 millions, including some of the Turkicized Finnic tribes of the Volga. Linguistically and politically they form one group with the Eastern Turks, with the exception of the Azerbeijan, who speak a Western Turkic language. But in physical type and culture they are all now mixed with Eastern Europeans, to a slightly less degree than the Osmanly are with the South-Eastern Europeans. The Pan-Turanian programme

---

[1] It must be noted that, according to M. Joseph Halévy, the Turanians of Avesta and of Shâh Naméh were the Semites of Syria, because Syria was called Althura . . . Tura (C. E. Ujfalvy, *Les Aryens*, p. 49).

includes these people, and there is some linguistic excuse for this in the case of the Azerbeijan. Before the present war representatives of many Russian Mahometans could be found at the Pan-Islamic Conferences in Turkey, and within Russia they formed a 'Russian Mussulman Party' in the Duma, but so far they have never been united on ground of racial or national community. Although these East European Turks will play an important rôle in the politics of the near future, and have already played their part in the Caucasus, they will not be dealt with here, since they are not typically representative of the Eastern Turks. Besides, the problems relating to them are beyond the boundary of Asia.

The classification here proposed differs from that given by Vambéry[1] in 1885, in that his first four groups, viz. Siberian Turks, Central Asiatic Turks, Volga Turks, and Pontus Turks, are grouped together under the name Eastern Turks, leaving his fifth group, Western Turks, unaltered.

The Eastern Turks.

Before tracing the Eastern Turks in history, some account must be given of them as they are at the present day. Politically, almost all of them are dependent on Russia; only some $1\frac{1}{2}$-2 millions are subject to China. Culturally and ethnically they fall into two groups, differing widely from each other.

The first group consists of the Turks of Turkestan and some of the Turks of the Caspian Steppe country. Since their appearance in this region they have been constantly under Iranian influence, and hence have

---

[1] A. Vambéry, *Das Türkenvolk*, Leipzig, 1885, pp. 85-6.

physically and culturally become Iranized. Considering also that they settled in the country which already in the time of the *Avesta* bore the name Iran (as opposed to Turan), there is ample justification for calling them the *Iranian Turks*.

The other group consists of the Turks—many of them called Tatars—of the Steppe country, Southern Siberia, Jungaria, and Northern Mongolia, including the Altai and Sayan Mountains. Thanks to the geographical structure of the country, these Turks have been more shut off from foreign influence than the first group, though they have always been to a certain extent under obligations to the culture of China, and lately to that of Russia also. These may be called the *Turanian Turks*.

The Eastern Turks in Asiatic Russia number altogether some eight millions,[1] of which the Iranian Turks account for about six millions. The Iranian Turks form 92 per cent. of the population of Turkestan. Out of the 60 per cent. of Turkic population in the Caspian Steppe country, about one-third may be regarded as Iranized.

The Turanian Turks form an unimportant percentage among the Russian, Mongols, and Chinese in the midst of whom they live; their number in south-western

[1] The statistics here given concerning the Turks of the Russian State are based on the census of 1897 and an additional local census of 1911. See *Asiatic Russia*, edited by the Immigration Committee, St. Petersburg, 1914, vol. I. It should be noted, however, that the later census shows an increase over the earlier one greater than can be accounted for by a natural increase in the birth-rate. This is probably due to the fact that the census of 1911 was carried out by more careful observers. It is more reliable as far as linguistic grouping goes, but its estimates of the number of people professing Russian Orthodoxy are less correct.

Siberia scarcely reaches half a million, and yet this is the region which has been a centre of gravity for the old Turkic culture. So if for political interest we must look to the Iranian Turks, for ethnological problems we turn chiefly to these other Turks, who are the truest Turanians.

Language.

Preparatory to dealing with the separate nations of which these two groups are composed, it will be necessary to pass in review the linguistic and religious position of all the Eastern Turks in Asia, for it seems that in many cases these two factors are the only guides by which we can arrive at the definition of a Turk.

According to Professor Beresin and the Turkic-Tatar scholar Mirza Kasem Beg,[1] the Turkic or Turko-Tatar languages may be divided as follows:

1. Jagatai (Chagatai),
2. Tatar,
3. Turkish.

The Jagatai and Tatar languages, with their many dialects, have closer resemblances between themselves than either of them have with the Turkish. The Turkish language is used by the Western Turks, and consists of the following dialects:

(a) Derbent,
(b) Aberdjan (Azerbeijan),
(c) Crimean,
(d) Anatolian,
(e) Rumelian (Constantinople). } [Osmanly.]

Of the other two, Jagatai appears to be the older, and

---

[1] Mirza A. Kasem Beg, transl. Dr. J. T. Zenker, *Allgemeine Grammatik der Türkisch-Tatarischen Sprache*, Leipzig, 1848, pp. xi-xiii.

it includes the most classical Turkic dialect, namely
Uigur. The dialects of Jagatai are :

(a) Uigur,	(d) Usbeg,
(b) Koman,	(e) Turkoman,[1]
(c) Jagatai (Chagatai),	(f) Kazan.

The dialects of Tatar are :

(a) Kirghis,	(e) Karachai,
(b) Bashkir,	(f) Kara-Kalpak,
(c) Nogai,	(g) Meshcherak,
(d) Kuman,	(h) Siberian.

The first mention in Chinese documents of the fact
that the Uigur, the Tu-kiu, and the Kirghis use the
same character, occurs in a passage relating to the
fourth century A.D. The earliest specimens known to
us of the Turkic-Uigur language and characters are
the inscriptions on the burial mounds in the Yenisei
valley, dating from about the seventh century A.D. The
late Professor Donner,[2] who has left us a study of
the origin of this alphabet, suggests that some early
phases of old Turkic writing are still missing, and may
possibly be found west or south of the Minusinsk
inscriptions, for the inscriptions found to the east of
Minusinsk along the River Orkhon in Northern Mongolia are later than those of the Yenisei. The reason
for such a supposition rests on the fact that the script
adopted by the old Uigur Turks was of Aramaean or
Proto-Pehlevi origin, of the type employed during the
dynasty of Arsaçides in Parthia (third century B.C. to
third century A.D.). It is not clear, pending further

---

[1] According to some scholars Turkoman belongs to the Western
Turkic linguistic branch, and thus stands near to Azerbeijan and
Osmanly. See A. Vambéry, *Das Türkenvolk*, p. 86.

[2] O. Donner, ' Sur l'origine de l'alphabet turc du Nord de l'Asie ',
J. Soc. Fin.-Ougr., 1896, XIV, pp. 1–7, 21–71.

discoveries, who used the Aramaean characters during the three or four centuries which divide the time of Arsasides (whose power was destroyed by Ardashir, founder of the Sassanian Empire in 220 A.D.) from that of the Yenisei inscriptions. The assumption is that in some remote parts of the Sassanian Empire the Aramaean characters still continued to exist for some time, and that the earliest Turkic writings are still undiscovered. In any case, Professor Donner was disposed to take the Aramaean rather than the Indo-Bactrian or Kharosthi as the prototype of the Yenisei writing.[1] The popular opinion current until recently, however, was that the Uigur obtained their written character from the Nestorian monks, who exercised considerable influence in Turanian lands from the fifth century A.D. onwards, and who themselves used a Syriac language. Though the influence of the Nestorian missionaries was doubtless very profound, and though their language was probably known to some of the Turks, especially to the Uigur and the Kirei, the Yenisei inscriptions seem to have been modelled on a Semitic writing more primitive than the Syriac of the fifth century A.D., or even than the character in use during the latter part of the Arsasides dynasty, i.e. the third century A.D.[2]

Here must be mentioned a suggestion coming from

---

[1] Professor F. W. K. Müller, of Berlin, advances a theory that the Uigur character, especially in its most archaic form, is an adaptation of the Soghdian ('Uigurica', *Abh. Akad.*, Berlin, 1908-10). M. Gauthiot, accepting this, says that the distinctive character of the Uigur inscriptions is due to the adaptation to the old Turkic language of the phonetic system of a quite different type of language, viz. North Iranian and Soghdian (R. Gauthiot, 'De l'Alphabet Sogdien', *J. A.*, Jan.-Feb., 1911, p. 90).

[2] O. Donner, *op. cit.*, p. 67.

the Russian and Sibiriak ethnographers of Central Asia.[1] They would derive the old Turkic character from the clan-crests, called *tamgas*. There is no doubt that some letters of the Yenisei and Orkhon inscriptions bear a close resemblance to various *tamgas*, but the influence may equally well be regarded as reciprocal, until it is proved that the Turkic *tamgas* are more ancient than the Aramaean character.

But, on the other hand, it is quite obvious that the *pisanitsy*, or pictographic writings found in various parts of Turan, are to be connected with the *tamgas*, and that they represent the direct influence of environment rather than that of an imported culture.

Until the discovery of the Yenisei inscriptions the oldest Turkic-Uigur document was the famous *Kudatku Bilik*, translated as 'The Art of Reigning' (L. Cahun[2]) or as 'The Book of Joy-giving Knowledge' (A. Vambéry[3]). It is an ancient poem, imbued with the spirit of Islam, written in 1069 (or perhaps in 1076), that is to say during the dynasty of the Ilekids, and ascribed to Yüsuf Khass Hajib. It was found in Semirechie. The Turkic-Uigur writing was in use sporadically among the Volga and Bokhara Turks until the fifteenth century.

As monuments in Jagatai proper, a dialect akin to Uigur, may be cited the Memoirs of Baber the Moghul in the sixteenth century, and the History of Abul Ghazi in the seventeenth. The Memoirs of Baber have been

[1] N. A. Aristoff, *Attempt at an Explanation of the Ethnic Composition of the Kirghis-Kaizak,* &c., pp. 410 ff. ;   N. Mallitski, *On the connexion between the Turkic ' tamga' and the Orkhon characters,* 1897-8, pp. 43-7.
[2] L. Cahun, *L'Introduction à l'histoire de l'Asie,* p. 45.
[3] A. Vambéry, *op. cit.,* p. 322.

frequently translated into many European languages.[1] The poet who perhaps most enriched the Jagatai literature was Mir Ali Shir Navaï, who lived during the Timurid dynasty.

It is interesting to note that among the latest documents in the older form of the Uigur written character are some letters sent by the Mongol Khans of Persia in the thirteenth century to the Pope of Rome, Philip le Bel King of France, and Edward I King of England, the object of which was to arrange an offensive alliance against the Saracens. There were as many as six Embassies exchanged. A number of the letters were written in Uigur with Latin translations, and the original Uigur manuscripts of some of these were found by M. Abel Rémusat in Paris.[2] It is possible that the

[1] The translations in English are as follows:
'Memoirs of Zehir-ed-Din Muhammed Baber, Emperor of Hindustan, written by himself, in the Jaghatai Turkic, and translated partly by the late John Leyden, partly by William Erskine', London, 1826.

'The Memoirs of Bābur; a new translation of the Bābur-nāma, incorporating Leyden and Erskine's of 1826 A.D.', by Annette S. Beveridge, London, 1912.

'Memoirs of Baber, Emperor of India, First of the Great Moghuls, being an abridgement with an introduction, supplementary notes, and some account of his successors', by Lieut.-Col. F. G. Talbot, London, 1909.

[2] Abel Rémusat, 'Mémoires sur les relations politiques des princes chrétiens et particulièrement des rois de France avec les empereurs mongols', *Mém. de l'Acad. des Inscr. et Belles-Lettres*, Pt. I, vol. vi, pp. 396–469; Pt. II, vol. vii, pp. 335–431. See also T. Hudson Turner, 'Unpublished Notices of the Times of Edward I and of his Relations with the Moghul Sovereign of Persia', *Arch. Jour.*, VIII, London, 1851, pp. 47–50; I. J. Schmidt, *Philologisch-kritische Zugabe zu den von H. Abel Rémusat bekannt gemachten in den königlich-französischen Archiven befindlichen zwei mongolischen Original-Briefen der Könige von Persien Argun und Oeldshaitu an Philipp den Schönen*, St. Petersburg, 1824.

originals of those sent to England may yet be found in some British collection. Some of the envoys were Uigur priests of Nestorian religion.[1]

Religion.

Among the Iranian Turks in Turkestan the almost universal religion is Mahometanism. Its adherents form 99 per cent. of the Turks in Ferghana (Kokand), 93 per cent. in Samarkand, 96 per cent. in Syr Daria, and 88 per cent. in Transcaspia (1897). They are mostly Sunnites, and of the Hanifite rite. It is recognized in the Mahometan world that nowhere else is there such strict adherence to the Koran and the Sunna as in this region, nowhere else are there so many religious orders and so many saints. This contemporary religious fanaticism, however, does not play the cultural rôle which it did when Mahometanism was introduced into this region in the tenth and eleventh centuries, as a rival to the earlier influences of Buddhism, Christianity, and the well-developed local animistic religion. At that time, under the influence of Iranian culture, Mahometanism meant also the development of science and art, literature and architecture. The present theologians of Turkestan have banished from their religion everything which is not in accordance with strict devotion and

---

[1] The Uigur manuscripts known to exist in European libraries are :

Kudatku Bilik (copy made in Herat in 1439) (Wiener Hofbibliothek).

Légende de Oghus Chan (Library of Charles Schefer of Paris).

Teskere-i-ewlija (Bibliothèque Nationale).

Miradj nameh (Berliner Bibliothek).

Yarlyk of Temir Kutlug (Wiener Hofbibliothek).

Yarlyk of Toktamysh (Moscow Library).

Application of the envoy of Chami, Babeke, to the Chinese Emperor, with Chinese translation (Asiatic Museum, Petrograd).

asceticism.[1] In a way, they play the rôle of Calvinists in the Mahometan world; on the other hand, the influence of Buddhism still remains in the towns, while in the mountains and steppes there still lives a strong animistic cult, sometimes intermixed with Mahometanism.

Mahometanism, though introduced among the upper classes in the tenth century, did not spread among the masses of Turkestan until the thirteenth to fifteenth centuries, and it is now known that in the twelfth and thirteenth centuries Christianity, especially Nestorian Christianity, was a great rival of Mahometanism in the western part of Turkestan.

The people of the eastern part of Turkestan, especially the Kirghis and various descendants of the Uigur, were never great adherents of Mahometanism. In general, it is the Sarts, the Usbegs, and the Tadjik who are the most devoted Mussulmans. Still, if we compare the number of Mahometans in Russian Central Asia in 1911 (8,223,982) with their number in 1897 (6,996,654), it appears that Mahometanism is still spreading in Turkestan, though its increase in Siberia is negligible (128,403 in 1911, against 126,587 in 1897). The nomads of the north-east—i. e. of Semirechie, Semipalatinsk, Akmolinsk, and Uralsk— have been but slightly affected by Mahometanism, and it is curious to know that some of the most Turkic sections of all the Eastern Turks, the Kaizak and the Kirghis, accepted it only after the Russian conquest in the eighteenth and nineteenth centuries, assisted by the Russian officials! They still follow their customary law, zang ('ādat in Arabian), and if they give it up it is to accept, not the Mahometan written law, sheriat,

---

[1] A. Vambéry, 'Muhammadanism in Asiatic Turkey', E. R. E., 1915, pp. 885-8.

but the Russian law.   The Turanian Turks are affected
by Mahometanism about as much as they are by Russian
Orthodoxy.   It would be misleading to give the official
estimate,[1] but about two-thirds of them still adhere to
the form of animistic religion known as Shamanism.
As far as the Turanian Turks are concerned, therefore,
Mahometanism fails as a guide for identifying the
Turk.

The religion of the Turks who were responsible for
the inscriptions found in the Yenisei and Orkhon valleys,
seems to have been the same Shamanism which is still
to be found in a comparatively vital state among many
Turanians, especially the Altai 'Tatars' and the Yakut.
If we take Shamanism as a form of animistic religion
which originated in Asia, and which differs from the
animistic religions of other parts of the world in its
conception of the gods and in the nature of its pro-
pitiatory ceremonies, then we shall not find in any other
part of Central and Northern Asia a more typical and
more highly developed form of it than among these
people.   At the same time it must be remembered that
Shamanistic conceptions underlie many of the high
religious systems of the Asiatic continent.

A strongly marked dualism is present, the good and
the evil deities being comparable in the various tribes,
though known under different names.   Taking the Altai
'Tatars' as typical Shamanists, their chief benevolent
god at the present time, as in the seventh century, and
possibly earlier,[2] is *Ulgen*.   The chief malevolent god
is *Erlik*.   The sphere of activity of the former, and all

[1] See note to p. 22.
[2] I. P.Melioranski, 'On the Orkhon and Yenisei Memorial Inscrip
tions', *J. Min. Educ.*, June, 1898, St. Petersburg.

the spirits dependent on him, is the region above the earth, and of the latter the region below the earth. Their realms meet *on* the earth. Erlik is sometimes represented as a bear, e. g. among the Altaians.[1] Generally speaking there is no animal worship, but some animals are venerated. The greatest veneration is shown to the bear, occasionally to the wolf, and of birds, to the eagle, the hawk, and the goose. These creatures, as well as some fish, play an important part in the Shamanistic ceremonies, for when the Shaman's spirit-assistants appear at his call, they are supposed to assume the forms of animals.[2] It is, however, not in this veneration, but rather in the use of the clan-crests or *tamgas*, that any approach to totemism among these people must be sought.

The sky, sometimes called *Tengri*, is venerated as being the home of the good spirits, and they themselves are sometimes called *Tengri* also. To ward off the destructive power of the malevolent god, and to ensure the protection of his benevolent rival, a caste of priests, called Shamans (the name varying according to the tribe), performs religious ceremonies in which the sacred drum (*tiungur*) plays an important rôle. In some tribes, e. g. the Yakut, there is a white Shaman who propitiates the good power, and a black Shaman who has to deal with the dark power. All these tribes believe in various lesser gods, among them a female deity who presides over birth. She is called *Umai* by the Altaians, *Ayisit* by the Yakut.[3]

---

[1] N. N. Kosmin, *Chern*, p. 102.

[2] M. A. Czaplicka, *Aboriginal Siberia*, Oxford, 1914, pp. 277–82.

[3] M. A. Czaplicka, *op. cit.*, p. 141, and Chaps. VII and VIII. See also 'The Influence of Environment upon the Religious Ideas and

To show the persistence of the Shamanistic cere-
monial, it is interesting to find that the rites connected
with the cult of the sky, as practised at the present day,
are strikingly similar to those of the eighth century.[1]
The ceremony of sacrificing to the sky is called among
the Turks of the Minusinsk District *Tigir Tayi*. It is
held every third year, usually towards the end of June.
Among most of these Turks, for instance the Beltir and
Kachints, it has the character of a strictly clan cere-
monial. Women are not allowed to take part in it, nor
even to help with the preparations. The spot chosen
is usually the top of the highest mountain in the neighbourhood on which birches are growing. Some of these
birches are sacred, and near them two fires are lighted,
one called *ulug ot*, 'the senior fire', and the other *kichig
ot*, 'the junior fire'. No one dares to approach the
'junior fire' from the east, and even from other directions
only the leaders of the ceremony are allowed access.
A ram or a he-goat is then sacrificed, care being taken
that no blood should be shed, and no cry heard from
the sacrificial animal. Similar precautions are taken in
the sacrifice of the horse to Ulgen among the Altaians.
Then the fore-quarters of the beast are boiled on the
'senior fire', while the hind-quarters, together with the
flesh of various non-sacrificial animals, are boiled on
the 'junior fire'. Meanwhile each head of a family ties
his *üldürbä*, that is, a long thread of flax with eagle
feathers attached to it, to the sacred birches. The ends
of these threads are kept in the hand, and the master of
the ceremonies begins the song to the sky, while the

Practices of the Aborigines of Northern Asia', *Folk-Lore*, March 31,
1914.
  [1] I. P. Melioranski, *op. cit.*, pp. 264-5.

others form a chorus.   The feathered thread is the road
by which the song rises to the sky.   The meat which
has been prepared on the 'senior fire' is taken out and
carried round in a circle, in the direction of the sun.
After that the meat, with all the articles used in its
preparation, is burnt on the 'senior fire', and if the
smoke goes straight to the sky it is a good omen for
the clan.   Then only is the meat which was prepared
on the 'junior fire' ceremonially eaten, after which all
the bones and remains of the feast have to be burnt on
the 'senior fire'.[1]

Ethnography.

The Iranian Turks.

The question now arises, What Turkic nations go to
form the group of Iranian Turks?

THE TURKOMANS.   Their number in Persia, Khiva,
and Bokhara is about 600,000.   Of these 290,000 (in
1911, as against 248,000 in 1897) are in Transcaspian
territory of Turkestan.   Among the Turkomans subject
to Russia must also be reckoned the Caucasian Turkomans, some 11,000.[2]

The Turkomans of Turkestan were subjugated by the
Russians in 1881 after a stubborn resistance.   The
Russians put a stop to their slave trade, and from that
time they began to be more settled and to take up
agriculture.   But even now a large proportion are still
nomadic horse-breeders, adhering to the customary law

[1] S. D. Maynagasheff, 'Sacrifice to the Sky among the Beltir',
*Literary Collection of the Anthropological Museum of the Acad. of
Science*, Petrograd, 1915, vol. III, pp. 93-102.
[2] The Turkomans of the Ottoman Empire, commonly called
Turkmen or Avshahr, are not dealt with here.

('*ādat*). In religion they are now all Mahometans, in language they belong to the Jagatai Turks. Clan division is still fairly strict among them, and migrations are usually carried out in clans. Their custom of endogamy may be regarded as having as its object the preservation of the purity of their race from foreign admixture. Since the women are inferior in numbers to the men, the *kalym* or bride-price is very high, and in some places the unmarried men form 27 per cent. of the population. Their clans are nine in number, two of them, however, being almost extinct. The chief clans are :

Chaudor, between Khiva and the Caspian ;

Yomut, on the south shore of the Caspian, and in south-west Khiva ;

Goklan, on Persian soil ;

Akhal and *Merv Tekkes*, in the Akhal and Merv oases ;

Sarik, on the middle Murgab ;

Salor, round Merv and in northern Persia ;

Ersari, on the middle Amu Daria, and near Khoya Salih.

Though linguistically and politically classified as Turks, in all these people the Iranian type predominates, in culture as well as in physique.

THE SARTS (1,847,000 in 1911, as against 1,458,000 in 1897) live in the Ferghana and Syr Daria territories, and are also to be found sporadically in other parts of Turkestan.

They are a mixture of the original Iranian inhabitants, the Tadjiks, with their Turanian conquerors, the Usbegs. In physical type they approach nearer to the Iranians. They live in villages, called *kishlak*, and their houses, called *sakla*, are made of a compound of wood and clay.

Though engaged chiefly in commerce, they are also successful agriculturists. They know the use of *aryk* or irrigation canals, and are reputed to be the best cultivators of cotton and fruit plantations. On the whole there is only one people who surpass them as agriculturists, namely the Tadjiks,[1] who are supposed to be pure Iranians.

The Sarts are Mahometans, Sunnites, many of them followers of the Sufi order. They adhere to the Mahometan written law (*sheriat*). They keep their women more strictly in seclusion than is the case among any other Turkic tribe. This is probably connected with the high degree of organization shown in their religious culture, which exceeds that of the other tribes. They have a great reverence for the Mussulman educational institutions usually to be found in connexion with the Sufi religious orders, and supported by public donations. There are three of these orders in Central Asia, the most ancient of them being in Ferghana. The educational institutions are divided into higher (*Medresse*) and lower (*Mektab*). Besides instruction in religious and legal subjects, the students are given some general knowledge based on mediaeval conceptions; thus Sart geography represents the world as being flat, and surrounded by mountains. In the lower

---

[1] The Tadjiks are the remnants ot the old Aryan population ot Central Asia, living chiefly in the Samarkand and Ferghana districts. In 1911 they numbered about 400,000, i. e. 67 per cent. of the total population. The Tadjiks living in the valleys and engaged in agriculture are now scarcely distinguishable in language and physique from their neighbours the Sarts, but the Mountain Tadjiks, or Galcha, are still using their Iranian language, and differ from the dark Turanians around them by reason of their light-coloured hair and skin.

classes some Arabic is taught; in the higher Persian is the language used, but neither of these languages is really mastered.[1] The Russian schools have had less success among the Sarts than among the Kaizak or the Kirghis.

THE TARANCHI or ILI-TATARS (83,000 in 1911 as against 70,000 in 1897) live in Semirechie and in the Transcaspian Territory, having migrated to Russian Turkestan from Eastern Turkestan at the same time as the Dungans, that is to say, when Kulja passed under Chinese rule.

In physical type, culture, language, and religion the Taranchi stand very near to the Sarts; the only difference seems to be in regard to the treatment of their women, who have much greater freedom than among the Sarts, and do not cover their faces. The Taranchi are agriculturists, cultivating especially vegetable gardens, but some of them incline towards commerce.

The Turkomans, Sarts, and Taranchi may be grouped together as the least Turkic of all the Iranian Turks, being now strongly under Persian, as they were in the past under Arabian, influence. And of course it must be remembered that all of them form as it were a stratum overlying the original 'Aryan' population, whose culture was of an Irano-Greek type. But of the three the Taranchi have the closest connexion with the Turanian Turks, being probably the descendants of the old Uigur in Eastern Turkestan.

The next to be considered are the Usbegs, and their kindred tribes the Kipchak, the Kaizak (Kaizak-Kirghis), and the Kara-Kalpak.

THE USBEGS (592,150 in 1911 as against 534,825 in

[1] *Asiatic Russia*, vol. I, p. 170.

1897) live in the Samarkand, in some parts of Syr Daria and Ferghana Territories, and in the Khanates of Khiva and Bokhara. With them can be classed the KIPCHAK (60,000 in 1911 as against 45,000 in 1897), who live in the Ferghana Territory. The word Kipchak is found as the name of a clan, or perhaps a moiety, among various Siberian and Turkestan Turks, such as the Altaians, the Telengit, the Kaizak of the Middle Orda, and the Usbegs.

The Usbegs form the ruling class in Bokhara, Khiva, and Kokand, occupying much the same position as do the Osmanly in Turkey. Some groups of Usbegs are to be found in Northern Afghanistan, and in the west of Eastern Turkestan. The name Usbeg is political, and is probably derived from Usbeg Khan of the Golden Horde (1312-40). The Usbegs are a mixture of three elements, Turkic, Iranian, and Mongol, but the Turkic element and Turanian traditions are predominant, except in the case of the Usbegs of Khiva, where the Iranian type predominates.

Since the Usbegs are in process of exchanging their nomad life for a sedentary one, their customary law ('ādat) is being replaced by the written law (sheriat). Father-right is very strong, but the women are freer than among the Tadjiks or the Sarts. Though they now live in clay and wood houses (sakla), their old felt tents (yurta) are still to be seen, especially in summer.

There is much ethnological evidence that the Usbegs belong to the same ethnic group as that people who are called by the Russians Kaizak-Kirghis, but who call themselves Kaizak. Both names—Kaizak and Usbeg— came into use only in the fourteenth and fifteenth centuries, and even now Usbegs and Kaizak have many clan, or perhaps moiety, names in common (Jalair, Kangli, Kipchak, Kereit, Konkrat, Naïman, Tabyn, Arghyn, Tama, and Tilaou[1]). If the name Usbeg is derived from *bek*, 'master of oneself', and the name Kaizak from the Turkic *káz*, 'steppe goose', and the Persian *zagh*, 'steppe crow',[2] with the metaphorical meaning, 'wanderers free as steppe birds', it seems possible that the origin of both names involves the same idea. Another derivation of Kaizak from *kázmak*, 'to dig', fails to commend itself, as the meaning of the word has no direct connexion with their mode of life, the Kaizak never appearing as agriculturists.

The Kaizak-Usbegs were probably bands of people who escaped from the strong state organization of the Turkic Empires of the thirteenth and fourteenth centuries, and reverted to a nomadic life and a nomadic culture, under conditions which led to their mixing freely with such nomads as the Western Mongols. In seeking for rich pastures they were obliged to live in a state of constant war with the people who inhabited the steppes before them. Historical evidence supports this hypothesis.[3] Their warlike disposition seems to have given rise to a Tadjik proverb, referring to the Kataghan, a tribe of Usbegs of the Kundar district: 'Where the hoof of the Kataghan's horse arrives, there the dead find no grave-cloth and the living no home'.[4]

---

[1] P. Kuznietsoff, *La Lutte des Civilisations et des Langues dans l'Asie centrale*, Paris, 1912, p. 60.

[2] In this part of the world a Turkic-Persian hybrid is not uncommon.

[3] V. V. Velyaminoff-Zernoff, *The Emperors and Princes of the line of Kasim*, 1860.

[4] R. B. Shaw, *A Sketch on the Turki Language as spoken in Eastern Turkistan*, Calcutta, 1880, p. 139.

In contrast to the origin of the Usbegs and the Kaizak is the origin of the real Kirghis, by which is meant the Eastern or Yenisei Kirghis, called by the Russians the Burut-Kirghis and the Kara-Kirghis. These have more right to be called Turanian Turks than the Kaizak, who may be said to stand between the two groups. They will therefore be dealt with under that head (Turanian).

THE KAIZAK live in the northern and eastern part of the Aral-Caspian basin, and in the Orenburg Steppes. Together with the Kara-Kirghis and some of the Yenisei Kirghis—i. e. all the people whom the Russians call Kirghis, and so include under one head in their census—they numbered 4,700,000 in 1911 as against 4,100,000 in 1897. Out of this total the non-Kaizak element may be reckoned at between 500,000 and 800,000 (in 1911).

The Kaizak say that they are sprung from the Usbegs, and that the Kara-Kirghis are sprung from dogs, but the Kara-Kirghis call themselves brothers of the Kaizak, and are in fact probably related to them, since the Kaizak have recruited themselves not only from the Usbegs but also from other Turkic states.

The Kaizak were divided by their Khan Tiavka in the thirteenth century into three 'hordes', called Ordas. This was done for administrative purposes, but since the death of Tiavka the history of each orda runs independently.

The ordas are:
1. Ulugh-yüz (Ulu-jus) or Great Orda, living in the neighbourhood of the rivers Chu and Talas, and subdivided into the Abdan and Dolat tribes.
2. Urta-yüz (Urta-jus) or Middle Orda, living between the rivers Tobol and Irtish and the Syr Daria,

and subdivided into the Arghyn, Naïman, Kip-.
chak, and Konkrat tribes.

3. Kichik-yüz (Kichik-jus) or Little Orda, living between
the Aral Sea and the lower Volga, and subdivided into the Alchin and Yabbas tribes.

At the present time the 'hordes' of the Kaizak inter-
mingle to a great extent, but class distinctions within
the hordes are still upheld. The nobility, called Tiuri
or Ak-sök, i. e. 'White Bones', trace their ancestry
from Jinghis Khan, notwithstanding that the latter was
a Mongol. All the other people are called Kara-sök,
i. e. 'Black Bones'. Some old legal customs still disregard the Russian law, as e. g. that of *baranta*, or
revenge for a wrong inflicted on one tribesman or clans-
man, by carrying away the culprit's or his clansmen's
herd.

Like the other Turks, the Kaizak base their social
structure upon a patriarchal system. It is very difficult
to define what should be called a clan among the Turks
of Central Asia, in the sense in which that term is used
in dealing with Africa and Australia. There seems to
be a conception of a political group, called among both
the Kirghis and the Kaizak *uruk* or *ru*, with its head,
bey, *bi*, or *serdar* (possibly a confederation of such clans
was once called *el*), while a group of families affiliated
by blood is called by the Kaizak *taypas* or *tayfa* (by the
Kirghis *kyrk*). The head of such a sub-clan, based on
blood relationship, is called *ak-sakal*. An amalgamation
of several sub-clans forms a *sök* (clan).

If a clan 'sök' increases in size, and wishes to divide
or to migrate, the departive group sometimes takes as a
name the word for the number of the sub-clans of which
it is composed, e. g. *On* ('ten'), *Yur* ('a hundred'); or

choose some characteristic trait of their group, e. g. Kaizak, 'Wanderers free as steppe birds', Kara-Sakal, 'Black Beards', Kara-Kalpak, 'Black Caps'. Sometimes they may adopt the name of their leader, e. g. Usbegs, Seljuk, or that of the most influential sub-clan, e. g. Sakhalar (the name of the nation called by the Russians the Yakut), though not all the members of this nation belong to the Sakhalar sub-clan. The clan-name Sakhalar (sing. Sakky) is to be found among many Turkic people of the Abakan and upper Yenisei, and it was probably only with the Russian advance at the end of the sixteenth and beginning of the seventeenth centuries that one group of the Sakhalar clan migrated towards Lake Baikal, and then northwards along the Lena, while a smaller group went directly northwards along the Yenisei. This would be about the time when the Burut-Kirghis migrated from the upper Yenisei to Jungaria.[1]

Thus in the case of these migrations the clan names are not sufficient guide in tracing the racial affinity of the people. More assistance is obtained from a study of their sub-clan crests, or *tamgas* (sing. *tamga, tamaga, tamka, dam-k'a, t'amga*), and their war-cries (*urany*, sing. *uran*). It is curious that these two most interesting sources of ethnological evidence have so far been only partly investigated, though considering the numerous divisions and subdivisions existing among the Turkic peoples, and the fact that the national names are, as has been seen, accidental and variable, any permanent means

[1] N. N. Kosmin, *D. A. Klements and the Historical and Ethnographical Investigation of the Minusinsk Country*, Irkutsk, 1916, pp. 13-15.

of throwing light on their racial relationships ought to be welcomed.

How complicated their tribal and clan subdivisions are is seen in the following table given by the Kaizak ethnologist Mustafa Chokayeff, to explain his own standing in the Kaizak nation.[1]   He belongs to—

Turkic race,
Kaizak nation,
Middle orda,
Kipchak tribe,
Toru-aibgyr clan,
Shashli sub-clan,
Boshai branch (in Russian *kolieno*),
Janay sub-branch (*podkolieno*).

The *tamga* may be regarded as the symbol of a sub-clan (*tayfa* among the Kaizak, *kyrk* among the Kirghis), a group of families affiliated by blood, because it is such groups which usually live together, and whose live stock, whether reindeer, horses, or dromedaries, are marked by this symbol.   The *tamga* appears also on their various belongings, as well as on the graves of deceased members of the clan.

The antiquity of these symbols can be judged from the fact that they are to be seen on the old Nestorian monuments, and on the monument to Khan Kul-Tegin in the valley of the Orkhon, on which the inscriptions are in old Turkic characters, dating from 732 A.D.[2] Those who boldly derive the old Turkic written

[1] A. N. Samoylovich, 'Prohibited words in the vocabulary of a married woman among the Kaizak', *L. A. T.*, vols. I–II, 1915, p. 162.

[2] N. A. Aristoff, *Attempt at an Explanation of the Ethnic Composition*, &c., 1894, p. 410 ; N. Mallitski, *On the connection between the Turkic 'tamga' and the Orkhon characters*, 1897–8, p. 43.

character from the clan *tamgas* would of course claim greater antiquity than that of Orkhon and Yenisei inscriptions.

According to tradition, the *tamga* was introduced among the Kaizak by their Khan Tiavka, because the Kaizak of his time were so rich in cattle that some device of this kind was necessary for the identification of the various herds. Some think that the origin of the *tamga* is to be sought in Mongolia, but as a matter of fact it occurs among the Turks no less frequently than among the Mongols and Tungus, because the custom of marking cattle is natural and common to most pastoral people. As may be expected, the pastoral Turks, such as the Kaizak and some of the Kirghis, have the *tamga* system much more highly developed than have the sedentary part of the Kirghis, the Altaians, and the forest and mountain Turks generally. Being either hunters or agriculturists, they have less need of the *tamga* for practical purposes. The study of the *tamgas* gives in many cases a clue to the composition of the tribe; for example, among the Kaizak there are to be found *tamgas* of various Turkic tribes of Asia, either in their original form or as composite signs, thus proving conclusively the mixed origin of that people.[1]

It is difficult to ascertain how far the *tamga* corresponds to a totem. Some *tamgas* seem to represent merely geometric designs: the Naïman clans had as their favourite *tamga* an angle, the Kirei use a square. Some of the Kaizak of the Middle Orda have *tamgas* representing a 'bird's rib' (*urdas bii*), a comb (*tarak*), and a forked stick (*selak*). Sometimes, however, the

[1] Aristoff, *op. cit.*, p. 421.

tamga plays more obviously the rôle of a totem. Among the Turks of the Minusinsk country there exist survivals of public clan sacrifices to the spirit-owner of the clan, for instance the horse, which appears also to be the clan *tamga.*

At the present time the *tamga* is usually cut or branded on the left side of the animal, i. e. the side from which the rider mounts, but the exact place where the mark is made differs among the various tribes.

The fact that the same *tamgas* are used on graves belonging to the same clan is of assistance in tracing the migration of clans, but it is only by considering the *tamga* on the one hand, and the *uran* or war-cry on the other, that the origin of a group can be traced. The *uran* was originally the common property of a political group, a larger unit than the group of blood-relations who owned the *tamga.* It often consists of the name of a well-known chief or hero, but since the Turkic tribes have ceased to lead a warrior's life the new generation scarcely remember the battle-cry of the clan, and hence the *uran* is more difficult of discovery than the *tamga.* Grodekoff,[1] perhaps the most successful of all the investigators along these lines, found that the chief *uran* of the Great Orda, namely, of the clans Jalair and Dulat, was 'Bahtyar', the name of one of the Kaizak heroes; the Kangli have a *uran* 'Bayterek', which is probably a corrupt form of the same name. This community of the *uran* confirms what is now known about the relationship between the Kangli and the Jalair. Sometimes the name of the clan is used as a *uran*, as

[1] *The Kirghis and Kara-Kirghis of the Syr Daria Territory,* 1829, pp. 2-3.

among the Seykym clan of the Kaizak, whose *uran* is also 'Seykym'.

Though the Kaizak belong geographically to the Iranized Turks, culturally they have on the whole much affinity with the Mongols. The majority are still nomadic cattle and horse breeders. Their method of cattle-keeping is a most luxurious one. They leave the cattle on the pastures the whole year round, hence their only care is to find a fresh pasture every season. The spring and autumn pastures may be the same. It is only recently, since more of the land has been claimed by the Russian Immigration Committee, that the Kaizak have begun to lay up winter stores for their cattle. Each clan has defined limits to its pasture lands. Under the old Russian system the pasture land used by the Kaizak belonged to the State, and they were granted the use of it, dividing it at their communal gatherings according to the number of people, cattle, and vehicles in each class. The permanent houses, gardens, arable land, and irrigation canals are hereditary.[1]

It is curious to note that the Kaizak, whose dwellings are so light and portable, bury their dead in solid structures of wood, clay, and brick. This custom also exists among the Kara-Kirghis, and was known to the old Yenisei-Kirghis. As it is not found among the non-Turkic population of Central Asia, it seems to indicate that those who practise it now are perhaps the nearest relatives of the people who built the old burial mounds of the Yenisei, called *kurgans*.

THE KARA-KALPAK ('Black Caps'), another Turkic tribe of the same group (134,313 in 1911 as against 111,799 in 1897), live in the Amu Daria district of the

---

[1] *Asiatic Russia*, vol. I, p. 159.

Syr Daria Territory, in the Kokand district of the Ferghana Territory, and some 20,000 in the Khanate of Khiva.

Half of them are settled agriculturists, the rest are still nomad cattle-breeders, their pasture lands being, however, more strictly fixed than among the Kaizak. Some of them are also engaged in trading. Of all the Kirghis group their language is the most nearly related to that of the Western Turks.[1]

This may be explained by the fact that they belong to the stream of Turks who participated in the westward migration some ten centuries ago.

Speaking of the origin of the Kara-Kalpak or Chornyie Klobuki, as they were called in Kieff-Russia, P. Golubowski[2] says that they were a mixture of Ghuz Turks, Pyechenyeg, and others, and that they formed that remnant of the Ghuz Turks who remained in Russia when the new wave of Turkic invaders from Asia—the Polovtsy—drove the other part of their tribe across the Danube. The remnants of the Ghuz, together, possibly, with other Turks, settled on the Russian borderlands, accepted Christianity, and were known as the Kara-Klobuk (Kara-Kalpak), while some of them moved back to Asia, and, according to V. Moshkoff, about 70,000 of them live until now in Bessarabia under the name of Ghaghauzy (Gagauzy).[3] Whether the Kara-Kalpak not living in Asia are the same as the Kara-

---

[1] A. Maksimoff, 'The Kara-Kalpak', vol. XXIII, p. 454, of the *Encyclopaedic Dictionary*, ed. Jeleznoff.

[2] *The Pyechenyegi, the Torki and the Polovtsy until the Tatar Invasion*, Kieff, 1884, p. 151.

[3] V. Moshkoff, *Examples of the Folk-Literature of the Turkic Tribes*, St. Petersburg, 1904, p. xxii.

Kalpak who in the eleventh century were the borderland population of Southern Russia, it is difficult to ascertain, but possibly they re-migrated to Asia from European Russia in the eighteenth century, where Howorth thinks they formed one tribe of the Nogai-Pyechenyeg on the Yaik River.[1]

The Turanian Turks.

It is impossible to draw a well-defined line between the Iranian and the Turanian groups of the Eastern Turks. Thus the Kaizak, who are here reckoned among the Iranian Turks, are in many respects closely allied to the Kara-Kirghis, who may be called the descendants of the Yenisei Kirghis. They have also affinities with the Turks of Eastern Turkestan, of Northern Mongolia, and of Siberia, all of whom might be called Turanian.

It is important to bear in mind that at present the adjective 'Turanian', as applied to these people, really means that they are under Mongolian, Chinese, and Tibetan cultural influences, while they have also retained to some extent the original traits of their pre-Mahometan Turkic culture. The Iranian group has fewer traits of this old Turkic culture left, owing to the predominance of Persian and Arabic cultural elements, and when we pass to the Western Turks, the infiltration of Mediterranean and Central European influence leaves few points of resemblance, other than language, between them and the Turanian Turks living one on each side of the main mass of Turkic-speaking peoples.

THE KIRGHIS, as has been said, are to be distinguished

[1] H. H. Howorth, *History of the Mongols,* vol. II, p. 5.

from the people erroneously called Kirghis, namely
the Kaizak, who were dealt with among the Iranian
Turks. The Kirghis, or 'Eastern Kirghis', are as a
matter of fact, together with the Altai 'Tatars' and the
Kirei, the truest representatives of the Turanian Turks.
The name seems to be derived[1] from *kir* (*kr*), 'cultivated
field', and shows that these people were originally
agriculturists, as indeed we know they were during
at least the period from the sixth century up to the
time when the occupation of the upper Yenisei, first by
the Mongol Altyn Khan, and then by the Russians,
forced many of them to migrate farther south, and to take
up a pastoral life. Even now part of them are agriculturists and hunters, and it is only that section which
was subjected to the most frequent migrations that have
adopted what may be called horse-culture. This may
be defined as a mode of life dependent on cattle and
especially horse breeding, hence their nomadic habits.
They use the horse for riding, he provides them with
food, and to a certain extent with clothing, while for
heavy draught work it is the dromedary which is
chiefly used.

The Kirghis are called by the Russians 'Eastern',
'Burut', 'Black' (Kara), or 'Mountain' Kirghis; the
latter is used to distinguish them from the Kaizak
Kirghis of the plains. Their home was since the
beginning of our era in the valley of the Yenisei,
whence they moved south under the advance of the

---

[1] Another derivation of the name is *kyrk kys*, meaning 'forty
girls', and the legend tracing the Kirghis from forty women from
China who married forty men of U-si seems to uphold this
(Schott, 'Über die ächten Kirgisen', *Abhandl. Berliner Akad.*, 1865,
p. 432). But as a matter of fact the name by which they call
themselves is not Kirghis but Krgyz.

Russians. Some few of them still live in the upper Yenisei valley, where they are mixed with the Abakan 'Tatars', but the majority of them are now to be found south of Yarkand, round by Pamir and Alai, to the north of Kashgar and Aksu (the Issyk-kul district). Many of them are known under their clan-names, others form the nation of the *Kara-Kirghis*.

The Kara-Kirghis fall into two branches, a right branch, called Ong, and a left, called Sol. The Ong branch is divided into two groups, Edigzne and Tagai. The Tagai group is composed of seven clans:[1]

1. Bugu (Stag), near the River Tekes, and to the east of Lake Issyk-kul.
2. Sary Bagish (Yellow Elk), to the south and west of Lake Issyk-kul.
3. Solto, south of the River Chu.
4. Sayak.
5. Cherik (Army) in Ferghana.
6. Chong Bagish (Great Elk), west of Kashgar.
7. Bassyz.

The Sol branch is less numerous, and lives chiefly along the River Talas. It includes three clans, Saru, Koshi, and Munduz.

All these Kirghis clans are related by intermarriage to the Naiman and the Kipchak, who, however, are reckoned to be quite a different nation.

It must be noted that Kirghis occurs also as a clan-name among the Usbegs and the Altaians.

The Kara-Kirghis have clan *tamgas* like the Kaizak, but the headship of their clan is a hereditary office, in contradistinction to the custom of the Kaizak, whose heads are elected. The head of the Kara-Kirghis clan is called *manap*, and the head of a confederation of

[1] Aristoff, *op. cit.*, p. 430.

clans is called *aga-manap*. A comparison of the social structure of the Kara-Kirghis with that of the Kaizak shows that the former is of a type more suited to the needs of a sedentary people, and the latter to those of nomads.

The comparative isolation of the Kirghis from any but Turkic tribes gives some assurance that their customs have more right than those of many other tribes to be taken as typically Turkic. A picture of their marriage ceremony may be of interest in this connexion.

In general the wife is purchased, but as the bride-price (*kalym*) is usually paid in instalments there exists a special *rite de passage* between the arrangement of the marriage and the final wedding ceremony. After the first part of the bride-price is paid, the bridegroom and his companions, bringing rich presents to the bride's family and to the match-makers, drive to the *aul* (village) of the bride, in the neighbourhood of which he halts. Meanwhile the *djinai* (female match-makers) prepare a special tent, to which they lead the bridegroom, while the bride is carried away from her parents to another tent belonging to some relative. Then a feast is held by the bride's parents, at which neither the bridegroom nor the bride is present. Late at night the *djinai* conduct the bride and bridegroom from their separate tents to the house of the bride's parents. The bride resists ceremonially, while the bridegroom is ceremonially hindered from reaching the house by the *djinai*, one of whom pretends to be a fierce dog, another a wild cow, and so on.

Early in the morning the bridegroom goes away, and for the whole day he must avoid his parents-in-law. This goes on for about a fortnight, after which the bridegroom leaves the *aul*. Some time after, when the whole *kalym* is paid, he returns to fetch his wife, who again pretends to defend herself, and to be loath to leave her parents' *aul*. There is a show of taking her away by force. The first stage of the marriage, when the bridegroom lives in the house of the bride's parents, in regard to whom he must observe the custom of avoidance, cannot be dispensed with even if the whole *kalym* is paid at once.

Among some other Turks, such as the Turkomans and the Kazan 'Tatars', the period during which the bride remains with her people after the first marriage ceremony extends over several months, or even a couple of years.

The Kirghis are strictly exogamous, as far as the blood-clan is concerned. Before marriage a young woman is allowed a good deal of freedom with the men of her own clan, but custom forbids her to meet men of other clans.[1]

THE SIBERIAN TURKS[2] fall into two groups, one consisting of the nation of the Yakut, the other of a conglomerate of clans and tribes known as the 'Siberian Tatars'; various branches of them are called according

[1] P., 'The Customs of the Kirghis of the Semipalatinsk Territory', *Russian Messenger*, 1878, No. 9, pp. 32-7; A. Levshin, *Description of the Kirghis-Kaizak Hordes and Steppes*, 1832, pp. 100-102; P. E. Makovyetski, *Materials for the Study of the Juridical Customs of the Kirghis*, 1890, pp. 16-19; N. Grodekoff, *The Kirghis and the Kara-Kirghis of the Syr Daria Territory*, pp. 63-5.

[2] To be distinguished from these Siberian Turks, who have been settled in the country since the very beginning of our era, are the 'Tatars' who migrated back from European Russia fairly recently. In 1897 the number of these in Asiatic Russia was 94,000, in 1911 they numbered 124,000. They are partly Nogai of the northern Caucasus, and partly Kazan 'Tatars', and many of them differ from the Russian colonists only in their Mahometan religion.

to their geographical distribution : the 'Baraba Tatars', the 'Altaians', the 'Abakan Tatars', and so on.

The *Yakut*, who are now the northernmost branch of Turkic-speaking people, live along the River Lena right up to the Arctic shore, and in the region between the Lena and the Yenisei as far south as Lake Baikal.   They are superior in numbers to all the 'Siberian Tatars' taken together.   In 1911 they numbered 245,000, as against 225,000 in 1897, while the 'Tatars' numbered 208,000 in 1911, plus some 4,000 people classed by the Russian officials as 'Turks of undefined nationality', as against 175,000 in 1897, plus some 3,000 'Turks of undefined nationality'.[1]

Under the influence of their new environment[2] the Yakut have been driven to take up reindeer-breeding and a nomadic tundra life, but in their social and religious institutions survivals of the more settled conditions of their southern home are still to be seen.[3]

Of all the Turks of Asia the Yakut are the most typical representatives of what may be spoken of as 'reindeer-culture'.[4]   The reindeer is to this region what the horse is to the Central Asian steppe-nomads.   It supplies food, clothes, bone-implements, and is used for draught work.   But while the people who have been living for a long time at the stage of reindeer-culture, such as the Koryak of the north-east or the Samoyed of the north-west, never use reindeer for riding, the Yakut ride their reindeer as their ancestors rode the horse, a practice which is looked upon with disfavour

[1] *Asiatic Russia*, vol. I, pp. 79–80.
[2] See p. 41.
[3] M. A. Czaplicka, *Aboriginal Siberia*, 1914, pp. 107, 277, 297.
[4] B. Laufer, 'The Reindeer and its Domestication', *Mem. of the Amer. Anthrop. Assoc.*, vol. IV, No. 2, 1917.

by their neighbours. It must be remembered that
while the reindeer is not known to the Turks of Tian-
Shan and the upper Yenisei, the latter people have
several other species of deer, especially the elk (*Cervus
alces*) and the maral (*Cervus elephas*). The domesticated
deer is rare.

Forming a wedge between the Tungusic and the
Palaeo-Siberian tribes, the Yakut impose their language,
together with many of their customs, on both these
groups, as well as on the Russian settlers. In religion
they are typical Shamanists.

On meeting a Yakut among the various Mongoloid
peoples of the north, one is at once struck with the
difference in his physiognomy. His hair and eyes are
darker, his nose narrower and better marked, and on
the whole he gives the impression of possessing
Southern, and one might almost say Semitic, characteristics. And yet he can hardly be suspected of having
any Arabic strain.

The *Siberian Tatars* live chiefly in the Tomsk and
Yeniseisk Governments. In the Tomsk Government,
70 per cent. of them do not know any language but
their own ; the remaining 30 per cent. speak Russian
also. In the Yeniseisk Government only 12 per cent.
speak the Russian language besides their own.

As to their religion some of them are Mahometans,
namely :

1. Tobolsk Tatars and 'Siberian Bokharians' of the
   Tobolsk district.
2. The Baraba Tatars of the Kainsk district.
3. The Tomsk Tatars of the Mariinsk district.
4. The Kuznietsk Tatars of the Kuznietsk and Barnaul
   district.

Others are still Shamanists or 'Christian-Shamanists',

people who mix their pagan practices with some of the Russian Orthodox Church beliefs. Those are:

5. The Forest (Chern) Tatars of the Biisk district.
6. The Teleut and Telengit of the Biisk and Kuznietsk districts.
7. The Kumandits (or 'White Kalmucks') of the Kuznietsk and Biisk districts.
8. The Shortes and Lebyedints of the Kuznietsk district.
9. The Kyzyl and Chulim natives of the Achinsk district.
10. The Abakan Tatars (Kachints, Koibal, Beltir, and Sagai) of the Minusinsk district.
11. The Karagass of the Nijneudinsk district of the government of Irkutsk.
12. The Kamashints of the Kansk district.

The *Teleut* of the Kuznietsk district are perhaps the most Russified, while the *Telengit*, along the rivers Biya and Katun, are very much mixed with the Mongols. The following tribes are said to be mixed with the Ugrian-Ostyak, the Yenisei-Ostyak, and the Samoyed, though in culture, language, and tradition they are now Turkic:

1, The Kamashints; 2, the Karagass; 3, the Koibal; 4, the Beltir; 5, the Kyzyl; 6, the Shortes; 7, the Kumandints.

The racial origin of these tribes has been defined, often superficially, merely judging from the names of their clans. Thus the Kyzyl (*Kysi*, 'man') are composed of ten classes: Kyzyl, Malo-Achin, Bolshe-Achin, Agy, Bassagar, Kamnar, Argyn, Kalmak, Kurchik, Shui. Of these, Argyn clan is said to be the remnant of the Kaizak of the Middle Orda, because those people have also had a clan of this name. Kalmak clan is also found among the Teleut, and Shui among Yenisei Ostyak, hence the admixture of the two races is attributed to Kyzyl by Radloff.[1]

Most of the Siberian Tatars, as well as Northern Uriankhai, call themselves Tuba, either exclusively or alongside with their tribal name, *Tuba* being the name of one of their clans. This name *Tuba, Tubas, Tupo* or *Doubo*, like the word *Tatar*, should be used with great caution, until its origin and meaning have been more clearly defined. It seems to have been adopted by the Chinese as a collective term for the people living in the Southern Yenisei Region, probably along the river of this name, the right tributary of the Yenisei. The Russian historians of Siberia, Miller[2] and Fischer,[3] mention the people of Tuba as paying tribute to the Mongol Altyn Khan, and opposing for a long time Russian conquest, but it is not clear whether this name had a racial meaning, designating, e. g., the extinct Arine, Kottes, &c., or the Samoyed, or was used only as a geographical term for all peoples living near the River Tuba. Now at any rate it does not seem to be limited entirely to the tribes whom one can suspect of having some Samoyed blood in them, for it is found among the Altaians, whom even Castrén and Kostroff with all their ' Pan-Samoyedic' theory could not call ' Tatarised Samoyed '. It is found moreover among the *Kachints*, who, according to Katanoff,[4] were Kuchum-Khan people, who moved to the River Kacha, near Krasnoyarsk, after the defeat of Kuchum, and farther

[1] A. A. Yariloff, *The Kyzyl and their Industry*, 1899, p. 1.
[2] G. F. Miller, *Description of the Tsardom of Siberia* (1750).
[3] J. E. Fischer, *Sibirische Geschichte* (1768).
[4] ' Legends relating to old deeds and old people among the tribes living near the Sayan Mountains', *Mem. I. R. G. S.*, vol. XXXIV, 1909, p. 280.

south later on.   But its distribution is still wider: the
eastern neighbours of the Uriankhai, the *Darkat* and
the *Uigur*, living on the shores of Lake Kossogol, have
a clan called Tuba, though no tribe here uses this name
for itself as a whole.   The Darkat now speak a Mongolian language, but in tradition they seem to have
more in common with the Turks than with the
Mongols.

The *Tuba* is not the only clan-name so widely spread;
there are others, such as Kirghis, Sokka, Oirat Ari,
&c., while some clan-names, such as Kaska among the
Kachints, are peculiar to one tribe.   On the whole,
the Siberian Tatars cannot be compared to the Kaizak
with regard to their memory of the tribal and clan past.
Katanoff[1] found that this lack of tradition seems to
characterize all the Turks known as 'Tatars'.   The
Kazan Tatars do not have any written or oral record
relating to the important fact of the fall of Kazan, under
the pressure of Ivan the Terrible, and the Tobolsk
Tatars scarcely have any records giving accounts of
the Tsar Kuchum and his wars with the Russians.
But perhaps the fault rests more with Kuchum's
personality, for it is not so much the events which are
important in history as the personality of heroes that
inspire the oral tradition.   Thus a certain hero Kangza,
unknown in history, has very many tales devoted to
him among the Teleut (Radloff), the Altaians (Vyerbitski),
and the Abakan Tatars (Katanoff).

Of all the Siberian Tatars the most interesting ethnologically are the *Chern* (in Russian) or *Black Forest*
'*Tatars*', also known as *Altaians*, though the name
Altaians is wider and includes also some other Tatars,
such as the Kumandints.   The Altaians call themselves

[1] *Op. cit.*, p. 267.

Iish Kysi (*Iish*, 'black forest', 'chern'; *Kysi*, 'men'). In language and religion they keep free from foreign admixture, they are therefore typical Turanian Turks. Their mode of life is sedentary whenever the environment allows them to practise agriculture. In religion they are Shamanists.

THE TURKS OF NORTH-WESTERN MONGOLIA AND EASTERN TURKESTAN. While the Altaians or Chern 'Tatars' occupy the Northern Altai, there lives in the Southern, so-called Little Altai, along the Black Irtish, in Jungaria and in Eastern Turkestan, another Turkic tribe, a rival of the Altaians as representative of the pure Turanian type. This is the tribe called *Kirei*, *Kerrit, Kerrait*, or *Kirai*. The chief distinction between the Kirei and the Altaians is now a religious one, the Kirei being Mahometans. We know that from the eleventh to the thirteenth centuries they were adherents of Christianity in the form of Nestorianism, and it is among them that the fabulous Christian king Prester John (probably the native king Ouang-Khan, a contemporary of Jinghis Khan) is said to have lived. In mode of life they are at present nomads, and are well known as hunters.[1]

The Kirei are sometimes called *Kirei-Kirghis*, and it is possible that in the period from the beginning of our era till the sixth century, when the Kirghis were spreading in the basin of the upper Yenisei, one clan, the Kirei, were left behind, and settled in the Kemchik valley. Again, when in the seventeenth century the Yenisei-Kirghis were retiring before the Russian advance, from the Minusinsk steppes southwards to Jungaria and Mongolia, some of them may have settled

---

[1] D. Carruthers, *Unknown Mongolia*, vol. II, pp. 351–5.

among the Kirei, who had meanwhile become to some extent Mongolized.[1]

To the south-west of the Kirei, in Kulja and in the western part of Chinese Turkestan, on the slopes of the Tian-Shan, live remnants of various Turanian Turks, sometimes called *Kashgarians*, many of whom are perhaps the direct descendants of the old Uigur, and possibly have also a strain of the pre-Turkic Aryan population of which traces are still to be found in Central Asia. In language, and probably in physical type, they are among the purest Turanians. Most of them, especially those who are Chinese subjects, are Mahometans. They are chiefly cattle-breeders. Such are the *Yerlik*, the *Kashgarlik*, and the *Yetisherlik*. Those subject to Russia number some 54,000 (in 1911). Since the great upheaval caused by the conquests of Jinghis Khan, and the migrations which followed, these people have remained stationary to a degree impossible anywhere but in the heart of the Asiatic continent, but it is not impossible that under a helpful and sympathetic government all of them, whether Russian or Chinese subjects, might awake to play their part in the future history of Asia.

The country to the east of the region occupied by the Chern 'Tatars' or Altaians, and to the south of that occupied by the Abakan 'Tatars', i. e. that part of the Yeniseisk Government between the Sayan Mountains and the Tannu Ola range, is called Uriankhai, and its 100,000 inhabitants are usually grouped together under the same name, Uriankhai, sometimes in its Chinese form, *Uriangut*. The northern part of the country, along the River Ussa, began to be colonized

---

[1] While Vambéry and Cahun reckon the Kirei as Turks, Skrine and Ross reckon them as Mongols. See note to p. 72.

by the Russians in 1856, and was practically annexed by them in 1886. The whole country became almost independent of China after Mongolia declared its independence in 1914, and the old Russian Government, intending to occupy this rich pasture land, had begun to colonize it energetically. This aroused some opposition among the natives, who, having scarcely felt their dependence on China, were not prepared to give up their best lands to the Russian Colonization Committee. Many Uriankhai have for the last three years been moving in clan order, with all their herds, into the steppes of Northern Mongolia. This is, in fact, the most recent *en masse* migration in Central Asia. It has ceased, however, since the Russian Revolution, owing to the influence exercised by Siberian scholars and public men, such as G. Potanin and A. Adrianoff, in the protection of the rights of the natives.[1]

The Uriankhai are sometimes called *Soyot* (sing. *Soyan*, from the clan-name *Saya*). But it is not certain whether this name ought to be applied to all of them. The name by which they call themselves in the North is *Tuba*.

According to the East Turkic scholar Katanoff, the language of the Uriankhai is Turko-Tatar,[2] but of course they are now mixed to a great extent with the Mongols. It must be remembered that Castrén and some of his followers are inclined to see in the Uriankhai members of the original Samoyed-Yeniseian race, who mixed with the Turks and adopted a Turkic language.[3]

[1] See articles in *Sibirskaya Jisn*, Feb. 26, 1916, May 3, 1917.

[2] E. K. Yakovleff, *Ethnographical Survey of the Native Population of the Valley of Southern Yenisei*, Minusinsk, 1900, p. 18.

[3] M. A. Castrén, *Nordische Reisen und Forschungen*, vol. IV, pp. 83-6; D. Carruthers, *op. cit.*, vol. I, pp. 20, 52-5, 200; vol. V, pp. 116-17.

That at one time a Samoyed group might have migrated
to the Soyot (Uriankhai) is not out of the question,
since many clan-names of the Samoyed and the Uriankhai are alike.   But no other signs of this relationship
can be found now, and the southernmost Turks, who
may have been originally Samoyed, are the Kamashints,
some of whom, at the time of Castrén's travels (1840–
50), were speaking a Samoyedic dialect.   When Radloff
visited them, however (about 1865), all signs of Samoyedic speech had disappeared, and only a Turkic dialect
was in use.

Radloff thinks that the Uriankhai are the forefathers
of the present Yakut,[1] which, however, sounds im-
probable, if only because the Uriankhai are almost the
most successful reindeer-breeders known, whilst the
Yakut learnt that art only after their migration to
the north.

The number of the Uriankhai is some 100,000.   Until
recently they formed one *aimak* or province of China.
They are subdivided into nine local groups (*khoshun*
or *kopun*), which again are divided into *sumo* or tribes.
The *sumo* is further subdivided into *sök*, clans, or
perhaps moieties.   The clan-names are mostly of Turkic
origin, many of them being found also among other
Turanian Turks, e.g. Irgit, Soyan, Kirghis, Kaizak,
Koeluk, Uigur, &c.

The Uriankhai living in the steppe country are mostly
cattle-breeders; some of them, however, depend chiefly
on hunting and fishing.   It is only in this region that
we find the breeding of horse, yak, and reindeer for

[1] Radloff, 'Die Jakutische Sprache', *Bull. I.A.S.*, 1908, pp. 54–6.
For opposite opinion see I. P. Silinich, 'On the question of the
physical type of the population of North-west Siberia', *Russ.
Anthr. J.*, Nos. 3–4, 1916, pp. 51–3.

draught purposes carried on together, and in a way it characterizes the Uriankhai, for they seem to combine the traits of the Mongol horse-nomads, the Turkic hunters and cattle-breeders, and the Tungus reindeer-breeders.

History.

The history of the Turks in Central Asia falls roughly into the following periods:

I. From the first vague mention of them in the Chinese annals of the Tang and Yu dynasties (2356–2200 B.C.), and the no less vague mention in the *Avesta* (if it is right to identify 'Tura' with Turks), to the middle of the sixth century A.D., when the name Tu-kiu (Turks) appears for the first time.

II. From the rise of the Tu-kiu, through the period of rapid independent development, to the Mongolian invasion in the thirteenth century.

III. From the thirteenth century through the period of the great migrations started by the Jinghis Khan conquests, and of the still independent Turkic states under Mongolian dynasties, to the beginning of the Russian advance in the seventeenth century.

IV. From the seventeenth century, through the period of the wars with Russia and of subsequent Russian rule, to the Russian Revolution of 1917.

First Period. The probable ancestors of the Turks lived to the north of China, and were mentioned by the Chinese chroniclers as long ago as the third millennium B.C. on account of their raids on China, but of course scarcely any mention is made by the Chinese of the Turks living to the far north and far west of China.

The first name now identified as that of the ancestors of the Turks is *Hiung-nu*. According to Professor Parker,[1] there exists 'a Hiung-nu tradition that about 1200 B. C. a (Chinese) royal personage who had most probably been misconducting himself fled to the nomads of the north and founded among them a sort of dynasty'. The Chinese are concerned with their neighbours on the north-west, the Hiung-nu, and on the north-east, the *Tung-hu* (subsequently Tungus), only so far as these barbarians annoyed them. The Emperors of the Tsin dynasty (255–209 B. C.) built the Great Wall to protect their northern frontiers, and this directed the strategic movements of the Hiung-nu in the second century B. C. towards the west. It is possible that some branches of them may have migrated westwards before the construction of the Great Wall, and then continued to develop quietly in their new home, otherwise it is hard to understand the high degree of organized culture in which we find them in the Altai and Yenisei region about 200 B. C.,[2] when we hear that the Kirghis and the Usuni were already there, and had found some remnants of still earlier Turkic immigrants. They may possibly have been in possession of this region already in the Bronze Age, unless, of course, we assume the independent origin of the Altai and Yenisei Turks, and take

---

[1] E. H. Parker, *A Thousand Years of the Tartars*, 1895, p. 3. Another Chinese translator, Father Jakinth Bichurin, gives a different version of the origin of the Hiung-nu dynasty: Shun-wei, son of the last emperor of the Hia dynasty, went in 1764 B. C. to Mongolia, and there started the Hiung-nu dynasty. Bichurin considers the Hiung-nu to be Mongols. (*Collection of Information concerning Peoples living in Central Asia*, 1851, vol. I.)

[2] N. A. Aristoff, *Attempt at an Explanation of the Ethnic Composition*, &c., p. 460.

the Hiung-nu as representing a stage when the easternmost Turks were not yet differentiated from the Mongols.

A more clearly defined stage is that of the Hun-nu Empire (possibly a form derived from Hiung-nu), which united under its domination most of the Turkic tribes of Central Asia. The reign of Mété (209-179 B.C.) seems to mark the climax of their power in Asia. The information gathered from the Chinese annals gives us the geographical distribution of the Turks of that time, who were divided into two hostile groups, Western and Eastern, both subject to Mété. The Eastern Turks were composed of the Uigur, between Tannu Ola and the Yellow River, and between the Tian-Shan and the basin of the Tarim. To the north of them lived the Din-lin (Telengit?), near Tannu Ola. The Kirghis (Khakas) lived along the Yenisei, and the Karluk and Tu-kiu in the Altai, and as far south as Tarbagatai.

The Western Turks comprised the Usun (Usuni), who lived to the south of Lake Balkash; the Kangli (Kan-giu), farther west as far as Amu Daria; the Yüe-Chi,[1] still farther to the south-west as far as the Caspian Sea; and the Yao-Chi, to the north of the last-named.

The Usun power in the western part of Turan (rivers Ili and Chu) dates chiefly from the end of the second century B.C. to the first century A.D. Since they found on their arrival the Kangli (Kan-giu) Turks settled in the Tian-Shan, it was with them that they struggled for the predominance, and both sides called for help either to the Chinese or to the Hun-nu.[2] But

---

[1] W. W. Radloff, *Concerning the Uigur*, 1893, p. 126.
[2] Aristoff, *op. cit.*, p. 461.

when both of them were subdued by the Hun-nu, their two tribes intermingled, and a part of them migrated to the northern outskirts of their territory, to escape the despotic rule of their conquerors, the Hun-nu. It is possible to look upon these groups as the earliest Kaizak organization, later imitated by the Cossacks.

All these probably Turkic tribes, and many remnants of 'Aryan' peoples and states in Central Asia, were under the rule of Mété,[1] who divided his empire into twenty-four parts, governed by six princes and six administrators. Within each part a strictly military organization prevailed, with units of 10, 100, 1000, and 10,000 men.

Nineteen of these twenty-four groups were composed of Uigur. Ten of them formed a confederation called On-Uigur, and nine another confederation called Togus-Uigur. The latter lived to the north of the On-Uigur. Professor Radloff thinks that as the bulk of the Hun-nu Empire was composed of On-Uigur, it is possible that the name Hun-nu is only a corrupt form of On-Uigur, On-Ui.[2]

The Chinese feared the power of the Hun-nu so much that about the middle of the second century B. C. they tried to make a defensive alliance with the Yüe-Chi, who, at the end of the pre-Christian era and the beginning of our own, formed one of the most powerful empires of Central Asia. Though that attempt failed, we hear that the Hun-nu, after having defeated the

---

[1] Though Professor Radloff reckoned the Yüe-Chi as a Turkic tribe, it is more probable that they were a Tung-hu tribe surrounded by Turkic people, with whom the Chinese confused them. They are later known as Kushan.

[2] Radloff, *op. cit.*, p. 127.

Wusun (Usuni) near Ili in 176 B.C., and the Yüe-Chi near the Tarim valley, were subsequently conquered by the Yüe-Chi at the end of the first century B.C., and that in the same century a Hun-nu prince submitted to China.[1]

Subsequently the eastern half of the Hun-nu Empire was divided into northern and southern parts, both of which had finally fallen by A.D. 215. The downfall of the Hun-nu Empire was thus due to the combined efforts of the Chinese and the Tung-hu, and indeed a Tung-hu power (Sien-pi, Toba, and Moyun) was then arising between China and the Turks.

It would seem as if the Hun-nu, their power in Asia ruined by all these defeats, migrated westwards in the second and third centuries, particularly the On-Uigur branch of them. Taking these to be the Huns who terrified Europe in the fifth century, we know that in A.D. 275 they were on the Volga, afterwards advancing farther west. At the same time another stream of the Hun-nu directed its course towards Transoxania, where they were known as the White Huns of Ephthalites. From there they successfully advanced on Persia and India, until in A.D. 528 their movement was checked by a confederation of Hindu princes.

Some of the tribes who entered into the composition of the Hun-nu Empire of Mété, and already at that period had a marked individuality, were the Khakas, later called Kirghis, and the Kiao-Che ('High-Carts'), later called Uigur. The Chinese historians say that the Kirghis and the Uigur (both of whom they call sometimes Ting-ling, sometimes Kankalis) use the same

---

[1] E. Chavannes, *Les Documents chinois découverts par Aurel Stein dans les sables du Turkestan oriental*, Oxford, 1913, p. vii.

language, and Professor Parker makes the suggestion that all the cart-using people of Hiung-nu origin north of the desert region of Issyk-Kul and Syr Daria were once called Ting-ling.[1]

How far the other tribes of Central Asia prominent towards the end of the pre-Christian era, for instance the Saka, were related to the Hun-nu it is difficult to ascertain, but in any case the 'Aryan' population of West Central Asia must have been considerably long after the Graeco-Bactrian kingdoms were destroyed by the Yüe-Chi. The lack of information about the linguistic affinities of these people makes it difficult to define them in the very early centuries of our era. It is known, for instance, that the Hun-nu used the Turkic language in the fourth century A. D.,[2] but whether it was their original language is not clear.

We hear that the Usuni (Wusun) of Ili and Balkash, and the Khakas (later Kirghis), were fair-haired and blue-eyed. This may be explained either by their contact with some 'Aryan' people, or by attributing to them an 'Aryan' origin. In 95 B. C. the Chinese said that the Khakas lived in the regions of the Kem and the upper Yenisei. Then again in the third century A. D. we hear about the 'blond Kirghis' (Kien-kun) as being very powerful and providing 20,000 men in time of war.[3] Of course, we have no proof that the fair Khakas of that time, and their kin the Uigur, were Turkic-speaking people, except that some names of objects and of the months mentioned by the Chinese

[1] Parker, *op. cit.*, p. 265.

[2] Barthold, review of Aristoff's *Attempt at an Explanation of the Ethnic Composition*, &c., p. 343.

[3] O. Donner, 'Sur l'origine de l'alphabet turc du Nord de l'Asie', *J. Soc. Fin.-Ougr.*, Helsingfors, 1896, XIV, p. 70.

in connexion with the Khakas are in a Turkic language.[1] After the ninth century the Chinese no longer speak of them as Khakas, but as Kili-ki-dze, which, according to Klements, is a Chinese pronunciation of the name Kirghis. The time of the greatest development of the Kirghis belongs to the seventh to ninth centuries, i. e. to the second period of Turkic history.

The Uigur are first heard of about the second century B. C., and the Chinese had constant relations with them from that time till the sixteenth century, so that the history of the Uigur runs through all the first three periods of Turkic history. But as the evolution of this important tribe is an essential part of the history of the Turks in Central Asia it will be useful to give here a consecutive account of them in some detail.

The Uigur were known to the Chinese under the names Hao-Hui, Kao-Che, Kan-Hui, Vei-He, U-He, U-Hu, Hon-He, and Hu. It was through the various Asiatic transliterations of the name Uigur that European writers came across it. The first mention of it is found in Ptolemy.[2] In its present form the name seems first to have been used in the Mahometan histories at the beginning of the thirteenth century.[3] Rashid al-Dīn says that in his time the name Uigur was applied to a large group of Turkic tribes living between the sources of the Yenisei and the Selenga. But after this, in fact until the seventeenth century, most of the Eastern Turks were known under this name.

While most Turkic scholars, such as Rashid al-Dīn,

---

[1] N. N. Kosmin, *D. A. Klements and Historical and Ethnographical Research in the Minusinsk Country*, Irkutsk, 1916, p. 7.

[2] *Serica*, Liber IV, p. 16, 3.

[3] Skrine and Ross, *op. cit.*, p. 96.

Abul Ghazi, Kasem Beg, Vambéry, Klaproth, and Schott, derive the name Uigur from a Turkic root, J. I. Schmidt refers it to the Mongolian language, and places the origin of the Uigur people in Tibet.[1] If we accept Professor Radloff's view that the bulk of the Hun-nu, or rather the southern branch of them, were the On-Uigur, then we know that most of them moved towards the west along the steppes lying north of Tian-Shan. But the people who played their part in the history of Central Asia were those of the On-Uigur who remained behind in Eastern Turkestan, especially in the basin of the Tarim, and the Togus-Uigur in the northern part of the present Mongolia. That branch of them who were already established near the Aral Sea in the second century A. D. are often called by their neighbours simply *On* or *Onlar* ('Ten').[2] Later, when after the death of Attila the Hunnic Empire broke into separate tribes, they again assumed their tribal names, viz. On-Uigur, Utigur, Sary-Uigur, Kotrigur, while the name Hun almost disappears. Of these tribes, the On-Uigur are known to have been in the north of the Caucasus in the seventh century, on their way back to Asia.[3]

It is difficult to follow the exact fate of these remnants of the Hun-nu Empire. Presumably a part of them settled among the Finnic tribes of the steppe forest near the Urals, but there is so far very little proof in support of the somewhat vague assumption that the

[1] *Forschungen auf dem Gebiete der Völker Mittelasiens*, St. Petersburg, 1824, p. 95.

[2] Among the Turks a confederation of tribes very often has as its name the number of the tribes composing it, e. g. Uz, 100, probably the same as Ghuz. Radloff, *op. cit.*, p. 128.

[3] Radloff, *op. cit.*, p. 128.

powerful Finnic state of Ugra, which in the tenth and eleventh centuries stretched between the Volga and the Urals, owes its name to the Uigur.

Of the Uigur who stayed in Asia, i. e. the Togus Uigur, we know that in the fifth century they emancipated themselves from the power of the Jwen-Jwen, and created an independent state called by the Chinese Hao-fu. At the time of the hegemony of the Tu-kiu the Uigur also were subdued to them. When in turn the leading rôle among the Turks of Central Asia passed to the Uigur dynasty (A. D. 744–847), the name of the state was again Togus-Uigur ('Nine Tribes'), though it was composed of more than that number of tribes. The capital of the Khagan of the Togus-Uigur was Karakorum on the River Orkhon. Some fourteen Khagans ruled during the period of Uigur power. When, in consequence of the intrigues of the Chinese with the other Turkic tribes, the Uigur dynasty and political power were undermined and finally overthrown at the hands of the Kirghis (A. D. 847), the Uigur culture, which was of a high order, still flourished in Western China, Eastern Turkestan, and the district of Hami. It was in that district that the later Uigur state, under the dynasty of the Arslan Khans, continued its existence, and curiously enough it enjoyed an independent and influential position, since its civilization spread among the nomadic Mongols, and even in Transoxania. This position the Uigur owed solely to their great ability, and to their sedentary agricultural mode of life, which raised them, as it did the Yenisei Kirghis, above their nomadic neighbours. They came under the influence of Buddhism, of Christianity, and later on of Islam. In the western part of the Uigur country a new political power, that of the Islamic Uigur dynasty of Ilek Khan, arose, and its domination spread as far as Bokhara. But the advance of the Kara-Kidan once more overthrew the power of the Uigur, who were obliged to recognize the suzerainty of the Kara-Kidan. These in their turn succumbed before Jinghis Khan. Yet even in the times of the Mongolic rule of Jinghis Khan the Uigur culture did not fail to make itself felt, and still later it was able to produce the well-known Nestorian patriarchs, Rabban Cauma and Jabalaha.[1]

Second Period. It is not easy to trace the history of any other Turkic tribe with the same continuity. Turning to the Tu-kiu, with whom begins the second period of the history of the Turks in Central Asia, we meet with them first about A. D. 550, at the time when the Sassanides were reigning in Persia, when we find them living, under the name of Assena, between the Altai and the Syr Daria.

Professor Parker derives the word Tu-kiu from the Turkic word *durkö*, meaning 'helmet', from the shape of the mountain to which the Turkic tribe of Assena migrated to escape from the despotic rule of the Sien-pi (Tung-hu). They seem, however, not to have been independent even there, since they had to serve the then powerful Jwen-Jwen as workers in iron.[2] They

---

[1] J. B. Chabot, *Histoire du Patriarche Mar Jabalaha III et du Moine Rabban Cauma*, traduite du Syriaque, 1893, vol. I, p. 578.

[2] The Jwen-Jwen (Zhu-Zhu) are possibly the ancestors of the Avars, who appeared in Europe in the sixth century, and forming a wedge between the Eastern and Western Slavs, soon amalgamated with them. Blochet identifies the name Jwen-Jwen with Ib-Ib, Ibim, Ibil, Ibir, from which he derives Sybir, Siberia, and he believes the Jwen-Jwen to be of Tungus stock, and identical with the Sien-pi ('Le Nom des Turcs dans l'Avesta', *J.R.A.S.*, 1915, p. 305).

adopted the name of the mountain Durkö as a tribal name.

There seems to be some confusion as to the geographical position of the mountain thus connected with the rise of the Durkö, Tu-kiu, or Turks. Professor Parker [1] places it not far from the city of Shan-tan in the modern province of Kan-su, which in the sixth century was called Kin-shan, i. e. 'Golden Mountains'. But the birthplace of the Turks is usually held to be the Altai Mountains, which are also called Kin-shan. Since when we first hear of the Turks they are expert metal-workers, it would seem that the Altai, with its incomparable mineral wealth, is more likely to be the Kin-shan of the Chinese sources. All modern archaeological and ethnological investigations support this view.

At the end of the fifth century the Tu-kiu became very prosperous, probably thanks to their metal industry and the richness of the mountains near which they settled, and in A. D. 530 their prince Tumen (Tumin) threw off the yoke of the Jwen-Jwen and soon subjugated all the Turkic states of Central Asia to himself, adopting the title of Il-Khagan.[2] For a short time—

[1] Parker, *op. cit.*, p. 178.

[2] It would seem that the title Khagan (Khan), usually so closely associated with the Turks, and occurring in the Turkic inscriptions of the Orkhon, is not Turkic, but Tungus. But this hypothesis of Blochet holds good only if it be assumed that the Jwen-Jwen were Tungus, and that Tumen used their title after taking the hegemony in Central Asia from them. The title used by the chiefs of the Huns was Chab-gu, and at the time when the Huns were at the height of their power the chiefs of the Jwen-Jwen Tungus adopted the title Chab-gu, until at the beginning of the fifth century they were strong enough to impose on other people their own title of Khagan, which was taken up by Tuimien in 552 (Blochet, *op. cit.*, p. 305).

from the middle of the sixth to the middle of the seventh centuries—the Turks of Central Asia were again united and independent, as at the time of Mété. Soon, however, the eastern part of the empire passed under Chinese domination. Then it again became independent under the Uigur dynasty (A. D. 744-847).

The western part of the Tumen Empire escaped the domination of the Chinese only to fall under Arabian influence, and subsequently under the intellectual supremacy of Iran, during the renaissance of Iranian culture under the dynasty of the Samanides in the tenth century. Thus the splendour of Transoxania at that time was obviously the work of the Persians, not of the Turks, who must be judged rather by the civilization of the Eastern Empires. It was from these Eastern Empires that the main migrations of the Turks of that epoch originated.

From the tenth to the thirteenth centuries the Turks under Karluk[1] and Seljuk advanced into Turkestan, increasing the Turkic population there and destroying the Iranian culture. Some of them pushed on farther towards Asia Minor, while others followed a northern route via the Caspian and Black Sea steppes.

Four main groups of Turkic invaders of Southern Russia can be distinguished between the ninth and the thirteenth centuries: the Pyechenyeg or Kangli, the Khazar (possibly the plural of Khazak, Kaizak), the Uz (Ghuz) or Turki, and the Kuman (Kipchak) or Polovtsy.[2]

[1] A. Vambéry identifies the people of Karluk with the tribe of Naiman, and says that they were Turks (*op. cit.*, p. 15). Cahun would also class the tribe of Naiman, as well as the other Christian tribe, the Kirei, as Turks (*op. cit.*, pp. 208-9), while Skrine and Ross class both Kirei and Naiman as Mongols (*op. cit.*, p. 152).

[2] P. Golubowski, *op. cit.*, p. 56. See p. 46.

When the Khazar appeared in Eastern Europe at the
end of the ninth century they pushed the Pyechenyeg,
who had already been there for about half a century,
towards the west. Again, the Pyechenyeg, as they
were forced westwards, drove before them, into the
Danube region, the Magyars, the Asiatic people who
preceded the Pyechenyeg in their westward migration.

The Kirghis appear again in this second period.
During the supremacy of the Karluk (from the middle
of the eighth to the middle of the twelfth centuries)
they occupied the country stretching from the Yenisei
to the westernmost part of Tian-Shan. Here they
developed almost independently of the Karluk. When
in the twelfth century the Kara-Kidan extended their
power over Tian-Shan, they had great trouble in subjugating the Kirghis.

Third Period. A new era in the history of the
Turks begins with the Jinghis Khan invasions at the
very beginning of the thirteenth century. It is still
a disputed point whether the Jinghis Khan invasions
can be called Mongol, or whether they were largely
Turkic, but carried out under the military supremacy
of a handful of Mongolian steppe nomads. It began,
as Professor Parker says, 'in the humblest way, grew
as it rolled over the plains like a huge snowball,
absorbing almost everything in its way'.[1]

Until then the main struggles of China had been
with the two neighbouring races, the Hiung-nu and the
Tung-hu, and it is somewhat obscure what position
the Mongols occupied towards these races. One thing
is certain, however, that culturally the Mongols were
the most backward people, since the Tung-hu were

[1] Parker, *op. cit.*, p. 303.

always influenced by Chinese civilization and the Hiung-nu by Chinese plus Iranian.[1]   This will explain why Jinghis Khan himself and all his dynasty were under obligations to Turkic culture.   We hear that Jinghis Khan had as preceptor for his sons a Uigur Turk named Tatatungo,[2] and in the religious and cultural toleration he is known to have shown to the conquered countries the preference was given to the Turks.   Two Turkic sovereigns contemporary with Jinghis Khan, Ouang Khan ('Prester John') of the Kirei and Tai-Yang-Khan of the Naïman, were devoted Nestorian Christians.

Thanks to the researches of Rashid al-Dīn, it is

[1] Such would be the view obtained from as independent a standpoint as possible. It must be remembered, however, that Mongolian scholars would be ready to find a much larger Mongol element present in pre-Jinghis Khan times, and would attribute the Jinghis Khan conquests to the genius of the Mongolic race. There are tribes, such as the ancient 'Tatars'—some of them, namely the Otui and Tokus 'Tatars', mentioned in the inscriptions of Bilghe Khan in the Orkhon valley as dependent on Turkic *ela* (confederacy)—whom Mongolian scholars such as Father Jakinth Bichurin would reckon with the Mongols, while the Turkic scholar N. A. Aristoff reckons them with the Turks.   And if a Tungus scholar cared to trace the origin of the name Tatar (a sub-division of Tatan) in the Chinese annals as translated by Bichurin, he would find that the name Tatan was adopted in the ninth century by a branch of the Mo-ho (Mokho) who were descendants of Sushen and Ilu, now recognized as being of Tungus race.   In the twelfth century the Tatan confederacy was composed of Mongol, Khere, Taigut, and Tatar tribes.   Bichurin gives Jinghis Khan as one of the four princes belonging to it.   (W. Thomsen, 'On the Orkhon and Yenisei Monuments with Inscriptions', *J. Min. Educ.*, June, 1898; J. Bichurin, *Notes on Mongolia*, vol. II, pt. iii, pp. 174-7; N. A. Aristoff, 'Notes on the Ethnic Composition of the Turkic Tribes and Nations', *L. A. T.*, 1896, III and IV, pp. 277-456.)

[2] Skrine and Ross, *op. cit.*, p. 155.

possible to obtain a clear idea of the tribes inhabiting Central Asia in his time. From his knowledge of them, and the information he collected, he divides them into three groups : (1) the Ogus Turks and their kindred, of purely Turkic blood; (2) the tribes which were taken for Mongols in the thirteenth century, but who were in fact Mongolized Turks; (3) the tribes of purely Mongol blood, who lived on the eastern and northern outskirts of the Turkic lands.[1]   Hence the tribes called pure Turks by Rashid al-Din probably inhabited the lands which are known to have recovered their Turkic features after the death of Jinghis Khan.

Of the states that arose after the death of Jinghis Khan in 1227 the most Turkic were the Middle Empire (Eastern and Western Turkestan), ruled over by his son Jagatai and his descendants, and Dasht-i-Kipchak, i. e. the country of the lower Volga, the North Caspian Steppes, the Aral Steppes, and Western Siberia, ruled over by another son, Juji, and his descendants.

Turkic in feeling and in culture as were Jagatai and his line, they were succeeded in 1360 by Timur, a chief of Moghulistan, purely Turkic in blood as in sympathies, who founded the brilliant Timurid dynasty.[2] ' The annals of this house were rendered illustrious by the names of poets, philosophers, and theologians which are still household words throughout the East.'[3] Among its famous members was the great general, philosopher, and writer Mirza Baber, whose Memoirs still remain as a monument in the Jagatai language.[4]

[1] Radloff, *Concerning the Uigur*, p. 1.
[2] L. Cahun (*op. cit.*) takes Timur to be a descendant of Jagatai.
[3] Skrine and Ross, *op. cit.*, p. 180.
[4] See p. 27.

The splendour of the Timurids was checked by the advance of the Kaizak-Usbegs at the end of the fifteenth and the beginning of the sixteenth centuries. These brought new blood, partly Turanian, partly Mongol, into a region which was becoming Iranized. The Usbegs, who claimed descent from Jinghis Khan through his son Juji, appeared in Transoxania about the time when the Turko-Tatars were losing their dominion over Muscovite Russia, forming, as it were, a returning wave of Turks, whose three hundred years of mastery in Eastern Europe proved a failure, in that they neither entirely subdued their Russian foes, nor entirely assimilated themselves with them.

The history of the Usbegs in Transoxania is the history of three separate Khanates, those of Bokhara, Khiva, and Kokand, for the Usbeg conquerors were never strong enough to form an empire equal to that of the Timurids or of Jinghis Khan, or perhaps had not enough of the spirit of unity and the power of organization so strongly developed among the Timurids to achieve such a task.

The Turks of the Altai and Western Siberia, who had succumbed to the power of Jinghis Khan after but slight resistance, became independent after the fall of the Golden Horde. Their western branch started an independent state along the River Ishim. In the middle of the fourteenth century they divided into two, one with its capital at Chingi-Tura (now Tiumien), and later at Isker (Sybir), and the other along the River Ishim. In the fifteenth century Khan Kuchum moved with his Kaizak from the Aral-Caspian steppes and overran both empires, creating a great Siberian Khanate from the Urals to the left tributaries of the Ob. In 1583

his capital Isker fell into the hands of the Cossacks
under Yermak.

Another Turkic state, which had also become independent after the death of Jinghis Khan, offered more
resistance to the Russians than did the Khanate of
Kuchum. This was a state of the Kirghis, or rather
a confederacy of four states,[1] including among its
kyshtymy (subjects, slaves) many Finnic and Samoyedic
peoples.

Very little is heard of the Kirghis from the thirteenth
to the fifteenth century. They appear again in the
fifteenth century at the time of the fall of the Jagatai
dynasty, when it is recorded that the Kaizak population
was enlarged by new additions from the Kangli and
Kipchak tribes. In the seventeenth century the Kirghis,
emancipated from the rule of the Jagatai, were employ-
ing the Kaizak in their fights against the Mongol
Kalmuck. It was probably then that the Kirghis and
the Kaizak began to intermix, and as the result of this
struggle with the Kalmuck part of the Kirghis and the
Kaizak migrated to Ferghana.

At the end of the sixteenth and the beginning of the
seventeenth centuries the Kirghis state on the Yenisei,
though its position was not to be compared with what
it was in the most flourishing period from the seventh
to the tenth centuries, still carried on the tradition of
the old Khakas, and was an agricultural state, highly
organized politically, if not strong in a military sense.
The first Russians to invade the Kirghis state in the
sixteenth and seventeenth centuries, namely the Cossacks
from Tomsk, made a distinction between these Kirghis

[1] The four states were Altir, Altisar, Isar, and Tuba or Tubiu.
(N. N. Kosmin, *op. cit.*, pp. 14-21. See also *Historical Documents*,
published by the Imperial Archaeological Commission.)

and the Kaizak whom they came across in their conquest of the Kuchum Khanate.[1] It was only subsequently that the Kaizak were named by the Russians Kirghis-Kaizak, and that the Kirghis of Yenisei, after their migration southwards before the Russian advance, became known as the Burut-Kirghis and the Kara-Kirghis.

Fourth Period. The fourth and last epoch in the history of the Turks in Central Asia begins with the Russian conquest of a more regular character than the exploits of the Volga Cossacks. In the north it began with the foundation of Tomsk (1604) on land wrung from the Kuchum Khanate, and it ended in 1647 with the foundation of Okhotsk on the Pacific. In the south the first milestone of the Russian advance was the destruction of the Khanate of Kazan in 1552; the Khanate of Astrakhan shared its fate in 1556. For a moment the Russian success was checked by the rising of the Yaik Cossacks, to whose efforts the previous advance was largely due. After the suppression of their rising these Cossacks, renamed the Ural Cossacks, again became a Russian weapon, moving against the Kaizak and the Turkic tribes of the steppes. Although the Kaizak were nominally subjugated in 1734 they were not really conquered until Russia became master of Turkestan, and there was a great rising against Russia in 1840, when Kenissari, the Sultan of the Great Orda, made another attempt to unite the Kaizak into one great independent nation. In 1864 the Russians succeeded in encircling the Kaizak territories with a line of military defences, thus cutting them

[1] See M. A. Czaplicka, 'The Evolution of the Cossack Communities', *J. Centr. As. S.*, May, 1918.

off from the other Central Asiatic powers, just as in the eighteenth century they succeeded in encircling the Finno-Turkic nation of the Bashkir between the Volga and the Urals.

The first Turkic intellectual centre to fall into Russian hands was Tashkent in 1865, and three years later the capital of the Iranian Turks, Samarkand (known to the Greeks as Marakanda, and captured by Alexander the Great in the fourth century B. C.), lost its independence. This decided the fate of Bokhara, which became a dependent state, and a little later, in 1875, Khiva succumbed also. The Khanate of Kokand, conquered in 1875, was renamed the Ferghana Territory. The next tribe to be subdued was the Turkomans, whose courageous and obstinate defence was broken by the fall of Gheok-Tepe in 1881. In 1895 the eastern boundary of Russian territory was fixed at the Pamir.

The Central Asiatic territories were never colonized to the same extent as Siberia, or even the Caspian Steppe country; they might be called dependencies rather than colonies. Economically during the last two decades these provinces have begun to increase their output of cotton, fruit, and other local products, but intellectually the Iranian Turks have vegetated in the antiquated remnants of the Arabo-Persian civilizations, influenced gradually by the slow, heavy progress of Russian culture. The Turanian Turks, in much greater political subjection than the Iranian, and economically entirely dependent on Russian colonization, have kept their primitive culture from spurious elements, either Arabo-Persian or Chinese, but they are, of all the Turks, the most amenable to the influence of Russian peasant life.

Archaeology.

Special attention is now being given by scholars to the archaeological remains of Turan, especially to those of Southern Siberia and Northern Mongolia. Although it is only recently that organized investigations have been carried out, they were already known to the early Russian travellers, for some mention of them is made by Witsen, who visited this region in 1692, while the next traveller, Dr. Messerschmidt (1720), speaks of the existence among the Russian settlers of the 'industry' of plundering the old graves for the sake of the iron, bronze and particularly gold objects found in them. The men engaged in this, called *bugrovshchiki*, would organize parties of between two and three hundred, and start on their expedition in the 'season of the hunter', i. e. in the spring, and return with their plunder in the autumn, living during the winter on the proceeds.

The fame of this old metal-work reached Peter the Great—the same emperor who, as the legend runs, used to summon Siberian shamans to his court. He issued a Ukaz prohibiting plundering, and ordered the local officials to purchase such objects. Though a certain number of them have thus been saved for European museums, plundering had not ceased even in the summer of 1915, when the author saw old bronze and iron in common use among the Russian settlers.

The early travellers give merely descriptive accounts, and archaeological investigations did not begin until the nineteenth century. Among those whose energies have been thus employed are such earnest workers as Radloff, Aspelin, Klements, Yadrintseff, Adrianoff, Tallgren, and Gränö.

To pass now to a short review of these antiquities. Though they consist chiefly of metal cultures, some mention must be made of the pre-metal remains.

There are remnants of Stone Age stations along the southern Yenisei and its tributaries, between Krasnoyarsk and Minusinsk, but nearer to Krasnoyarsk than to Minusinsk. According to Adrianoff[1] they may be ascribed to the Neolithic period, but another Russian scholar, Savyenkoff, would place them in the Palaeolithic period.[2] It seems, however, fairly certain that although some of the implements found by Savyenkoff in Bazaikha, on Mount Afontova near Krasnoyarsk, and in other places, may be of Palaeolithic type (according to the catalogue of the Peter the Great Museum in Petrograd they are of Mousterian and Aurignacian types), the stations are more accurately described as Neolithic. Many of them might be called kitchen-middens. In any case the Stone Age remains lie outside the scope of this essay, though stone implements have been found together with the bronze, copper, and gold objects of the succeeding age, and even with objects of the Iron Age.

Burial-mounds, called kurgans, are spread in hundreds and thousands from the River Irtish to the River Orkhon. Judging from the objects found in these kurgans they belong either to the Bronze or to the Iron Age. Connected with the kurgans are the stone figures called by the Russians *baby* (sing. *baba*), and by the Turkic natives *koyotash*, and also the stone

---

[1] A. V. Adrianoff, *Sketches of the Minusinsk Country*, 1904.
[2] I. T. Savyenkoff, *The Stone Age in the Minusinsk Country*, 1896, and *The Palaeolithic Epoch in the Neighbourhood of Krasnoyarsk*, 1892.

memorial tablets covered with inscriptions in the Old Turkic language, called Uigur, many of which have now been deciphered. Independently of these inscriptions, there are on the cliffs and rocks of this region traces of pictographic writings, so far uninterpreted.[1] Russian investigators call the Old Turkic characters 'runic inscriptions', and the pictographs *pisanitsy*. In addition to all this, there are remnants of irrigation canals, copper-mines, and fortresses, these last called by the natives *shibe*.

Generally speaking, all these antiquities of the Metal Ages, known by the Russians under the vague appellations of 'Chud' or 'Tuba' remains, fall into two groups:

1. Remains of the Bronze Age, including copper and gold objects, the burial masks, the remnants of mines, and some of the pictographs.

2. Remains of the Iron Age, with which must be reckoned the stone memorial tablets with inscriptions, the stone figures, and the remnants of fortresses.

The Bronze Age of this region is divided by Tallgren[2] into the following periods:

I. Period dating (possibly from about 3000 B.C.) to 1000 B.C. No kurgans of this period are yet known. Chief implements : daggers, light

[1] N. S. Voronyeis, 'Rock Pictures found on the frontier of Turgai and Syr Daria Territories along the River Lack-Pay', *Russ. Anthr. J.*, 1916, Nos. iii and iv, pp. 57-61 ; A. V. Adrianoff, 'Preliminary Information regarding the Pisanitsy collected in the Minusinsk Country in summer 1907', *Bull. Russ. Committee*, 1908, No. viii, p. 37.

[2] A. M. Tallgren, *Collection Tovostine*, Helsingfors, 1917, p. 20.

spears, and socketed celts. Ornament purely geometric.

II. Period dating between 1000 and 500 B. C. No kurgans of this period are yet known. Chief implements : socketed double - looped celts, daggers, knives in great number. Ornament partly geometric, partly zoomorphic. Figures of animals as handles of daggers.

III. Period after 500 B. C. Kurgans, or burial-places surrrounded by quadrangular stones. Ornament chiefly zoomorphic ; towards the end of the period vegetable ornament appears. Contact with Scythian art is strongly noticeable.

The majority of the bronze objects found in this region belong to the third period. Here also must be placed the collection of knives of various shapes almost unknown in Scythia. A common type is a knife with a well-formed ring at the end, recalling the Chinese knife which degenerated into the round copper ' cash ', but to the same period belongs a type of dagger with a heart-shaped guard, reminiscent of the Scythic dagger of Eastern Europe.

As far as the Iron Age is concerned, its place is usually defined by the dates of the historical events mentioned in the inscriptions. The greater number of the graves of this period are estimated to belong to the time between the sixth and seventh centuries A. D. But the Iron Age must have started much earlier, as we know from the Chinese histories that in the second century B. C. the Hiung-nu, then living to the north of the Chinese, were using iron implements.[1] Judging from the forms of the implements, the early Iron Age

[1] A. V. Adrianoff, *Sketches of the Minusinsk Country*, p. 5.

of this region seems to be a continuation of the Bronze Age in another material. It is only in the late Iron period that new forms appear,[1] and hence it is probable that while the early Iron was evolved by the people responsible for the Bronze culture, the late Iron culture may have been brought by some new-comers, possibly, though not necessarily, of another race.

The honour of having first deciphered the Old Turkic inscriptions belongs to the Danish scholar Professor Vilhelm Thomsen, of Copenhagen,[2] working in 1893, and the investigation was continued by Professor Wilhelm Radloff of Petrograd[3] from 1894 onwards.

The Yenisei inscriptions are chiefly funeral tributes to deceased Khans or *Khagans* of the 'Kyrgys' (Kirghis); those of the River Orkhon in North-West Mongolia, which, judging from the more finished form of the writing, are of later date, contain historical and ethnographical information, and are ascribed to the Tu-kiu. Thus our knowledge of the Turanian Turks, which has been obtained by analysing the often confusing annals

---

[1] W. W. Radloff, 'Siberian Antiquities', *Materials for the Archaeology of Russia*, St. Petersburg, 1888, 1891, 1894, 1902; *Aus Sibirien*, vol. II, chap. vii; F. R. Martin, *L'Âge du bronze au musée de Minoussinsk*, Stockholm, 1893; D. A. Klements, *Antiquities of the Minusinsk Museum. The Remains of the Metal Ages*, Tomsk, 1886; I. P. Kuznietsoff-Krasnoyarski, *The Minusinsk Antiquities, Copper, Bronze, and Transitional Periods*, Tomsk, 1908; J. R. Aspelin, *Antiquités du Nord Finno-Ougrien*, Helsingfors, 1877.

[2] *Inscriptions de l'Iénissei recueillies et publiées par la Société Finlandaise d'Archéologie*, 1889; *Inscriptions de l'Orkhon recueillies par l'expédition finnoise 1890 et publiées par la Société Finno-Ougrienne*, 1892; V. Thomsen, 'Inscriptions de l'Orkhon déchiffrées', *Mém. Soc. Fin.-Ougr.*, V; N. Yadrintseff, *Ancient Monuments and Inscriptions in Siberia*, Literary Collection, 1885.

[3] W. W. Radloff, P. Melioranski, &c., *Collection of Documents of the Orkhon Expedition*, 1897.

of Chinese historians, has been amplified, and difficult points to some extent cleared up, by the interpretation of these inscriptions.

The older type of inscriptions is engraved; the later type is written on the stone, in some cases even in colours, but the art of using colours was apparently introduced by the Mongols and the Chinese. The Orkhon inscriptions are bilingual, the second language being Chinese.

The richest collections of objects of both Bronze and Iron cultures are to be found in the Minusinsk Museum, and in the Petrograd and Moscow Museums. Next to these come the Museums of Tomsk and Krasnoyarsk. The beginning of the excavation of the kurgans dates from about 1881; among the last thorough investigations are those of A. M. Tallgren (1915) in the Minusinsk region, and of A. V. Adrianoff in the Uriankhai country.

Several attempts have been made to classify the various types of kurgans. Radloff[1] distinguishes as many as ten types; these, however, are not sufficiently clearly differentiated to admit of their being referred to ten distinct cultures. A broader division, based on the more apparent external differences between them, is into two groups. The graves of the first group have their surface level with the surface of the ground, and are surrounded by quadrangular stone slabs. They are usually associated with the Bronze culture, and the implements they contain are such as would be characteristic of a more or less settled population. The graves of the second group are covered with a raised mound, and are often surrounded by high slabs of stone resembling monoliths, which sometimes reach a height

[1] W. W. Radloff, *Aus Sibirien*, vol. II, pp. 68-143.

of ten feet. These graves are usually associated with the Iron Age, and contain a large number of weapons of war. To the former type may be added the large mounds, called by the local natives *Chaa-tas*, which are collective graves, but usually contain one grave situated a little apart from the others, and showing much more finished workmanship. Graves of the first type are found especially on the banks of the upper Yenisei, and in the Abakan and Minusinsk Steppes. Graves of the second type occur in the basins of the Irtish and the Tobol, and also side by side with those of the first type in the Abakan and Minusinsk Steppes, so that the classification cannot be pressed too far. Until further investigations provide sufficient ground for making a more detailed division, Tallgren, following Castrén and Aspelin, proposes to keep to this dual grouping.[1]

It is not possible in this essay to go into further details with regard to the archaeology of this region, but, accepting the conclusions of the archaeologists, an endeavour will be made to trace the course of culture contact during the Bronze and Iron Ages, beginning with a consideration of the question how far the Siberian culture can be compared with similar cultures of corresponding periods elsewhere.

As we know, the kurgans of the later, i.e. the Iron Period, are not confined to these regions, but stretch all along Southern and Central Russia, Lithuania, and Poland, as far as the Vistula. Yet the kurgans of the Irtish-Orkhon region have their own characteristic features, which permit of their being treated separately.

As to the other centres of the Bronze culture, the Kama-Ural centre is sometimes considered to be the prolongation of the Minusinsk centre. But Tallgren,

[1] Tallgren, *op. cit.*, p. 14.

after comparing the objects found in both regions, comes to the conclusion that the two groups are quite independent, and that what features they have in common are due to the fact that they were both influenced by the same civilization from the south and west.[1] E. H. Minns lays stress on the resemblance between the Bronze culture of Minusinsk and that of the Scythians.[2] While agreeing with Minns that the resemblance is considerable, Tallgren sees also a great difference, namely, that the Iranian influence coming from Turkestan at that time was stronger in Turan than in Scythia. In any case it is not the Scythian bronze that influenced the Minusinsk bronze, but rather the reverse.[3]

Just as the late Professor Donner looked upon the region of the ancient Sogdia, Bactris, and Iran as possibly hiding the earliest form of the Yenisei inscriptions, Tallgren looks upon it as the place where the Bronze culture of Minusinsk originated. From this archaeological evidence it would seem that the people of Turan took their knowledge of bronze-working from

[1] Tallgren, op. cit., p. 9.

[2] Ellis H. Minns, Scythians and Greeks, p. 241: 'The resemblances between the culture I have called Scythic and that of the early inhabitants of Siberia ... are so great that it is impossible to treat the archaeology of South Russia without touching that of Siberia.' Thus Minns approaches the question of the Siberian remains from the study of Scythic remains, while Tallgren adopts the opposite method of taking the Minusinsk culture as the standard and comparing the other with it. This is the method that I have tried to follow in ethnographical questions, for it is always safer to define the Asiats in Asia before attempting to define the Asiats who invaded Europe. Recently a book appeared (J. Strzygowski, Altai-Iran und Völkerwanderung, Leipzig, 1917) which on its purely archaeological merit deserves to be placed next to Tallgren's and Minns's valuable contributions, but the tendency of the author is strikingly Pan-German, and this prevents him from confining the subject within its proper geographical limits.

[3] Tallgren, op. cit., p. 11.

Iranian Turkestan, and developed it themselves. The Chinese influence, which was so powerful in the Iron Age, is not so noticeable in the Bronze Age. Thus, for instance, zinc, which enters into the composition of the bronze implements of Minusinsk,[1] does not occur in the bronze of China.[2] One of the most remarkable resemblances emphasized by Tallgren is that between the Minusinsk bronze and the products of the La Tène Celtic civilization. This is especially significant in the decorative motives, such as the geometrical patterns and the form of the handles of daggers.[3]

A few words must be said about the attempts at the representation of human figures in this old culture of the Minusinsk region. While geometric, zoomorphic, and, later on, plant ornament reaches a high stage of development, representations of the human form are rare and obscure. In the Bronze Age we find scarcely any. One of the few which were found forms the handle of a knife, and recalls a human figure now in the collection of the British Museum. Perhaps the most successful attempts at giving an idea of the human face are the burial masks found in some kurgany associated with the late Bronze Age, especially the gypsum casts.

Even during the Iron Age little progress is made in this form of ornamentation, but from this era onwards we have numerous stone figures, whose object is probably the same as that of the masks of the earlier period,

[1] H. Struwe, 'Analyse verschiedener antiken Bronzen und Eisen aus Abakan und Jenissei', *Bull. I. A. S.*, St. Petersburg, 1866, X, pp. 282-9; Brandenburg and Ivanowski, *Transactions of the Commission for the Chemical Technical Analysis of Ancient Bronze*, St. Petersburg, 1882.

[2] Tallgren, *op. cit.*, p. 34.

[3] *Ibid.*, p. 11.

namely, to picture the dead person.   The figures, some
of which reach a height of three to four feet, are made
of rude stone blocks, and almost all of them are
characterized by the curious position of the hands,
clasping in front a cup, or cup-like object.   While the
general appearance of the figure is highly conventional-
ized, the faces differ greatly.   They are of both sexes;
in fact the female sex predominates.   Only some of them
show Mongolian traits.   Stone figures of similar appearance are found in Southern Russia, where they coincide
with the belt known for its Scythic remains.   These,
however, are of much later date, since we know that
some of the Turkic tribes who invaded Russia before
the time of Jinghis Khan, such, for instance, as the
Polovtsy (Cumans), were in the habit of erecting such
figures.[1]   Though the custom of placing a small wooden
figure of the deceased on the grave is known to many
Turkic and Finnic tribes in Siberia, these old stones
are taken by the modern natives for images of gods,
and sacrifices are often offered to them.

The burial masks have, so far as is known at present,
a very limited distribution.   They have been found on
Tagara Island quite close to Minusinsk, and at a spot
about sixty versts to the south-east (Salt Lake).[2]   Altogether not more than twenty masks are known from
this region.   But some have been found also in the
Graeco-Scythic tombs of the Crimea at Glinishche.
The masks are either white or coloured, and are
found associated with the skull, or, in cases where the

[1] Minns, *op. cit.*, p. 240.
[2] K. I. Goroshchenko, 'Burial masks of gypsum and a special
type of trepanation in the Kurgans of the Minusinsk District',
Bull. of Tenth Arch. Congress in Riga, 1896, p. 4.

skull is missing, separately on a specially erected stone slab.   In some cases it seems likely that the masks had been broken or partially burnt, together with other objects belonging to the dead person.   In one kurgan at Salt Lake we find, besides the plaster covering the skull, clay and gypsum covering the first five vertebrae also; in this case the mask has not been taken from the face of the deceased, but covers the skull on a foundation of clay moulded to imitate the features. Thus we have to deal with two types of mask in this region.   One is a plaster cast of gypsum, taken from the face of the deceased by the modern method of making a mould and taking a cast from it.   Such masks are typical of the kurgans of Tagara Island, and are associated with the custom of burning the body and burying the ashes, or of burying the whole corpse in a standing position.   The ashes are often buried along-side of the skull and the mask, and obviously the mask must have been taken immediately after death.

The other type, found in the kurgans called *Chaa-tas,* or communal kurgans, near the Salt Lake, is, properly speaking, not a mask but an artificial reconstruction of the face of the deceased superimposed upon the skeleton.   This type is connected with the custom of burying the skeleton in a standing position,[1] and it must be supposed, therefore, that after death the corpse was left either outside the kurgan or in a temporary grave until the flesh had completely disappeared from the bones.[2]   And indeed this custom corresponds to what we know from Chinese and Greek writers about the burial customs of the old Turks.   ' If a man die in spring or summer they wait for the leaves to fall,

[1] Goroshchenko, *op. cit.*, p. 3.   [2] *Ibid.*, p. 9.

if in autumn or winter they wait for leaves and flowers to come out. Then they dig a ditch and bury him.'[1] In fact, in the difficult task of disentangling the Hiung-nu (Turks) and the Tung-hu (Tungus) tribes in the Chinese annals, one of the safest guides is the burial customs of these peoples, since the Tung-hu buried their dead, as they do sometimes now, on a high platform, while the Hiung-nu left the body in the tent or outside the tent for a long time. To this custom is due the fact that so few kurgans include the complete skeleton. The frequent absence of the skull, where the mask replaces it, may, however, be explained by the custom of keeping the skull among the living as a memento.

Moreover, the fact that some of the skulls found in the same communal kurgans have undergone post-humous trepanning in the region of the temple suggests that the skull was not left for the flesh on it to decay naturally, but that artificial means were employed to prepare it for the final burial ceremony. After the skull had been thus cleaned of all its soft tissues, all the openings were plugged with clay, and then the features of the face were reconstructed. In most cases a layer of clay covers the calvaria also. Sometimes a coating of gypsum is put on the top of the clay.

The artificial method of cleaning the skull and then reconstructing the features, so well known among various primitives of Melanesia and, as has been pointed out to me by Mr. Henry Balfour, also of Mexico, might very well be taken for the genuine custom of the aborigines of the country, which were doubtless of Turkic race, while the more refined

[1] Minns, *op. cit.*, p. 94.

gypsum casts may have been introduced by the people who brought the Bronze culture to this region.   In support of the first part of this statement it is worthy of mention that Father Bichurin, whose translations of the Chinese annals have been made use of extensively in this investigation, says that a people living in Southern Mongolia, and possibly contemporary with the construction of these kurgans, had the custom of 'tearing off the skin from the dead', which seems to be a direct reference to this second mode of burial as being prevalent in Central Asia.[1]

Goroshchenko, the Siberian anthropologist to whose thorough study of the osteology of the kurgans the author is indebted, thinks that the masks of the Chaa-tas type developed out of the casts of the Tagara type. But if we consider the archaeological remains there seems to be very little to show the difference in age between these two groups of kurgans, both of them differing from other Bronze Age kurgans in this, that they include both bronze and iron implements.[2]   They should therefore be ascribed to the late Bronze Age type.

There is no doubt that the clear and refined features of the masks of the Tagara type, some of which can be seen in the Helsingfors and Moscow Museums, approach the 'Aryan' type—to retain this unsatisfactory but convenient term—while the masks of the Chaa-tas, with broader face and coarse features, approach the Mongolian type.   But it is possible that the difference is merely superficial, and is explained by the different

[1] Father Jakinth Bichurin, *Collection of Information concerning Peoples living in Central Asia*, vol. III, pp. 197-9.
[2] K. I. Goroshchenko, *Skulls from the Kurgans of the Minusinsk District*, 1900, pp. 8-9.

method of construction. The face as reconstructed on a skull would naturally be coarser than the mask taken from a face, unless of course the constructor were a master more skilled in the moulding of human features than was the man of the Bronze Age of Minusinsk.

It is noteworthy that the craniometric measurements of skulls found in these kurgans do not give us evidence to support the theory of two distinct physical races. The results of these measurements are summed up by Goroshchenko as follows:[1] that the type of these skulls shows great uniformity with that of other Bronze Age skulls, that they resemble the skulls of the older kurgans of the Moscow Government, and that they do not correspond with any measurements of skulls on living people of the modern population of this region, whether Mongol or Turk. The most striking feature of these skulls is their long-headedness. Out of 96 skulls of the kurgans of the Minusinsk region, 42 were dolicho-cephalic and 21 sub-dolichocephalic.[2]

This brings us to this most unsettled problem: the definition of the physique of the Turks of Central Asia.

[1] Goroshchenko, *op. cit.*, pp. 7-8.
[2] *Ibid.*, p. 30. The measurements of the male skulls of the two groups of kurgans where the masks were found give the following result (Table II):

Cephalic Index.

Tagara Kurgans . . . . 74.6 (16 measurements)
Chaa-tas . . . . 73.2 (13   „   )

Horizontal Circumference.

Tagara Kurgans . . . . 522 (18 measurements)
Chaa-tas . . . . 527 (14   „   )

Altitudinal (Height) Index.

Tagara Kurgans . . . . 76 (6 measurements)
Chaa-tas . . . . 72.5 (10   „   )

As has been said in dealing with the history and archaeology, the mention of fair-haired and blue-eyed people[1] leads us to the conclusion that this type must have entered into the composition of the modern Turk of Central Asia. Besides, nothing else was to be expected in the region of Altai and Sayan, considering how close this region is to the Amu-Daria (Oxus) and Tarim valleys, where it is fairly certain that the brachy-cephalic Alpine type of Western Europe originated. Whoever studies the altogether insufficient anthropometric data of Central Asia must necessarily wonder with Joyce 'whether indeed the race is not the result of an admixture in varying proportion, according to locality, of Aryan and Mongol stocks'.[2] Even if we agree that the Central Asiatic Turks have their individuality historically and ethnologically, this is not necessarily associated with a distinct physical race. And yet, although the amount of research as yet accomplished, and perhaps also the present state of anthropology, is not such as to justify us in speaking of a separate Turkic race or sub-race, there seems to be some national type, or types, which we can distinguish in the Turks when we meet them outside their proper territory. Thus, the Yakut, who have now inhabited the Arctic region for several hundred years, stand out amongst the other Arctic peoples on account of what might be called their Southern type. The admixture of the 'Tatar' blood of Southern Yenisei in the Samoyed of the Ob is also clearly apparent.

[1] A. V. Adrianoff, *Sketches of the Minusinsk Country*, p. 7 ; G. E. Grum-Grzymailo, *Description of Travels in Western China*, ch. viii, 1896-7.

[2] T. A. Joyce, 'On the Physical Anthropology of the Oases of Khotan and Keriya', *J. A. I.*, 1903, vol. XXXIII, p. 315.

Among the earliest investigators of the anthropology of Central Asia is the well-known Hungarian scholar Ujfalvy.[1] Then there should be mentioned Grenard,[2] Troll,[3] Shishoff,[4] and Goroshchenko.[5] The Russian anthropologist Ivanowski,[6] who is responsible for a compilation containing a greater number of anthropometric data than that of any other living anthropologist, distinguishes what he calls the Central Asiatic anthropological type. He defines its characteristics as follows: dark-coloured hair and eyes, light hair and eyes being exceptional; stature of the majority medium, with a tendency towards high stature among the Kaizak of the Middle Orda, the town Taranchi, and some Sarts; the head is brachycephalic (broad-headed) or hyperbrachycephalic; the nose among the majority is leptorrhine (narrow), broad noses being met with chiefly among the Kaizak of the Middle Orda; the trunk is long and the chest dimensions are medium, with a tendency to very small. Taking this as the standard, we see that the Kara-Kirghis differ from it by being

[1] C. E. Ujfalvy, *Essai d'une Carte ethnographique de l'Asie centrale; Les Aryens au nord et au sud de l'Hindou Kouch*, 1896; *Expédition scientifique en Russie, Sibérie et dans le Turkestan*, 1878.

[2] F. Grenard, 'Le Turkestan et le Tibet', in *Mission scientifique dans la Haute Asie*, 1890–5; J. L. Dutrueil de Rhins, pt. II.

[3] Troll, 'Individual-Aufnahmen central-asiatischer Eingeborner', *Z. f. E.*, 1890, pt. iii.

[4] A. Shishoff, *The Sarts*, vol. III, Anthropology, 1905.

[5] K. I. Goroshchenko and A. A. Ivanowski, 'The Natives of the Yenisei', *Russ. Anthr. J.*, 1907, Nos. i, ii; K. I. Goroshchenko, 'Materials for the anthropology of Siberia', *Bull. Krasn. S. E. Sib. Sect. I. R. G. S.*, vol. I, No. ii, 1905.

[6] A. A. Ivanowski, *Anthropological Composition of the Population of Russia*, 1904, pp. 207–8; and *Population of the World*, 1911, pp. 391–2.

less dark in colouring, taller, with a longer face; the Yakut approach nearer in type to the Mongol-Buriat; while the 'Tatars' of Southern Yenisei stand nearer to the Samoyed.[1] This similarity must naturally be attributed to later admixture.

There are no anthropometric data regarding the various Altaian Turks (namely, the Chern 'Tatars', Kumandints, Teleut, Teles, Altaian Oirot, same as Altai Kalmuck, and the Chu Telengit). We have, however, most valuable observations about their physical type by the late Siberian scholar Yadrintseff. In an essay

[1] Some of the chief measurements of the Turks of Central Asia, based on the work of Ivanowski (*Population of the World*) and Joyce (*op. cit.*):

Tribe.	Stature (medium).	Ceph. Ind.	Height Index.	Full-face Index.	Nasal Index.	Authority.
Taranchi	(374) 1646	(368) 86.4	(107) 74.5			Ujf.
Sarts	(238) 1677	(223) 83.6			(104) 61.5	Blag. / Shi. / Troll
Kaizak and Kipchak	(418) 1644	(405) 87.0		Ivanowski's index is from margin of hair to mental.	(172) 68.9	Tr. / Ujf.
Usbegs	(292) 1675	(282) 86.1			(13) 69.0	Tr. / Ujf.
Kara-Kirghis	(83) 1676	(78) 85.9			(47) 75.9	Tr. / Ujf.
Soyot	(72) 1597		(72) 71.4		(72) 70.2	Goros. / Ivan.
Sagai	(60) 1620	(60) 80.8			(60) 73.0	Goros. / Ivan.
Kachints	(42) 1619	(34) 82.4			(34) 78.0	Goros. / Ivan.
Beltir	(78) 1607	(74) 79.5			(73) 78.0	Goros. / Ivan.
Khotanese	(19) 1645	(22) 84.4		(23) 87.4	(23) 71.7	Stein
Keriyans	(15) 1589	(16) 86.9		(16) 82.4	(16) 81.1	Stein

For the measurements of the Yakut see 'Report of the Expedition to the Yenisei', by M. A. Czaplicka and H. U. Hall (to be published shortly).

on the Altaians, published in 1881,[1] he says that many Altaians who have as yet had no contact with the colonists resemble in their type the Caucasians (Aryans). Blue eyes, chestnut and fair hair, and non-prominent cheek-bones are often met with, especially among the Kumandints.[2] And yet no record is known that the Aryans ever spread as far as the Altai Mountains; on the other hand, we know of the close association of the Turkic race with this region. The only plausible suggestion, therefore, is that the prehistoric contact of the Turks and Aryans, which brought the knowledge of bronze to Turan, affected the physical type of the Asiatic Turks just as it affected their nomad life, leading them to settle down to agriculture.

When remains of two archaeological periods are found in one place the popular conclusion is that the later culture was brought to that place by the later comers. For a long time the archaeology of the Minusinsk district was treated in accordance with this rule. The Bronze period of the region was ascribed to some local autochthonous people. They were said to be peaceful, since there are hardly any weapons among the remains of this period. From the abundant remains of implements connected with agriculture and mining they were put down as agriculturists and miners, and finally they were described as democratic, because we find at that time communal graves and graves of common people generally, while in the Iron Age it is mostly the chiefs who enjoyed the privilege of burial in a kurgan. On the other hand, the Iron Age people were supposed

---

[1] N. M. Yadrintseff, 'On the Altaians and the Chern Tatars', *Bull. I. R. G. S.*, 1881.

[2] *Ibid.*, pp. 5–7.

to have been warlike nomads, who left behind them many weapons of war, who lived on their horses, and who were more or less like the nomad Scythians of the Greeks. The Bronze Age people are often set down as Finno-Samoyedic, or vaguely as Palaeo-Yeniseians, while the Iron Age people are set down as Turks. But a closer study of the region shows that the problem is not yet solved, and it may be stated as follows : Were the Bronze Age people quite different from the Iron Age people, and what is the relation of either or both of them to the remnants of the Turanians now living in this region ?

The solution of this problem has usually been sought by the historical method of investigation, that is to say, by quoting disconnected facts obtained from free translations of the Chinese writers, who could not, of course, have a very intimate acquaintance with regions so far away. Again, in dealing with the present natives it has usually been linguistic considerations that have been taken as a basis for determining racial affinities.[1] But with all respect to the Chinese annals (which may perhaps one day be given to Europe in a full and authoritative translation), it would seem that as we are now able to read the history of these people from their archaeology and from their own inscriptions, it is possible to adopt an archaeological method, and to compare the results thus obtained with those arrived at by ethnological research. This provides a means of checking the work done by the historical method.

We have no direct information from the Chinese or any other sources as to the Bronze Age people of this

[1] This has been the case especially since the famous linguistic researches of Castrén some fifty years ago.

region having been overrun by steppe nomads belonging to the Age of Iron. Archaeological evidence proves that the first period of the Iron Age evolved naturally out of the Age of Bronze, while the fact that the second period of the Iron Age is, as it were, interrupted by a new influx of Iron civilization—possibly owing to an invasion—does not necessarily mean that the invaders were of quite different race; they may have been of the same race but of more pastoral habits, and this may also account for the fact that the invasion escaped the comments of foreign historians. Since it is established that the late Iron Age is to be ascribed to the Turks, and that the early Iron Age does not differ sufficiently from it to warrant the assumption that these two stages of the Iron Age are the product of two different races, it follows that the Bronze Age people may well have been of Turkic, or at least Turkic-Iranian (Turkic-Aryan ?) origin. However, even if we go so far as to assume an association between the Old Turkic race and the Bronze remains, it is necessary at the same time to remember that the knowledge of bronze-working and the types of implements produced were obtained from some centre of 'Aryan' culture, just as the characters of the inscriptions were borrowed from Semitic.

The ability of the old Turks to develop these borrowed arts is surprising, in view of the fact that no later Turks in Central Asia have reached so high a standard of civilization, but the explanation may possibly be that the Turks of that time were freer from Mongolian admixture than they have been since the thirteenth century, and that the 'Aryan' element in Central Asia was, at the time of this old culture, very considerable.

In his recent book on the archaeology of this region Tallgren says: 'The people who developed the Bronze Age civilization of the Upper Yenisei might have been Turc or else Indo-European.'[1] He rejects the idea that they may have been some Palaeo-Siberian people of the same stock of the Ostyak of the Yenisei, who still live in this region, since, as he very rightly says, they could only produce 'une civilisation des non-civilisés', and even if it were right to call them autochthones of the country they could never play any part in its history. The author's personal knowledge of these people corroborates Tallgren's opinion.

The forests of Altai have been regarded by many prominent scholars of Siberia[2] as a natural environment for the beginning of settled life. Whether as cattle-breeders, as agriculturists, or as miners and smiths, the Altaians must always have been more settled than the people of the Caspian-Aral steppe. A study of the implements, both ancient and modern, bears out the hypothesis that we have here to do with a continuous sedentary culture. Furthermore, the continuation of the pictographs through both Bronze and Iron Ages points in the same direction, and the *tamga* or tribal (clan ?) marks found on the implements and gravestones of both periods may still be seen at the present day on the reindeer and implements of the modern natives.

But though the passing of the Bronze Age into the Iron Age may have been a process of natural evolution

[1] *Op. cit.*, p. 30.
[2] N. N. Kosmin, 'Chern', *Sibirskiya Zapiski*, Aug. 1916, No. 3, pp. 95–112; *D. A. Klements and Historical and Ethnographical Research in the Minusinsk Country*; N. M. Yadrintseff, *On the Altaians and the Chern Tatars*.

of the same people, this does not exclude the fact that about the middle of the Iron Age some invasion took place, which gave rise to wars, and to a correspondingly great development of implements of war. There is, however, as has been said, no proof that these invaders were of different race from the men of the Bronze and early Iron Ages, but as they came from a steppe environment they may quite well have brought other customs with them. Some fall in the scale of culture may also have occurred as a result of a decrease in, or perhaps entire absence of, contact with the people (probably Aryan) who must have influenced the Yenisei Bronze culture. But though changes there were, they were not fundamental, since the general culture was never destroyed, as it was after the Kalmuck of the Russian conquests.

The Yenisei and Orkhon inscriptions so far known were written at the time when the supposed Turkic invaders were settling in the land they had conquered from the autochthones, but they certainly do not show the spirit of unacclimatized new-comers. The Turks of that time speak of themselves as inhabitants of the forest, not of the steppe. It is the dense forest *yish* (the same as *Chern*, 'black forest') that is constantly referred to in the Orkhon inscriptions.[1] The Orkhon Tu-kiu, when describing their fights with the Kirghis or other Turks, always say that these took place in the *yish*, and that their country, as well as the country of the Kirghis, is the *yish*. Judging from the original names of the rivers flowing in the forest regions of the upper Yenisei, they were all named by the Turks.

---

[1] The present Altaian 'Tatars' call themselves 'Tuba', 'Tubalar', or 'Yish-kis'.

The Russians who first colonized this country from the north took up the name Yenisei from the Tungus, whom they met first; they came in contact with the Southern Turks only after they had subjugated the Tungus. But even now, in the upper Yenisei region, the Yenisei is known as the Ulu-Kem, which again is formed by the junction of two streams with Turkic names, Bii-Kem (Bei-Kem) and Kha-Kem (Hua-Kem). These names recall the terms for the two chief rivers of the Altai, Biya (Bi) and Katun (Khatun), which were probably also named by the Turks.

The dense forests of this region made communication between various tribes more difficult than it would have been in the open steppe. Hence arose the necessity of making on the bark of trees, or the flat surface of the rock, signs conveying various kinds of information. These signs, called by the Russians *myety*, gave rise to the pictographic writings called *pisanitsy*. Some of them seem to have been a means of conveying tribal information and a chronicle of events, others to have been connected with the religious cult, and these latter are very much like some of the pictures on the modern shaman's drum.[1] Still others may be nothing more than tribal *tamgas*. Great numbers of such engraved or painted pictographs are met with in the forest region of the northern Altai and upper Yenisei, while they are never found in the open steppes, where communication can be carried on much more easily by means of messengers on horseback or by smoke signals, and where chronicles are handed down by word of mouth.

[1] N. M. Yadrintseff, *The Ancient Monuments and Inscriptions in Siberia*, pp. 456, 476.

Curiously enough, it is recorded in the old Russian Cossack reports of the seventeenth and eighteenth centuries, made accessible of late years, that the Kirghis, who were then fighting with the Mongolians of Jungaria, tried to communicate with the Cossacks, and to show them tracks through the forest, by means of such pictographic signs.[1]

In comparing the life of the old inhabitants of this region with that of the modern population it is natural to begin by considering the form of their dwellings. Unfortunately there are no indications as to the type of habitation of the people of the Bronze or the Iron Ages. The region furnishes, however, such a collection of various types of dwelling, that it is not fanciful to assume a long evolutionary development. First there is the very primitive tent, *suyulta*, or *alenchek* if covered with birch bark. Then there are quadrangular wooden dwellings called *aida*, still without windows. Next come wooden structures covered with earth, and provided with a window. These are called *kuzenek*, and in them a clay stove, *chuval*, has already replaced the smoke-hole of the more primitive types. There is an elaborated form, called *spa*, in which the whole structure is raised higher from the ground, and given a hexagonal shape, with a sloping roof. Within, it has a kind of small vestibule. The tent also has its line of development, for the use of such of the population as devote their attention to cattle-breeding, and hence are seasonal

---

[1] *Memoirs of Siberian History, Seventeenth Century*, vol. I, No. 58. N. N. Kosmin, in one of his recent journeys in the Amyl Taiga of the Minusinsk country, records that his Tatar guide, on striking camp left behind a notched stick, the notches on which indicated : ' Five of us slept here one night and went away in two boats ' (N. N. Kosmin, *Chern*, p. 99).

nomads. This, in its most elaborate form, is spherical, and resembles to some extent the so-called Kirghis, or properly speaking Kaizak, tent, from which, however, it differs in having a conical top instead of being built round a circular frame. There also exist hexagonal, octagonal, and polygonal varieties. These are usually covered with felt, and are called *yurta*.[1]

As regards the botanical environment, more data are available for comparison. There are certain forest plants, very plentiful in the Altai and Sayan Mountains, whose roots are much esteemed as food by the modern Turks, as they seem to have been by the ancient. Among them are *sarana* (*Lilium Martagon*), *kandyk* (*Erithronium dens canis*), and *cheremsha* (*Allium ursinum*). So characteristic are these roots as articles of food among the present-day Turks that the names for the different times of the year are taken from the plants that are then in season. Thus Bes-ai is 'the month of *kandyk*' (May), and Ak-sep-ai is 'the month of *sarana*' (June).

The agriculture carried on in the clearings of the forest was in the olden days similar to what it was at the time when the Russians first occupied the country. Barley seems to have been the chief product. On spots where the cattle have been pastured for some time the modern Altaians grow hemp. The vegetable ornament found in the late Bronze Age, and in abundance in the Iron Age, proves that the ancient inhabitants knew and used the same plants as are utilized by the present natives.

Among the agricultural implements found in the

---

[1] N. M. Yadrintseff, *On the Altaians and the Chern Tatars*, p. 8.

kurgans are some which are in use up to the present time among the Tatars. Such are the *ozyp*, a kind of hoe used for digging up roots, and the *obyl*, a kind of primitive plough, which, if it has shafts, is called *andazyn*. Instead of a harrow they now use the trunk of a small tree with stumps of the branches left projecting. Many of the present Tatars, for instance those along the River Chu, reap their corn by tearing it off in handfuls; only in some places is a knife with a curved handle used for this purpose. No threshing implement occurs either in the graves or among the present inhabitants, but possibly in the olden days, as in some places up to modern times, there existed the practice of singeing the straw in order to dry it, when the grain can be separated by stirring it with a stick. There are not found, either in the graves or among the Southern Altaians, the typical mill-stones which are used by the Chern Tatars, but flat slabs of stone are met with between which the grain is rubbed. The remains of the irrigation canals, called *aryk*, show that they were more elaborate in the Bronze and Iron periods than their modern substitutes, sometimes called *sugak*. It is not known in what way land was fertilized in the olden days, but at the time of the arrival of the Russians, and to a certain extent until now, the natives chose old camping sites on which to sow their grain.[1]

While some Turkic tribes, for instance the Kaizak, even now do not trouble to lay up winter stores for their cattle, the Altaians twist up straw into rolls, and store it in that way, which is also convenient for carrying.[2] Among the forest Tatars hay is prepared

[1] Yadrintseff, *op. cit.*, p. 11.
[2] *Ibid.*

by being hung in bundles from the branches of trees.[1]

As for the animal world, there is a record that the Cossack Ataman Vasili Tumenets,[2] who passed through the land of Tuba on his way to Mongolia in 1616, found these people in possession of horses and reindeer, but without cattle or sheep. It is interesting to note that in all the archaeological remains both of the Iron and of the Bronze periods, a great many different species of deer are represented. Among the present Turkic tribes the deer, *syn*, is still the most popular animal. The horse and the goat are also favourite motives in the bronze zoomorphic ornament, and the mountain eagle and the swan are the most frequently represented birds. All this seems to prove that the metal-workers must have lived in the same environment as the modern inhabitants. But we find in the Bronze Age also representations of animals not known to frequent the upper Yenisei, such as the dromedary and the donkey.[3] This would point to Southern influence, or at least to contact with a Southern people during the Bronze Age.

Thus it becomes clear that the people who were responsible for the early pictographs, and possibly for the bronze implements, as well as the people responsible for the Uigur inscriptions and the iron implements, are connected with the present remnants of the local Turkic population in the way in which they reacted to their botanical and zoological environment. No such similarity can be traced between the ancient inhabitants

---

[1] N. N. Kosmin, *Chern*, p. 98.
[2] A. V. Adrianoff, *Sketches of the Minusinsk Country*, 1904, p. 5.
[3] Kosmin, *ibid.*

and other sections of the modern population such as the Ostyak or the Samoyed.

Finally, it is curious that among the many primitive races of Northern and Central Asia only two tribes have a reputation as iron-workers, the Yakut and the Kuznietsk 'Tatars'—from *kuzniets* (Russian), 'smith'. At the time of the Russian conquest the latter were paying tribute to China with iron implements of their own manufacture. It seems impossible to dissociate these people, whose original home was in the region of the Iron Age remains, from the ancient iron-workers. Of course, it is more difficult to trace their ancestry further back, though there is no evidence to prove that the Bronze Age people were of a different race from the people of the Iron Age.

The presence of rich mineral deposits in the country of the old Turks gave rise to an extensive mining industry, the high value of which, added to the richness of the animal and vegetable world, made the population of the *yish* self-satisfied, and disinclined to leave their lands. The Orkhon inscriptions contain many allusions to 'the benevolent earth and waters of the Turks', and unfriendly comments on the people who migrate from the forests and mountains to the open plain, take up Chinese trade, and develop the war instinct. I will allow myself to quote one of the most instructive passages of the Orkhon inscriptions. The author addresses his tribesmen: 'Whence came your lust for warfare? Ye went away, ye people of Utukan Yish, some to the west and some to the east, but all that ye found there, in the place to which ye came, amounts to this, that your blood was shed like water, and your bones heaped up in mountains; your strong sons are now serfs, and your clean daughters are fallen into slavery.'[1] Surely this quotation does not bear out the idea cherished by some scholars, that the Turanian Turks, at the time when they enter history, were very similar to the Mongols, that is, were warlike nomads of the steppes. Such a description would to a great extent be applicable to the border population of the Kirghis, the nomadic Kaizak. But to judge the old Turks by the Kaizak would be equivalent to estimating the culture of modern Russia by that of the European Kaizaks or Cossacks.

Even if we find among some Turkic tribes of the present day a tradition of their having been originally steppe nomads, this notion may be classified with another fictitious Turkic tradition, namely, that which provides them with a descent from the Mongol Jinghis Khan.

Some Conclusions.

From this review of the archaeological, historical, and ethnological evidence, it seems obvious that the Turanian Turks may be considered to be a remnant of the old Turkic race which has passed through various changes in Central Asia, having been originally known as Hiung-nu. The Turks, who are here called Iranian, have lost to a much greater extent than the Turanians the line of genealogical continuity with the Hiung-nu, or even the Tu-kiu. Still more is this the case with those Turks who have passed through several more 'racial filtrations' and environmental influences, namely, the Azerbeijan and the Osmanly Turks. In fact, were it not for their Turkic language, the Osmanly would have to be classified among the

[1] Kosmin, *op. cit.*, p. 106.

Europeans 'by adoption', like the Hungarians or the Bulgarians.

It is not the author's aim to append a political moral to a work whose object is to show the unscientific character of one of those high-sounding terms that begin with 'Pan-'. To wish for conquest and expansion is one thing; to claim a land on grounds of ethnical and traditional continuity is quite another. Linguistic relationship has often been used—and abused—as a plea for subjugating a weaker race to a stronger. The fact remains, however, that if there is no other community than a distant relationship in language, there need be no community of interest at all. Of course, the Turkic people of Central Asia, who, though numerous, are divided into small nations, may be at the mercy of a stronger invader; and, should the course of this war or of the Russian Revolution bring about such a situation, they may be subdued to such a power in a political way. But to speak of the Osmanlis and the Turanian Turks as a racial and cultural unity would be by a stroke of the pen, or by means of a propagandist pamphlet, to wipe away all the invasions, migrations, massacres, and fusions which for twenty centuries have played havoc with that part of the world.

It is now clear that Asia cannot in the future be artificially divided from her peninsula Europe, and that she will rapidly return to conditions similar to those which existed before our era, when the White and Yellow races met on the heights of Turan. Of course, the plan for a 'Middle-Asia' involves fewer practical difficulties than that for a 'Mittel-Europa', in so far as the national consciousness of the Central Asiatic Turks is weaker than that of the Central European neighbours of Germany.   But is it feasible that any single power or any single European culture should have the monopoly of Central Asia? Before such a state of affairs could disturb the balance of Europe, it would surely disturb the balance of the power that made the attempt. For the utmost effort on the part of a highly organized European or Asiatic Government would be needed in order to bring about any permanent unity of feeling throughout that vast continent; and until this consummation is reached no economic advantage can follow either for the aboriginal people or for any others.

Throughout its whole history, except perhaps for a period between the fourteenth and seventeenth centuries, Central Asia has been the scene of the mingling of various cultural and political influences. The scientific investigations carried on there of late years give an excellent illustration of this. An example is afforded by the monumental explorations of Sir Aurel Stein. Though the explorations themselves were carried on under the British flag, yet in the preparation of the results for publication men of almost every European nationality have been engaged.[1] The archaeological trophies brought home at various times by Sir Aurel Stein are as rich and varied as the influences to which Central Asia has in the course of its history been subjected. Hence no single man, not even a single nation, would be qualified to undertake a thorough digest of this material. And we see here a wonderful collaboration of European scholars: a Dane, Professor Thomsen of Copenhagen; Frenchmen, MM. Chavannes,

[1] Sylvain Lévi, 'Central Asian Studies', *J.R.A.S.*, 1914, pp. 953-64.

Gauthiot,[1] Pelliot; a Belgian, M. La Vallée Poussin; Germans, Professors von Le Coq and F. W. K. Müller; a Russian, Professor Radloff; and Englishmen, Sir Aurel Stein, Dr. Hoernle, and Dr. Cowley. Will any League of Nations bring about a harmony more complete than this, which has been proved to be possible among scientific men of all nationalities in their work on Central Asia? Could the voice of such unbiased scholars be heard in the Council Chambers of the diplomatists, it might not be too much to hope that the same international collaboration which has proved of such benefit in the sphere of scientific research may likewise become possible in the politics of the future.

[1] Whose most regrettable death at the Front was announced some time ago.

APPENDIX A

WHEN speaking of 'Central Asian riches', it is understood to mean all the natural resources found in what is called Russian Central Asia. In particular, one stretch of land deserves the reputation of possessing a value surpassing all known colonial possessions. This is the part inhabited by various Turkic-speaking people, stretching from the mouth of the Ob on the Arctic, through the forest, agricultural and cattle-breeding regions of Western Siberia, the Steppe country and Turkestan, as far south as the frontiers of Persia.

In commercial value this area represents—rich fishing in the sub-Arctic region; rare fur animals in the forest region; valuable timber, of which in Western Siberia alone some 110 million dessiatins were registered by the Russian Government; rich cornfields, almost half of which are occupied by wheat; steppes swarming with cattle, and lakes abundant in fish; mountains rich in minerals; and finally, the irrigated fields of Turkestan covered with cotton plantations, not to mention such promising industries as butter and eggs, fruit and vegetables.

As to the minerals, the 'Golden' or Altai Mountains, as well as the Northern Steppes are equally rich in gold, silver, iron, coal, copper, and almost all known mineral resources. However, in the production of gold it is Eastern Siberia which occupies first place in the Russian Empire (in 1910 it produced 2,828 puds; in 1914, 2,729 puds); the second place belongs to the Ural Mountains (in 1910, 642 puds; in 1914, 299 puds), and Western Siberia stands third (in 1910, 416 puds; in 1914, 133 puds). This can be accounted for chiefly by the lack of enterprise and capital. The chief deposits of gold in Western Siberia are in the following districts: 1, Tomsk; 2, Krasnoyarsk-Achinsk; 3, Southern Steppes; 4, Yenisei; 5, Altai; 6, Minusinsk; 7, Northern Steppes. Probably some gold deposits could be found in Bokhara and Turkestan.

The silver deposits are found in great number in the Altai and north of Semipalatinsk. The richest deposits of coal, iron, and copper are found in the district between Novo-Nikolaevsk, Tomsk, Barnaul, and Kuznietsk; also in the region of Semipalatinsk. The Kuznietsk basin alone occupies some 15,000 sq. klm.

The best-known oilfields are situated on the western coast of the Caspian. But it is possible that the Transcaspian oilfields, now almost entirely limited to Chikishliar and some other points along the railway, may prove to be no less abundant. In Ferghana the oilfields are being exploited in four regions: 1, Shar-Su; 2, Maili-Su; 3, Chimionand; 4, Sel-Kokko, but so far the export is fairly limited; in 1914 it amounted to some 2,000,000 puds.

But it is cereals that form the most important product of export from Western Siberia, and 90 per cent. of the population is devoted to agriculture. Agriculture is found chiefly between 60° of N. lat. and 50° of S. lat. Beyond these limits the country is only half agricultural; while fishing, shooting, and cattle-breeding is carried on alongside. Out of some 12 million dess. occupied by cornfields in Asiatic Russia in 1911, some $4\frac{1}{2}$ millions were situated in Western Siberia, $2\frac{1}{2}$ millions in the Steppe country, and $3\frac{1}{2}$ millions in Turkestan. The chief centres of the corn export are Novo-Nikolaevsk, Omsk, Kurgan, Pyetukhovo, Barnaul, and Semipalatinsk. In 1906–10 average early export = 93,014·4 thousand puds.

Closely connected with agriculture is sheep-breeding, which is especially carried on in the Kirghis Steppes. While in European Russia at the outbreak of war for a hundred inhabitants there were only 32 sheep, in Russian Central Asia it amounted to some 200. The area of pasture land in Western Siberia amounted to some six million dess.; in the Steppe country some three million, and in Turkestan half

a million.   Next to sheep in importance is the breeding of
horses and cows.   In the cattle-breeding area the butter
industry is very successfully carried on, especially in the
governments of Tomsk and Tobolsk, and the chief centres
of its export are Barnaul, Omsk, and Kurgan.   In 1913 the
exports equalled 4·9 million puds as against 1·7 million puds
in 1903.   Closely allied to these industries is the export of
live stock, bacon, game, wool, hair, skins and furs.   But
although they occupy a considerable place, it is the corn which
comes first in quantity and cotton first in value among all
Central Asiatic products.   The pre-war export along the
railway shows the following proportion between the various
goods :   Corn, 35·6 per cent. (of all exported goods); cotton,
4·3 per cent. ; butter, 1·5 per cent. ; fish, 1·2 per cent. ; meat,
1·0 per cent.

In the production of corn Western Siberian ranks first ;
7 per cent. of the native population scarcely take any part
in this industry ; while out of 93 per cent. of European
population, 87 per cent. is composed of Great Russians, on
whom agriculture chiefly depends.   The cattle- and especially
sheep-breeding depend to a great extent on the Kirghis and
other Turkic tribes, forming 50 per cent. of the population
in the Akmolinsk and 85 per cent. in the Semipalatinsk
territories.   But it is the cotton industry which almost
entirely rests upon the native (Sarts and other Turkic tribes)
labour.

The cotton industry is closely connected with irrigation,
and again the irrigation canals form the most valuable
possession of the natives.   The canals seem to have been
much more numerous in ancient times, and the remnants of
them are found even in such barren deserts as Kizyl-Kumakh
or Gary-ishek-otran.   The native law codes (*shariat* as well
as '*ādat*) recognize that the water is common property, which
cannot be sold or bought, and that the land belongs to him
who irrigates it.   To look after the equal use of the irrigation
canals, called *aryka*, an elder, called *mirab*, is chosen from
among one settlement, and over several *mirabs* an *aryk-*

aksakala is elected, looking after the whole system of the chief canal. The lands irrigated by the natives in Turkestan (including Transcaspia), Bokhara, and Khiva equal 4,758,000 dess., or 2·6 per cent. of all the area. Since the Russian occupation, many attempts were made at reconstructing some of the ancient canals on modern lines. As the result of this, in the last few years before the war the Murgab canals were accomplished, irrigating some 25,000 dess., and the Romanoff canal, irrigating some 65,000 dess., in the north-eastern part of the Golodnaya ('Hunger') Steppe. A plan for irrigating a further four million dess. has been drafted.

No doubt this energy of the Russian administration was guided by appreciation of the immense value of the cotton industry. In 1913 some 550,000 dess., including the vassal Khanates, was under cotton plantations, realizing about 13½ million puds of cotton fibre (in 1914 some 675,000 dess., realizing some 13·9 million puds). Ferghana, which, it must be remembered, is the best-irrigated province, produced 75 per cent. of all cotton. Next comes the Tashkent district of Syr-Daria territory; the Katta-Kurgan, Khojent, and Samarkand districts of Samarkand territory; and the Merv and Tejent districts of the Transcaspian territory. It is owing to Russian influence that the old Central Asian specie of cotton (*Gossypium herbaceum*, L.) was almost entirely replaced by the American specie (*Gossypium hirsutum*, L.). The cotton plantations form a chief revenue of the Central Asiatic people, and were designated almost entirely for export. At the outbreak of war Russia occupied fifth place in cotton production (after U.S.A., Great Britain, Egypt, and China), and fourth place in cotton manufacture (after Great Britain, U.S.A., and Germany), and only one-fifth of her cotton was grown outside Central Asia (in Transcaucasia).

Other industries which might have a prosperous future are the rice and tobacco plantations and the rearing of silk-worms (at present Turkestan produces about 100,000 puds of dry cocoons per annum).

It has been said that this rich area has no communication

with the world outside, and difficult communications within. It is true that the only sea-outlet is through the mouths of the Ob and the Yenisei; but with the recent re-opening of the Kara Sea route the northern river-ways have a great commercial value. This will especially be the case when, on the completion of the Ob–Arctic Ocean Railway, there will be no necessity to cross the Kara Sea with its dangerous straits.

Within this region the communication is carried on—

(a) By means of natural roads, of which there are some 109,000 versts in Siberia, and 58,000 versts in Russian Central Asia, not counting the secondary roads.

(b) By means of river-ways, in which especially Western Siberia is very well endowed. The basin of the River Ob alone is navigable for a distance of some 15,000 versts, while some 16,000 more is passable for floating. Turkestan, with its two chief rivers Syr-Daria and Amu-Daria, has much more limited river communications; Amu-Daria is navigable for a distance of some 1,400 versts, but for steam-ships only 800 versts. Syr-Daria could be made navigable for a distance of 1,200 versts, but at present the river is more important for irrigation purposes. The southern rivers are free from ice for about six months in the year, while the rivers north of the Altai Mountains are navigable from three to four months a year.

(c) The railway is, of course, the most important means of communication, and each new line causes a great industrial and social upheaval in the district. The Trans-Siberian has only a relative value, and much greater importance is attached to the southern line of the Trans-Siberian (Chelyabinsk–Omsk) and the new branches; the Altai (Novo-Nikolaevsk–Biisk–Semipalatinsk) and the Minusinsk (Achinsk–Minusinsk). The Central Asiatic (Krasnovodsk–Andijan), covering 2,368 versts, and the Tashkent Railway (Orenburg–Tashkent), covering some 1,756 versts, unite to some extent Russian Central Asia with Western Siberia. A line between Semipalatinsk and some point on the Tashkent Railway will be of enormous importance for the further development of Western Siberia, the Steppe country and Inner Turkestan, and would thus help the communications between the northern and southern part of this rich area, which so far is carried on partly by means of river-ways (Ob, Irtish), and chiefly above the old caravan route. Out of two most important old roads in Central Asia, the first one—Orenburg–Tashkent—was utilized for the Tashkent Railway; the second—Tashkent-Semi-palatinsk—is awaiting the same fate. It is the most lively route along which the post, the passenger and goods traffic is carried on. It starts at Kabul-Sai (some 120 versts north of Tashkent), and passes through Chimkent, Aulieata, Pishnek, Viernyi, Kopal, and Sergiupol (the latter lies 272 versts south-east of Semipalatinsk). Branches of smaller roads connect this big route with Pjevalsk and Kulja.

The last plan of the old Russian administration was to connect European Russia with Turkestan by a second line parallel to the Tashkent line, i. e. along the River Amu-Daria.

Western Siberia has gained enormous experience during the present war. At the first stage of the war she was the chief storing-place for army supplies. After the Russian retreat many industries from Poland and Western Russia were transferred here owing to the abundance of coal and other cheap raw products in Western Siberia.

See:

Statistical Year Book, edited by the Minister of the Interior (Russ. Petrograd, 1910–16).

Torgovo-Promyshlennaya Gazeta (Russ. Petrograd, 1910–17).

Asiatic Russia, edited by the Immigration Committee (Russ. St. Petersburg, 1914).

Siberia, by P. M. Golovacheff (Russ. Moscow, 1914).

Economic Geography of Siberia, by P. M. Golovacheff (Russ. Moscow, 1914).

Russian Year Book, edited by N. Peacock (London, 1910–16).

Times Russian Supplement (1914–16).

Department of Customs. Revue of the foreign trade of Russia through her European and Asiatic Frontiers (Russ. St. P., 1912).

Malakhowski, N. Statistics concerning transport of goods on the Central-Asiatic and the Tashkent Railways (Russ. St. P., 1914).

APPENDIX B

THE ambitious plans of the Germans for the conquest of the East had as their first aim the plan of the Berlin–Bagdad railway. When the British successes cut short this plan and Southern Russia became the prey of German influence, the Berlin–Bagdad was put aside by some, in favour of a plan to revive the ancient route through the highlands of Central Asia: Berlin–Bokhara–Pekin. Whatever the ultimate fate of the German activity in the East may be, it has at least served to force the Pan-Turanian question upon the attention of the British public. See articles in *The Round Table*, No. 29, December 1917; in *The Times*, January 3rd, 5th, and 7th, 1918; in *The Quarterly Review*, No. 455, April 1918; in *The Round Table*, No. 31, June 1918; and in *Land and Water*, July 4, 1918.

Meanwhile, the Treaty of Brest-Litovsk, which ceded to Turkey the territories of Ardahan, Batum, and Kars (belonging to Russia since 1877), was the first step towards the realization of the Pan-Turanian dream. The population of the district—Armenians (two millions), Georgians (two millions), Tatars (two millions), and Russians (one million)—refused to recognize the Treaty (see *The New Europe*, July 25, 1918). However, the Caucasian Tatars soon deserted the cause of the 'Transcaucasian Republic' for that of the advancing Osmanly. The Georgian-Armenian forces were defeated, and the country was split into 'independent' Georgia (May 26, 1918) with its capital in Tiflis, 'independent' Armenia, consisting of the Armenian lands round Erivan, and an 'independent' North Azerbeijan, the capital of which, Tabriz, was occupied by the Turks.

This easy success inflamed the desire for conquest of the Turkic militarists. The popular paper of the Committee of Union and Progress, *Tasvir-i-Efkiar*, on April 15 contained the following passage (quoted in *The Cambridge Magazine*, August 24, 1918):

'To penetrate in one direction into Egypt, and to open the road to the 300,000,000 (*sic*) of our co-religionists, on

the other side to advance to Kars and Tiflis, to liberate
the Caucasus from Russian barbarism, and to occupy
Tabriz and Teheran, to open a road to those Mussulman
countries such as Afghanistan and India—this is the task we
have assumed.   This task, *with the aid of Allah*, with the
assistance of our Prophet, and thanks to the union imposed
on us by our religion, we will carry through to the end . . .'

It is noteworthy that the Turkish desire for expansion in
the East was supported in the Press of opposite political
opinions.   Thus *Tasvir-i-Efkiar*, *Sabah*, and the Government
organ *Tanin* supported it just as much as the papers of the
Opposition, *Ikdam* and *Zeman*, though the latter Press was
not so particular as to whether they would use the Central
Powers or the Allies' support in carrying out their designs
(see *The New Europe*, August 15, 1918).   The German-Russian
Supplementary Treaty added to the clash between the Osmanly
and German Eastern policy (*The Times*, Sept. 10, 1918).   Germany is aware that her political and commercial interests in
the East depend to some extent on the goodwill of the non-
Turkic inhabitants of Transcaucasia, Persia, and Turkestan,
whom the Osmanly tend to disregard.   Also, it was against her
aims to distract the Osmanly armies from the re-conquest of
Arabia, Mesopotamia, Syria, and Palestine.   This accounts for
the warm protection which Berlin has shown towards the new
Georgian Republic (see *The Times*, June 19, 1918), and the
indignation of the German Press with 'the growing demands
of the Pan-Turks' (*Münchener Post*, June 19, 1918; *Deutsche
Tageszeitung*, June 5, 1918; and *Kreuzzeitung*, July 16,
1918).   The *Frankfurter Zeitung* (May 28, 1918, quoted by the
Cambridge Magazine, July 27, 1918) argues that 'the Bagdad
Railway is of infinitesimal value compared to the traffic which
needs organizing from the Black Sea into the interior of
Asia.   These routes are destined to revolutionize the trade-
map of the world.'

There is no doubt that the presence of British forces
in Near Asia was the only obstacle to the German plan for
connecting Berlin with Bagdad, or even with Simla.   But
while the German papers played about with such schemes as
Berlin–Bagdad and Hamburg–Herat—schemes which under
the circumstances sound most fantastic—their commercial

agents were fully awake to the opportunities afforded to them by the Brest-Litovsk Treaty.

The immediate danger of Pan-Turanianism has dispersed with the collapse of Turkey. The character of the Allies' armistice with Turkey announced by the Press Bureau on November 1, 1918, shows complete military collapse, as the result of which the Ottoman Empire falls out of the Great War. Still, it is doubtful whether the mischief done by the spoken and written word will be remedied as rapidly as that of military action, so there yet remains a great need for making clear the true ethnological facts of the problem.

Then only the Osmanly and Pan-Turanian designs will be discredited in Central Asia, just as the Pan-Mahometan propaganda which Osmanly have carried on in Egypt and Arabia was exposed by the subsequent British successes. However, the greatest military and political successes of the Allies will not bring peace to the life of the Turks of Central Asia as long as the Russian element of the East is in a ferment. For it must be remembered that Bolshevism, Social-Revolutionism, Monarchism, and other propagandas have been at work there, and though the social upheaval in Central Asia does not reach such tragic expression as it does in Russia, no military or political settlement can be final before the social revolution has its *dénouement*. One can even prophesy that the Pan-Turanian problem will remain one of the burning questions long after the peace settlement is achieved in Europe and Asia. It is possible that with the great economic changes which can be expected in that part of the world, Central Asia will become part of a large confederate state before its peoples develop a feeling of national unity in the European sense of the word, thus exchanging their tribal for a republican mode of life.[1]

[1] I take the opportunity of thanking my friend Mr. Harold Williams, Ph.D., for his kindness in reading the chapter on the Pan-Turanian Movement and Appendix B.

BIBLIOGRAPHICAL MATERIAL

RELATING TO THE EARLY TURKS AND THE PRESENT TURKS OF CENTRAL ASIA

THIS bibliography is to the author's knowledge the first attempt to bring together a list of works relating to the origin of the Turks and their life in Central Asia from the earliest times up to the present day, and covering their history, ethnology, and archaeology. A somewhat vague suggestion of a work of this kind was made as far back as 1879 by the great Central Asian scholar Ujfalvy, who, in the second volume of his *Expédition scientifique française en Russie, en Sibérie et dans le Turkestan*, says, 'On pourrait écrire un livre sur la bibliographie de cette contrée, et il est bien naturel que les auteurs russes occupent dans cette bibliographie la place la plus importante' (p. xii). As will be seen from the bibliography, the scientific data has increased since that time both in quality and quantity.

Chinese, Persian, and Turkish sources are given only so far as they have been translated into English or some other European language. Existing bibliographies dealing with special aspects of the subject have been laid under contribution, and the data verified so far as the books are available in this country.

The greatest debt is due to A. N. Samoylovich's *Materials for an Index of the Literature relating to the Yenisei-Orkhon Inscription* (1912[1]; in Russian), from which some two hundred titles were taken and revised, and, to a certain extent, also to Inostrantseff and Smirnoff's *Materials for the Bibliography of the Mussulman Archaeology* (1906 ; in Russian).

The author is fully aware of the shortcomings of the present

---

[1] This bibliography, again, is to some extent based on *Orientalische Bibliographie*, begründet von F. A. Müller, bearbeitet und herausgegeben von Dr. L. Scherman, Berlin, 1888–1915.

collection, the probable omission of some valuable works on this subject, and the arrangement of the material merely in alphabetical order. At the present stage of research it is often difficult to isolate the Turks from other peoples in Central Asia without injuring the subject. It is, moreover, impossible to define which works are historical, which ethnological, and which archaeological. However, even in this crude form these bibliographical materials may serve as a starting-point for further research.

The following abbreviations have been used throughout the bibliography :

Bab. Orient. Rec. = Babylonian and Oriental Record. London.

J. R. G. S. = Journal of the Royal Geographical Society. London.

J. R. A. S. = Journal of the Royal Asiatic Society. London.

J. R. A. I. = Journal of the Royal Anthropological Institute. London.

J. Centr. As. S. = Journal of the Central Asian Society, London.

A. R. = The Asiatic Review (formerly ' The Asiatic Quarterly Review '). London.

E. R. E. = Hastings' Encyclopaedia of Religion and Ethics. Aberdeen.

Bull. Soc. Antiqu. = Bulletins de la Société Antiquarienne de France. Paris.

Rev. Or. = Revue Orientale pour les Études Oural-Altaïques. Paris.

J. A. = Journal Asiatique. Paris.

M. O. = Le Monde Oriental. Paris.

Le Muséon = Le Muséon. Paris.

La Géographie = La Géographie. Paris.

Rev. Numis. = Revue Numismatique. Paris.

Bull. Éc. Franç. = Bulletins de l'École française de l'Extrême Orient. Paris.

N. E. = Notices et Extraits des Manuscrits de la Bibliothèque du Roi, Ac. des Inscriptions et Belles-Lettres. Paris.

E. I. = The Encyclopaedia of Islam. Leyden and London.

O. B. = Orientalische Bibliographie. Berlin.

L. Z. = Literarischer Zodiacus. Leipzig.

Z. D. M. G. = Zeitschrift der Deutschen Morgenländischen Gesell-schaft. Leipzig.

W. Z. K. M. = Wiener Zeitschrift für die Kunde des Morgenlandes. Vienna.

Z. f. E. = Zeitschrift für Ethnologie.   Berlin.

T. P. = T'oung Pao.   Leyden.

K. S. = Keleti Szemle.   Budapest.

J. Soc. Fin.-Ougr. = Journal de la Société Finno-Ougrienne. Helsingfors.

Mém. Soc. Fin.-Ougr. = Mémoires de la Société Finno-Ougrienne. Helsingfors.

L. A. T. = Living Ancient Times.   Живая Старина.   Petrograd.

Russ. Anthr. J. = Russian Anthropological Journal.   Русскій Антро- пологическій Журналъ.   Petrograd.

Mess. I. R. G. S. = Messenger of the Imperial Russian Geographical Society.   Вѣстникъ Императорскаго Русскаго Географическаго Общества.   Petrograd.

Ethn. Rev. = Ethnographical Review.   Этнографическое Обозрѣніе. Moscow.

Government News (preceded by the name of the Government in question).   Губернскія Вѣдомости.

Oren. Gov. News = Orenburg Government News.   Оренбургскія Губернскія Вѣдомости.   Orenburg.

Tob. Gov. News = Tobolsk Government News.   Тобольскія Губерн- скія Вѣдомости.   Tobolsk.

Semip. Terr. News = Semipalatinsk Territory News.   Семипалатин- скія Областныя Вѣдомости.   Semipalatinsk.

Turk. News = Turkestan News.   Туркестанскія Вѣдомости. Tashkent.

J. Min. Int. = Journal of the Ministry of the Interior.   Журналъ Министерства Внутреннихъ Дѣлъ.   Petrograd.

J. Min. Educ. = Journal of the Ministry of Education.   Журналъ Министерства Народнаго Просвѣщенія.   Petrograd.

J. Min. Prop. State = Journal of the Ministry of the Property of the State.   Журналъ Министерства Государственныхъ Имуществъ. Petrograd.

Mem. I. A. S. = Memoirs of the Imperial Academy of Science. Записки Императорской Академіи Наукъ.   Petrograd.

Bull. I. A. S. = Bulletins of the Imperial Academy of Science. Извѣстія Императорской Академіи Наукъ. Petrograd.

Bull. Soc. F. S. Anthr. E. = Bulletins of the Society of the Friends of Science, Anthropology and Ethnography at the Imp. University of Moscow. Извѣстія Общества Любителей Естествознанія, Антропологіи и Этнографіи при Импер. Московскомъ Университетѣ. Moscow.

Bull. Russ. Committee = Bulletins of the Russian Committee for the Study of Central and Eastern Asia with regard to its history, archaeology, linguistics and ethnography. Извѣстія Русскаго Комитета для изученія Средней и Восточной Азіи, въ историческомъ, археологическомъ, лингвистическомъ и этнографическомъ отношеніяхъ. Petrograd.

Proc. Turk. Circle F. Arch. = Proceedings of the Turkestan Circle of the Friends of Archaeology. Протоколы Туркестанскаго Кружка Любителей Археологіи. Tashkent.

Mem. Ural S. F. S. = Memoirs of the Ural Society of Friends of Science. Записки Уральскаго Общества Любителей Естествознанія. Ekaterinburg.

Bull. S. Arch. H. E. I. Univ. Kaz. = Bulletins of the Society of Archaeology, History and Ethnography at the Imperial University of Kazan. Извѣстія Общества Археологіи, Исторіи и Этнографіи при Императорскомъ Казанскомъ Университетѣ. Kazan.

Rep. I. Russ. Hist. Museum = Reports of the Imperial Russian Historical Museum. Отчеты Императорскаго Русскаго Историческаго Музея. Moscow.

Rep. I. Arch. Commission = Reports of the Imperial Archaeological Commission of the Russian Historical Museum : the Moscow Popular and Rumyantseff Museums. Отчеты Императорской Археологической Коммиссіи Московскаго Публичнаго и Румянцевскаго Музеевъ, Импер. Россійскаго Историческаго Музея. Moscow.

Bull. I. Arch. Commission = Bulletins of the Imperial Archaeological Commission of the Russian Historical Museum : the Moscow Popular and Rumyantseff Museums. Извѣстія Императорской Археологической Коммиссіи Московскаго Публичнаго и Румянцевскаго Музеевъ, Импер. Россійскаго Историческаго Музея. Moscow.

Mem. I. R. Arch. S. = Memoirs of the Imperial Russian Archaeological Society. Записки Императорскаго Русскаго Археологическаго Общества. Petrograd.

Bull. I. R. Arch. S. = Bulletins of the Imperial Russian Archaeological Society. Извѣстія Императорскаго Русскаго Археологическаго Общества. Petrograd.

Trans. E. Sect. I. R. Arch. S. = Transactions of the Eastern Section of the Imperial Russian Archaeological Society. Труды Восточнаго Отдѣла Императорскаго Русскаго Археологическаго Общества. Petrograd.

Mem. E. Sect. I. R. Arch. S. = Memoirs of the Eastern Section of the Imperial Russian Archaeological Society. Записки Восточнаго Отдѣла Императорскаго Русскаго Археологическаго Общества. Petrograd.

Mem. Russ. and Slav. Arch. Sect. I. R. Arch. S. = Memoirs of the Russian and Slavonic Archaeology Section of the Imperial Russian Archaeological Society. Записки Отдѣла Русской и Славянской Археологіи Императорскаго Русскаго Археологическаго Общества. Petrograd.

Trans. I. Moscow Arch. S. = Transactions of the Imperial Moscow Archaeological Society. Труды Императорскаго Московскаго Археологическаго Общества. Moscow.

Trans. E. Comm. I. Moscow Arch. S. = Transactions of the Eastern Commission of the Imperial Moscow Archaeological Society. Труды Восточной Коммиссіи Императорскаго Московскаго Археологическаго Общества. Moscow.

Mem. I. R. G. S. = Memoirs of the Imperial Russian Geographical Society: section of Ethnography. Записки Императорскаго Русскаго Географическаго Общества: по отдѣленію Этнографіи. Petrograd.

Bull. I. R. G. S. = Bulletins of the Imperial Russian Geographical Society: section of Ethnography. Извѣстія Императорскаго Русскаго Географическаго Общества: по отдѣленію Этнографіи. Petrograd.

Mem. Sib. Sect. I. R. G. S. = Memoirs of the Siberian Section of

the Imperial Russian Geographical Society. Записки Сибирскаго Отдѣла Императорскаго Русскаго Географическаго Общества.
Petrograd.

Bull. Sib. Sect. I. R. G. S. = Bulletins of the Siberian Section of
the Imperial Russian Geographical Society. Извѣстія Сибирскаго Отдѣла Императорскаго Русскаго Географическаго Общества.
Petrograd.

Mem. W. Sib. Sect. I. R. G. S. = Memoirs of the West Siberian
Section of the Imperial Russian Geographical Society. Записки
Западно-Сибирскаго Отдѣла Императорскаго Русскаго Географи-
ческаго Общества. Omsk.

Bull. W. Sib. Sect. I. R. G. S. = Bulletins of the West Siberian
Section of the Imperial Russian Geographical Society. Извѣстія
Западно-Сибирскаго Отдѣла Императорскаго Русскаго Географи-
ческаго Общества. Omsk.

Mem. Semip. S. W. Sib. Sect. I. R. G. S. = Memoirs of the Semipalatinsk Sub-section of the West Siberian Section of the
Imperial Russian Geographical Society. Записки Семипала-
тинскаго Подотдѣла Западно-Сибирскаго Отдѣла Императорскаго
Русскаго Географическаго Общества. Semipalatinsk.

Mem. E. Sib. Sect. I. R. G. S. = Memoirs of the East Siberian Section
of the Imperial Russian Geographical Society. Записки
Восточно-Сибирскаго Отдѣла Императорскаго Русскаго Географическаго Общества. Irkutsk.

Bull. E. Sib. Sect. I. R. G. S. = Bulletins of the East Siberian Section
of the Imperial Russian Geographical Society. Извѣстія
Восточно-Сибирскаго Отдѣла Императорскаго Русскаго Географическаго Общества. Irkutsk.

Trans. E. Sib. Sect. I. R. G. S. = Transactions of the East Siberian
Section of the Imperial Russian Geographical Society. Труды
Восточно-Сибирскаго Отдѣла Императорскаго Русскаго Геогра-
фическаго Общества. Irkutsk.

Mem. Krasn. S. E. Sib. Sect. I. R. G. S. = Memoirs of the Krasnoyarsk Sub-section of the East Siberian Section of the Imperial
Russian Geographical Society. Записки Красноярскаго Подотдѣла Восточно-Сибирскаго Отдѣла Императорскаго Русскаго
Географическаго Общества. Irkutsk.

Trans. T.-K. S. Amur Sect. I. R. G. S.=Transactions of the Troits-
kosavsk-Kiakhta Sub-section of the Amur Section of the
Imperial Russian Geographical Society. Турды Троицкосавско-
Кяхтинскаго Подотдѣла Амурскаго Отдѣла Императорскаго
Русскаго Географическаго Общества. Troitskosavsk.

Mem. Cauc. Sect. I. R. G. S. = Memoirs of the Caucasian Section
of the Imperial Russian Geographical Society. Записки
Кавказскаго Отдѣла Императорскаго Русскаго Географическаго
Общества. Tiflis.

Bull. Turk. Sect. I. R. G. S. = Bulletins of the Turkestan Section
of the Imperial Russian Geographical Society. Извѣстія
Туркестанскаго Отдѣла Императорскаго Русскаго Географическаго Общества. Tashkent.

Mem. Oren. Sect. I. R. G. S. = Memoirs of the Orenburg Section
of the Imperial Russian Geographical Society. Записки
Оренбургскаго Отдѣла Императорскаго Русскаго Географическаго
Общества. Orenburg.

The abbreviations of other publications used throughout the
bibliography need no further explanation.

To facilitate the use of the bibliography relating to the Turkic
tribes at present inhabiting Central Asia, a table is appended giving
the main existing groups and the names of modern authorities
on each of them. The titles of the works will be found in the
bibliography.

Altaians (including the Telengit, the Kyzyl, and the Chulim
natives).—Adrianoff, Aristoff, Castrén, Gorokhoff, Kalacheff,
Korsh, Kosmin, Kostroff, Lutsyenko, Radloff, Shchukin, Shvetsoff, Shvetsova, Vambéry, Vyerbitski, Yadrintseff, Yariloff.

Beltir.—Adrianoff, Goroshchenko, Kostroff, Katanoff, Yakovleff.

Kachints.—Adrianoff, Castrén, Goroshchenko, Karatanoff, Katanoff, Kostroff, Ostrovskikh, Yakovleff, Stepanoff.

Kaizak.—Alektoroff, Aristoff, Castrén, Czaplicka, Daulbaeff, Geins,
Grodekoff, Ibrahimoff, Kazantseff, Kharusin, Krassovski,
Kustanaeff, Kittary, Levanewski, Levshin, Medvyedski, Meyer,
Mikhailoff, Nazaroff, Nikolski, Potanin, Radloff, Reypolski,
Schmidt, Troll, Ujfalvy, Velyaminoff-Zernoff, Wulfson, Ya-
drintseff, Yevreinoff, Zeeland, Zelenin.

Kamashints.—Castrén, Kostroff, Donner, Radloff, Stepanoff.

Karagass.—Katanoff, Prelovski, Radloff, Shtubendorff, Vasilyeff, Zaleski.

Karakalpak.—Maksimoff, Radloff, Castrén.

Kashgarians.—Ujfalvy.

Khotanians.—Joyce (Stein).

Kirei (Kerians, Kerraits).—Carruthers, Joyce (Stein), Kohn.

Kirghis (Kara-Kirghis, Burut).—Alektoroff, Aristoff, Castrén, Chermak, Czaplicka, Divayeff, Geins, Golubyeff, Grodekoff, Ivanowski, Kharuzin, Kosmin, Krasnoff, Nazaroff, Nikolski, Potanin, Radloff, Shkapski, Troll, Tronoff, Ujfalvy, Vambéry, Valikhanoff, Venyukoff, Wulfson, Yadrintseff, Yastreboff, Zagrajski.

Koibal.—Castrén, Goroshchenko, Kostroff, Radloff, Yakovleff.

Kumandints.—Radloff, Sherr.

Sagai.—Adrianoff, Castrén, Goroshchenko, Radloff, Yakovleff.

Sarts.—Mayeff, Nalivkin, Ostroumoff, Shishoff, Sorokin, Troll, Ujfalvy, Vambéry, Wulfson, Yaworski.

Soyot (Uriankhai).—Adrianoff, Africanoff, Carruthers, Castrén, Fabritsius, Goroshchenko, Ivanowski, Katanoff, Maltseff, Olsen, Ostrovskikh, Shishmaryeff, Silinich, Yadrintseff.

Taranchi.—Geins, Gorbachoff, Khoroshkhin.

Tatars (Siberian Turks).—Adrianoff, Castrén, Czaplicka (and Hall), Golovacheff, Goroshchenko, Katanoff, Kosmin, Kostroff, Kuznietsoff, Maloff, Middendorff, Radloff, Stepanoff, Ujfalvy, Yadrintseff, Yakovleff, Yushloff.

Turkomans.—Arkhipoff, Bode, Galkin, Ilyenko, Ivanowki, Kuropatkin, Lessar, Neboksin, Tarnowski, Ujfalvy, Yaworski.

Usbegs.—Bogdanoff, Grebyenkin, Khoroshikhin, Malyeff, Radloff, Troll, Ujfalvy, Vambéry, Velyaminoff-Zernoff, Zaborovski.

Yakut.—Clark, Jochelson-Brodsky, Jochelson, Maak, Middendorff, Piekarski, Priklonski, Shchukin, Sieroszewski, Troshchanski, Wrangell.

BIBLIOGRAPHY

Abercromby, J. Note on the Yenisei Inscriptions. Bab. Orient. Rec., 1891, V, pt. ii, pp. 25–30 ; pt. iii, p. 72.

Abramoff, N. A.   Ancient Settlements in the Yalutoroff District of the Tobolsk Government.   Mess. I. R. G. S., 1854, X, pt. v, p. 77. — *Абрамовъ, Н. А.* Древнія городища въ Ялуторовскомъ округѣ, Тобольской губ.

—— Short description of a burial monument in Kozukurpyech, in the Kirghis Steppe under Siberian administration. Bull. I. R. Arch. S., 1859, I, p. 247. — Краткое описаніе надмогильнаго памятника Козу-Курпеча въ Киргизской степи Сибирскаго Вѣдомства.

—— Kurgans and Settlements in the Tiumien, Yalutoroff and Kurgan Districts of the Tobolsk Government.   Bull. I. R. Arch. S., 1861, II, pp. 220–28. — Курганы и городища въ Тюменьскомъ, Ялуторовскомъ и Курганскомъ округахъ, Тобольской губ.

—— On ancient stone structures.   Tob. Gov. News, 1864, Nos. 44, 45. — О старинныхъ каменныхъ строеніяхъ.

—— Ancient fortress along the River Chingilda.   Tob. Gov. News, 1867, No. 50. — Древнее укрѣпленіе при рѣчкѣ Чингильдѣ.

—— Ancient kurgans and fortresses in Semipalatinsk and Semirechensk Territories. Bull. I. R. Arch. S., 1872, VII, pp. 190–298 ; 1877, VIII, pp. 60–63. — Древніе курганы и укрѣпленія въ Семипалатинской и Семирѣченской областяхъ.

Abu-Halib-Hussein : *see* Timur.

Abul-Gazy-Bahadur Khan (Aboulgasi Bahadour Chan).   Histoire des Mongols et des Tartares, publiée, traduite et annotée par le baron Desmaisons.   St. P., 1871–4.

　English trans. by Col. W. Miles, London, 1838.

　Latin trans. by C. M. Fraehn, Kazan, 1825.

　German trans. by D. G. Messerschmidt, Göttingen, 1780.

Abu-Takhir-Hadja. 'Samaria', description of the antiquities and of Mussulman churches of Samarkand. Translated by V. L. Vyatkin. A reference book of the Samarkand Territory, 1898. Repr. Samarkand, 1899. — *Абу-Тахиръ-Ходжа.* „Самарія", описаніе древностей и мусульманскихъ святынь Самарканда, переводъ В. Л. Вяткина.

—— 'Samaria', Tadjik text prepared for publication by N. I. Veselovski. St. P., 1904. — „Самарія", Таджицкій текстъ, приготовленный къ печати Н. И. Веселовскимъ.

A. Ch. 'Mezar'. Picturesque Russia, I, 1901. — *А. Ч.* Могила „Мазаръ".

Adler, B. Der Nordasiatische Pfeil. Beitrag zur Kenntnis der Anthropogeographie des asiatischen Nordens. Suppl. Intern. Arch. f. Ethnol., XIV.

Adrianoff, A. V. Travels in the Kuznietsk Country. Bull. I. R. G. S., 1881, XVII. — *Адріановъ, А. В.* Путешествіе въ Кузнецкій край.

—— Travels to the Altai and beyond the Sayan Mountains in 1881. Omsk, 1888. — Путешествіе на Алтай и за Саяны въ 1881.

—— Extracts from the diaries of the excavations of the Kurgans. Minusinsk, 1900. — Выборки изъ дневниковъ курганныхъ раскопокъ.

—— Sketches of the Minusinsk Country. Tomsk, 1904. — Очерки Минусинскаго края.

—— Preliminary information about the investigation into the 'pisanitsy' of the Minusinsk Country in 1894. Bull. Russ. Committee, No. 4, 1904, pp. 25–34. — Предварительныя свѣдѣнія о собираніи писаницъ въ Минусинскомъ краѣ лѣтомъ 1904 командированнымъ комитетомъ А. В. Адріановымъ.

—— 'Pisanitsa Boyarskaya' from the report of A. V. Adrianoff. Bull. Russ. Committee, No. 6, 1906, pp. 53–9. — Писаница Боярская изъ отчета А. В. Адріанова.

—— Investigations into the 'pisanitsy' of the Minusinsk Country in summer 1907. Bull. Russ. Committee, No. 8, 1908, pp. 37–47. — Обслѣдованіе писаницъ въ Минусинскомъ краѣ лѣтомъ 1907.

—— Report on the excavation of the cave in Mt. Tepsea in 1908. Bull.Russ.Committee, No. 10, 1910, pp. 34–40.—Отчетъ о раскопкѣ пещеры въ горѣ Тепсеѣ 1908.

—— Report on the investigation of the 'pisanitsy' of the Achinsk District of the Minusinsk Country. Bull. Russ. Committee, No. 10, 1910, pp. 41–53. — Отчетъ по обслѣдованію писаницъ Ачинскаго округа (Минусинскаго края).

—— The 'Pisanitsy' along the R. Mana. Mem. Russ. and Slav. Arch. Sect. I. R. Arch. S., IX, pp. 1–34. — Писаницы по рѣкѣ Манѣ.

Afanasieff, F. Contribution to the prehistoric archaeology of Siberia. Archaeological Bulletins and Notices, VI, p. 56. — Афанасьевъ, Ф. Къ доисторической археологіи Сибири.

Afrikanoff, A. M. The Uriankhai Country and its Inhabitants. Bull. E. Sib. Sect. I. R. G. S., XXI, No. 5, 1890. — Африкановъ, А. М. Урянхайская земля и ея обитатели.

Ahmed Arabshah : see Vattier.

Ahmed Ibn Yusuf (Abul Abbas): see Rasmussen, J. L.

Aksy. Antiquities from the ruins of the city of Aksy, in the Chutsk district of the Ferghana Territory. Mem. I. A. S., XXXVIII, 1881, p. 81. — Аксы. Древности изъ развалинъ г. Аксывъ, Чутскомъ уѣздѣ Ферганской области.

Alberts, O. Der türkische Text der bilingualen Inschriften der Mongolei. Halle, 1900.

Aleksandroff. Concerning the ruins of the city of Jankent. Turk. News, 1885, IV, pp. 45–6. — Александровъ. О развалинахъ гор. Джанкента.

Alektoroff, A. E. Sketches of the Middle Orda of the Kirghis (Kaizak). Bull. Oren. Sect. I. R. G. S., 1893, II; 1894, III. — Алекторовъ, А. Е. Очерки Внутренней Киргизской [Кайсацкой] Орды.

Alektoroff, A. E. Index of books, articles and notes on the Kirghis. Bull. S. Arch. H. E. I. Univ. Kaz., 1900, XVI–XX. — Указатель книгъ, журнальныхъ и газетныхъ статей и замѣтокъ о Киргизахъ.

—— Baksa. From the Kirghis (Kaizak) superstitions. Bull. S. Arch. H. E. I. Univ. Kaz., 1900, XVI. — Бакса. Изъ міра Кир-гизскихъ суевѣрій.

A. M. L. Expeditions to the Orkhon. Ency. of Andreevski, 1st ed., 1897, XLIII, p. 227 ; dealing with the expeditions of Paderin (1871); Yadrintseff (1889); Heikel (1890); Radloff (1891). — *А. М. Л.* Орхонскія экспедиціи.

Aminoff, Baron. Remains of sedentary life in the Jizako-Chinask Golodnaya Steppe. Turk. News, No. 27, 1873. — *Аминовъ, баронъ.* Памятники бывшей осѣдлости въ Джизако-Чиназской Голодной степи.

Anciens caractères. Anciens caractères, trouvés sur des pierres de taille et des monuments au bord de l'Orkhon dans la Mongolie orientale par l'expédition de M. N. Jadrintseff en 1889. Ed. by the I. R. Arch. S., St. P., 1890.

Andreas, F. C. Zwei soghdische Exkurse zu Vilhelm Thomsen. Sitzb. K. Preuss. Ak. Wiss., 1910, pp. 307–14.

Andree, R. Spielzeugparallelen. Globus, 1893, 64, p. iii.

Andreyeff, M. S. Places of archaeological interest in Turkestan. Proc. Turk. Circle F. Arch., 1895–6, I. — *Андреевъ, М. С.* Мѣстности Туркестана интересныя въ археологическомъ отношеніи.

—— Translation of the inscriptions from the burial monuments brought by N. F. Sitnyakowski from Shakhrisab and Khitab. Proc. Turk. Circle F. Arch., 1899–1900, V, pp. 104–15. — Переводъ списковъ съ надгробныхъ надписей привезенныхъ Н. Ф. Ситняковскимъ изъ Шахрисябза и Китаба.

Angren. Places of archaeological interest in the valley of the river Angren, in the Tashkent district. Bull. S. Arch. H. E. I. Univ. Kaz., 1893, XI, pp. 568–9. — *Ангренъ.* Мѣстности въ долинѣ р. Ангрена, интересныя въ археологическомъ отношеніи (въ Ташкентскомъ уѣздѣ).

Anichkoff, I. Archaeological journey to the village of Biish-Agach, of the Aulieata district. Proc. Turk. Circle F. Arch., 1895-6, I, pp. 1-11. — *Аничковъ, И.* Археологическая поѣздка въ селеніе Бишъ-Агачъ, Ауліеатинскаго уѣзда.

—— Concerning places of archaeological interest in the Kazalinsk district. Proc. Turk. Circle F. Arch., 1897-8, III, pp. 51-5. — О нѣкоторыхъ мѣстностяхъ Казалинскаго уѣзда, интересныхъ въ археологическомъ отношеніи.

—— Court in Khazaraspa. Proc. Turk. Circle F. Arch., 1898-9, IV, pp. 9-14. — Дворецъ въ Хазараспѣ.

Anikovski, A. Excav ions of the anc ient kurgan burial in the Turgai Territory, Aktyubin District. Proc. Turk. Circle F. Arch., 1902-3, VIII, pp. 95-105. — *Аниковскій, А.* Раскопки древнихъ кургановъ-могильниковъ въ Тургайской области въ Актюбинскомъ уѣздѣ.

—— Ancient burial-kurgans in the Kustanai district of the Turgai Territory. Proc. Turk. Circle F. Arch., 1902-3, VIII, pp. 84-94. — Древніе курганы-могильники въ Кустанайскомъ уѣздѣ Тургайской области.

Annau. Mosque in Annau. ‘Annual’ for 1883, p. 329. St. P., 1883. — *Аннау.* Мечетъ въ Аннау.

Anuchin, D. On ancient bows and arrows. Trans. of the Fifth Arch. Congress in Tiflis, 1881. — *Анучинъ, Д.* О древнемъ лукѣ и стрѣлахъ.

—— On some remarkable stone objects in Siberia. Trans. of the Sixth Arch. Congress in Odessa, 1884, I. — О нѣкоторыхъ своеобразныхъ каменныхъ издѣліяхъ изъ Сибири.

—— Notice sur quelques épées anciennes en bronze, trouvées dans la Russie méridionale et en Sibérie. Compte-rendu du Congr. Intern. Arch. à Moscou, 341, 1892.

Appelgren-Kivalo, Hj. Vogelkopf und Hirsch als Ornaments-motive in der Vorzeit Sibiriens. Finnisch-Ugrische Forschungen, 1912, XII.

Arandarenko, A. The kurgan of Chulak in the Turkestan Territory. Year-book of the Turkestan Statistical Committee. St. P., 1873. — *Арандаренко, А.* Чулакъ курганъ (Туркестанской Области).

Archaeology in the Transcaspian Country. Proc. Turk. Circle F. Arch., 1899–1900, V, pp. 66–8. — Археологія въ Закаспійскомъ краѣ.

Aristoff, N. A. Attempt at an explanation of the ethnic composition of the Kirghis-Kaizak of the Great Orda, and of the Kara-Kirghis based on clan traditions and on the existing clan divisions, on the clan ' tamga ', and also on historical documents and on the anthropological investigations. L. A. T., 1894, I, pp. 391–486. — *Аристовъ, Н. А.* Опытъ выясненія этническаго состава Киргизъ-Казаковъ Большой Орды и Каракиргизовъ на основаніи: родословныхъ сказаній и свѣдѣній о существующихъ родовыхъ дѣленіяхъ и о родовыхъ тамгахъ, а также историческихъ данныхъ и антропологическихъ изслѣдованій.

—— Notes on the Ethnic Composition of the Turkic tribes and nations, and information about their number. L. A. T., 1896, III–IV, repr. St. P., 1897, *see* Barthold, V. V. — Замѣтки объ этническомъ составѣ тюркскихъ племенъ и народностей и свѣдѣнія объ ихъ численности.

Arkhipoff, A. P. Three days in the aul of Yusup-Kadi. Geographical News, 1848, pp. 193–203. — *Архиповъ, А. П.* Три дня въ аулѣ Юсупъ-Кади.

—— Ethnographic sketch of the Nogai and Turkomans. Caucasian Calendar, 1859, pt. iii. — Этнографическій очеркъ Ногайцевъ и Туркменъ.

Arne, T. J. La Suède et l'Orient. Archives d'études orientales, publiées par J. A. Lundell, vol. VIII. Upsala, 1914.

Arnold, T. W. : *see* Houtsma.

Asiatic Russia. Edited by the Immigration Committee of the Department of Agriculture. St. P., 1914. — *Азіатская Россія.* Изданіе Переселенческаго Управленія Главнаго Управленія Землеустройства и Земледѣлія.

Aspelin, J. R. Sur l'âge du Bronze Altaï-ouralien. Compte-rendu du Congrès international d'Archéologie à Stockholm, 1874, I, p. 562.

—— Antiquités du Nord Finno-Ougrien, Helsingfors, 1877–84.

—— Suomalais-ugrilaisen muinaistutkinnon alkeita. Helsinki, 1875.

—— Anteckningar om den finska hästens ursprung. Kalender för finsk trafsport 1887.

—— Fels- und Stein-Inschriften am oberen Jenisci. Z. f. E., 1887, XIX, pt. vi, pp. 529–31.

—— Die Jenisei-Inschriften. Z. f. E., 1889, XXI, pt. vi, pp. 744–6.

—— Inscriptions de l'Yénissei recueillies et publiées par la Société Finlandaise d'Archéologie. Helsingfors, 1889.

—— Types de peuples de l'ancienne Asie Centrale. Souvenir de l'Iénisséi, dédié à la Société Impériale d'Archéologie de Moscou. Helsingfors, 1890.

—— Die Steppengräber im Kreise Minssinsk am Jenissei. Finnisch-Ugrische Forschungen, XII, 1. Helsingfors, 1912.

Asret, a Mohammedan church in Turkestan. 'Reference sheet of the town of Kazan', 1867, No. 5. — *Азретъ,* магометанская святыня въ Туркестанѣ.

Atkinson, J.: *see* Firdausī.

Atkinson, T. W. Oriental and Western Siberia. London, 1858.

Aulya, a Kirghis temple 'Aulya' near Lake Jektybay. Bull. S. Arch. H. E. I. Univ. Kaz., 1893, XI, p. 295.—*Аулья,* Киргизская святыня „ Аулья " вблизи Джектыбайскаго озера.

Auteroche, C. J d'. Voyage en Sibérie fait par ordre du roi en 1761. Paris, 1768.

Avvakum (Archimandrite). On an inscription found on a rock at the cave of Mangut. Mem. Sib. Sect. I. R. G. S., 1856, II, pp. 87–9. — *Аввакумъ, Архимандритъ.* О надписи, находя-щейся на скалѣ у Мангутской пещеры.

—— On an inscription on a gravestone situated on the banks of the Amur, not far from its mouth. Mem. Sib. Sect. I. R. G. S., 1856, II, pp. 78–9.—О надписи на каменномъ памятникѣ, находя-щемся на берегу рѣки Амура, недалеко отъ впаденія ея въ море.

B. M., Review of V. Thomsen's 'Inscriptions de l'Orkhon déchiffrées', 1894, I.   Journ. des Savants, 1900, p. 443.

Baber: *see* Vyatkin, V. L.; Erskine, W.; Beveridge, A. S.; Talbot, A. S.; and Courteille, de P.

Babinger, Fr. Ein schriftgeschichtliches Rätsel. Rev. Or., 1913, XIV, pp. 4–19.

Bang, W.   Review of V. Thomsen's 'Inscriptions de l'Orkhon déchiffrées' (1894). Litt. Centralblatt, 1900, pp. 537–9.

—— Zu den köktürkischen Inschriften und den türkischen Turfan-Fragmenten. W. Z. K. M., 1909, XXIII, pp. 415–19.

—— Review of W. W. Radloff's 'Die alttürkischen Inschriften der Mongolei', Neue Folge, 1897. T. P., 1897, VIII, p. 533.

—— Turkologische Epikrisen. Heidelberg, 1910.

—— Zur köktürkischen Inschrift I. E. 19–21. T. P., 1896, VII, p. 611.

—— Zur Erklärung der köktürkischen Inschriften. W. Z. K. M., 1898, XII, pp. 34–54.

—— Zu den köktürkischen Inschriften. T.P., 1898, IX, pp. 117–41.

—— Über die köktürkische Inschrift auf der Südseite des Kül-Tägin Denkmals. Leipzig, 1896.

—— Zu den Kök-Türk-Inschriften der Mongolei. T. P., 1896, VII, pp. 325–55.

—— Köktürkisches. W. Z. K. M., 1897, XI, pp. 192–200.

Barshchevski, L. S.   Collection of antiquities from Afrosyab and other places in Central Asia. Archaeological Bulletins and Notes, 1895, III, pp. 19–20. St. P. — *Барщевскій, Л. С.* Коллекція древностей изъ Афросіаба и другихъ мѣстъ Средней Азіи.

Barthold, V. V.   Christianity in Turkestan in the pre-Mongol period. H. P. 1893. — *Бартольдъ, В. В.* О Христіанствѣ въ Туркестанѣ въ до-Монгольскій періодъ.

—— Report of the Commission to Central Asia. Mem. E.
Sect. I. R. Arch. S., 1894, VIII, pp. 339–44; 1904, XV,
pp. 173 ff. — Отчетъ о командировкѣ въ Среднюю Азію.

—— Report of a journey to Central Asia with a scientific object,
in 1893–4. Mem. I. A. S., 1897, VIII, I, No. 4. — Отчетъ
о поѣздкѣ въ Среднюю Азію съ научною цѣлью, 1893–4.

—— Die historische Bedeutung der alttürkischen Inschriften. In
'Die alttürkischen Inschriften der Mongolei' of W. W. Radloff.
Neue Folge, 1897.

—— Gravestone inscription of 660 A.H. (=1262 A.D.) in Aulie-Ata
in the Semirechie territory. Mem. E. Sect. I. R. Arch. S.,
XII, pt. v, p. 189. — Надгробная надпись 660 г. X. (=1262 по
Р. X.) изъ г. Аулiе-Ата Семирѣченской обл.

—— Review of 'Samaria' by Abu-Takhir-Hadja. Mem. E. Sect.
I. R. Arch. S., 1899, XII, pp. 0123–0125. — Рецензія книги
Абу-Тахиръ-Ходжа „ Самарія ".

—— Die alttürkischen Inschriften und die arabischen Quellen.
'Die alttürkischen Inschriften der Mongolei' of W. W. Radloff.
Zweite Folge, 1899.

—— Mosque in Bibi-Khanym. 'Russian Turkestan', 1899,
No. 34. — Мечеть Биби-Ханымъ.

—— Review of Aristoff's 'Notes on the Ethnic Composition of the
Turkic tribes and nations, and information about their number'.
Mem. E. Sect. I. R. Arch. S., 1899, XI, 1–4, pp. 341–60. —
Рецензія книги Аристова: „ Замѣтки объ этническомъ составѣ
тюркскихъ племенъ и народностей и свѣдѣнія объ ихъ
численности ".

—— Vilhelm Ludwig Peter Thomsen. Ency. Andreevski, 1st
ed. Vol. LXVI, 1901, p. 482. — Вильгельмъ-Людвигъ-Петеръ
Томсенъ.

—— Merverrud. Mem. E. Sect. I. R. Arch. S., 1902, XIV,
pp. 028–038. — Мерверрудъ.

—— New investigation into the Orkhon inscriptions. J. Min. Educ.,
1902, pp. 231–325. — Новыя изслѣдованія объ Орхонскихъ
надписяхъ.

Barthold, V. V. Review of E. Chavannes' 'Documents sur les Tou-Kiue occidentaux'. Collection of Documents of the Orkhon Expedition, VI, 1903, in Mem. E. Sect. I. R. Arch. S., XV, 0162–0185. — Рецензія книги Chavannes, E.: Documents sur les Tou-Kiue (Turks) occidentaux.

——— The system of numerals of the Orkhon inscriptions used in the modern dialect. Mem. E. Sect. I. R. Arch. S., 1906, pt. XVII, pp. 0171–3. — Система счисленія Орхонскихъ надписей въ современномъ діалектѣ.

——— Turkestan at the time of the Mongol invasion. I, 1896; II, 1900, St. P. — Туркестанъ въ эпоху монгольскаго завоеванія.

——— History of the study of the East in Europe and in Russia. Man. Orient. Stud. St. Pet. Univ., 1911, No. 38. — Исторія изученія Востока въ Европѣ и въ Россіи.

Bartholomew, J. G. Literary and Historical Atlas of Asia. London, 1912.

Basset, R.: *see* Houtsma.

Baye, Baron de. Rapport sur les découvertes faites par M. Savenkov dans la Sibérie Orientale. Paris, 1894.

Bayer, Th. S. Vetus inscriptio prussica. Commentarii Academiae Scient. Imp. Petropolitanae, 1729, II, pp. 470–81.

Bayjumuroff, D. The Kyzyl-Gyanch Court (in the Karkalinsk district). Proc. Turk. Circle F. Arch., 1899–1900, V, pp. 90–3. — *Байжумуровъ, Д.* Кызылъ-Гянчскій дворецъ (въ Каркаралинскомъ уѣздѣ).

Beauvois, E. Review of V. Thomsen's 'Inscriptions de l'Orkhon déchiffrées' (1894). In Revue critique, 1897, XLIII, pp. 268–70.

Bekchurin, Mir Salikh. Ancient mosque of Asret situated in Turkestan. Collection of Military Essays, 1866, No. 8, pp. 209–19. — *Бекчуринъ, Миръ Салихъ.* Описаніе мечети Азрета находящейся въ Туркестанъ.

Bell, M. S. The great Central Asian trade route from Pekin to Kashgar. Proc. R. G. S., 1890, XII, pp. 57–93.

Bellew, H. W. The History of Kashgaria. Calcutta, 1875.

——— Kashmir and Kashgar. London, 1875.

Bergeron, P. Voyages faits principalement en Asie dans les xiiᵉ, xiiiᵉ, xivᵉ et xvᵉ siècles. [Benjamin de Tudelle, Jean de Plancarpin, Père Ascelin, Guillaume de Rubruquius, Marco Polo, Hayton, Jean de Mandeville.] La Haye, 1735.

Bergmann, B. F. B. Nomadische Streifereien unter den Kalmuken in den Jahren 1802 und 1803. Riga, 1804–5.

Besthorn, R. Review of V. Thomsen's 'Déchiffrement des inscriptions de l'Orkhon et de Jénisséi' (1894). Nationaltidende, 1894, No. 6393.

—— Review of V. Thomsen's 'Inscriptions de l'Orkhon déchiffrées' (1894). Nationaltidende, 1896, No. 7126.

Beveridge, A. S. The Memoirs of Bābur; a new translation of the Bābur-nāma, incorporating Leyden and Erskine's of A. D. 1826. London, 1912.

Bichurin (Father Jakinth). Notes on Mongolia. St. P., 1828. — Бичуринъ, Отецъ Іакинѳъ. Записки о Монголіи.

—— Collection of information concerning peoples living in Central Asia in ancient days. St. P., 1851. — Собраніе свѣдѣній о Народахъ обитавшихъ въ Средней Азіи въ древнія времена.

—— see Klaproth, H. J. von.

Biddulph, J. Tribes of the Hindoo-Koosh. Calcutta, 1880.

Blagovyeshchenski, Y. Die wirtschaftliche Entwicklung Turkestans. 'Rechts- und Staatswiss. Studien'. Heft 46.

Blanc, E. Antiquités de Samarkande. Revue des Deux Mondes, 15 février 1893.

—— Mausolée de Tamerlan à Samarkande. Comptes-rendus de l'Acad. des Inscriptions et Belles-Lettres, 1896, pp. 272–303. Paris.

—— Sur les inscriptions des principaux sarcophages dans le Mausolée de Tamerlan à Samarkande. Comptes-rendus de l'Acad. des Inscriptions et Belles-Lettres, 1896, XXIV, p. 272.

Blochet, E. Les inscriptions de Samarkande. Le Goûr-i-mīr ou Tombeau de Tamerlan. Revue Archéologique, sér. 3, 1897, XXX, pp. 67 ff., 202 ff.

Blochet, E.   Le nom des Turcs dans l'Avesta.   J. R. A. S., 1915, pp. 305–9.

—— Les inscriptions turques de l'Orkhon. Revue Archéologique, sér. 3, pt. XXXII (1898), pp. 356–82; pt. XXXIII (1898), pp. 352–65.

—— *see* Rashid al-Dīn Tabīb.

Bobrinski, Count A. A.   Collection of archaeological essays presented to Count A. A. Bobrinski on the twenty-fifth anniversary of his presidency of the Imperial Archaeological Commission.   St. P., 1911. — *Бобринскій, Графъ А. А.* Сборникъ археологическихъ статей, поднесенный Гр. А. А. Бобринскому въ день 25 лѣтія предсѣдательства его въ И. Арх. Коммиссіи.

Bode, Baron K.   On the Turkoman clans of Yamud and Goklan. Mem. I. R. G. S., 1847, II, pp. 203–32. — *Боде, Баронъ К.* О Туркменскихъ поколѣніяхъ Ямудахъ и Гокланахъ.

—— Sketches of the land of the Turkomans and the south-eastern shore of the Caspian Sea.   Otechestvyennya Zapiski, 1856, CVII. — Очерки Туркменской земли и юго-восточнаго прибрежья Каспійскаго моря.

Böhtlingk, O.   Ueber die Sprache der Jakuten.   *See* Middendorff, Reise in den äussersten Norden.

Bogdanoff, A. P., and **Deniker, J.**   Notes anthropométriques sur les Indigènes du Turkestan.   L'Anthropologie, 1891.

Bogdanoff, A. P.   The skulls from the kurgans of the Tarsk district, Tobolsk Government.   Russ. Anthr. J., 1917, XXXI, pts. 1–6. — *Богдановъ, А. П.*   Курганные черепа Тарскаго округа, Тобольской Губерніи.

Bogolubski, I. S.   Investigation into the antiquities of the Minusinsk district in 1881.   Bull. E. Sib. Sect. I. R. G. S., XIII, pp. 43–6. — *Боголюбскій, И. С.*   Изслѣдованіе древностей Минусинскаго округа въ 1881.

Bonaparte, Prince Roland.   Documents de l'époque mongole des XIIIe et XIVe siècles.   (Lithographed) Paris, 1895.

Bonin, Charles-Eudes.   Voyage de Pékin au Turkestan Russe par la Mongolie, le Koukou-nor, le Lop-nor et la Dzoungarie. La Géographie, Paris, vol. III (1901), pp. 115–22, 169–80.

Bonvalot, G. Les ruines de la vallée du Sourkhane. Revue d'Anthropologie, 1883, II, pp. 385 ff.

——— En Asie centrale. De Moscou à Bactriane. Paris, 1884.

——— Du Kohistan à la Caspienne. Paris, 1885.

——— Du Caucase aux Indes à travers le Pamir. Paris, 1888.

Borg, K. F. von der. Denkwürdigkeiten über die Mongolei. Translation of Bichurin's Notes on Mongolia. Berlin, 1822.

Borrodaile, A. A. Notes of a Journey in Northern Mongolia in 1893. Geogr. Journ., Nov. 1903, XXII.

Bouillane de Lacoste : *see* Lacoste.

Boyer. Discovery of a buried town built by Afrosyab in the district of Shakh-yara in Turkestan. Novorossiiski Telegraph, 1891, No. 5083. — *Бойеръ.* Открытіе въ Туркестанѣ, въ окрестностяхъ Шахъ-яра, подземнаго города, построеннаго Афросіабомъ.

Bretschneider, E. Notes on Chinese mediaeval travellers to the West. Shanghai, 1875.

——— Notes on the mediaeval geography and history of Central and Western Asia. Journ. of the North China Branch of the R. A. S., 1876, pp. 190 ff.

——— Mediaeval researches frcm Eastern Asiatic sources, fragments towards the knowledge of the geography and history of Central and Western Asia from the 13th to the 17th centuries. Truebner's Oriental Series, London, 1888.

Brown, R. The Yenisei inscriptions. Bab. Orient. Rec., 1889–90. IV, pp. 231–8.

——— The Yenisei inscriptions. Academy, 1890, XXXVII, pp. 103, &c.; XXXVIII, p. 251.

Bruce, C. D. Chinese Turkestan. J. Centr. As. S., 1907.

Brunnhoffer, H. Archaeological objects and aims of Russia in Central Asia. Bull. S. Arch. H. E. I. Univ. Kaz., 1892, X, pp. 240–2. — *Бруннгоферъ, Г.* Археологическія задачи и цѣли Россіи въ центральной Азіи.

Bryanoff, A.   Excavations in Kishlak-Aksa.   Turk. News, 1882, No. 26. — *Брянов, А.*   Раскопки въ Кишлякѣ-Аксы.

—— Traces of the ancient town of Kasan in the Ferghana district. Proc. Turk. Circle F. Arch., 1898–9, IV, pp. 142–53. — О слѣдахъ древняго города Касана въ Ферганской области.

Burana.   A column on the R. Burana in the Tokmak district, and legends of the Kirghis and Sart relating to it.   Transactions of the Fourth Archaeological Congress, 1884, I, p. lxiv. — *Бурана.*   Колонна при р. Буранѣ въ Токмакскомъ уѣздѣ и соединенныя съ этимъ памятникомѣ легенды Киргизовъ и Сартовъ.

Burns, A.   Travels into Bokhara . . . 1831–2.   London, 1835.

Byelkin, D. Z. : *see* Obrucheff.

Cahun, L.   Formation territoriale de l'Asie.   Timour et le Second Empire Mongol.   In L'Histoire générale, edited by E. Lavisse and A. Rambaud.

—— Origine des nations turques — Tchingiz-Khan et l'Empire Mongol.   In L'Histoire générale, edited by E. Lavisse and A. Rambaud.

—— Introduction à l'Histoire de l'Asie.   Turcs et Mongols des Origines à 1405.   Paris, 1896.

Campbell, C. W.   Report by C. W. Campbell, His Majesty's Consul at Wuchow, on a journey in Mongolia.   Blue Book, Series China, 1904, No. 1.

Campbell, J.   Siberian inscriptions.   Transactions of the Canadian Institute, III, p. 20.

Capus.   Le Toit du Monde.   Paris, 1890.

Carpini, John of Plano : *see* Yule.

Carruthers, D.   Unknown Mongolia.   London, 1913.

Castagné, J. A.   Antiquités des steppes Kirghises et du pays d'Orenburg.   Paris, 1910.

Castrén, M. A.   Nordiska Resor och Forskningar.   Helsingfors, 1852–70.

—— Nordische Reisen und Forschungen.   I. Reiseerinnerungen aus den Jahren 1838–44 (1853).   II. Reiseberichte u. Briefe aus d. J. 1845–8 (1856).   III. Vorlesungen über Finnische

Mythologie (1853). IV. Ethnologische Vorlesungen (1857). V. Kleinere Schriften (1862). VI. Versuch einer Ostjakischen Sprachlehre (1849). VII. Grammatik der Samojedischen Sprachen (1854). VIII. Wörterverzeichniss aus den Samojedischen Sprachen (1855). IX. Grundzüge einer Tungusischen Sprachlehre (1856). X. Versuch einer Burjatischen Sprachlehre (1857). XI. Versuch einer Koibalischen und Karagassischen Sprachlehre nebst Wörterverzeichnissen aus den Tatarischen Mundarten des Minussinschen Kreises (1857). XII. Versuch einer Jenissei-Ostjakischen und Kottischen Sprachlehre (1858). St. Petersburg.

Chabot, J. B. Histoire du Patriarche Mar Jabalaha III et du Moine Rabban Çauma. Traduite du Syriaque. Revue de l'Orient Latin, 1893, I and II.

Chaffanjou, J. Rapport sur une mission scientifique dans l'Asie centrale et la Sibérie. Archives des missions scientifiques, 1899, sér. 4, IX, pp. 51–101. Paris.

Chalon, P. F. En Mongolie: le pays des Saiotes. Revue de Géographie, 1904, LIV.

Chardin, J. Voyage en Perse et autres lieux de l'Orient. Amsterdam, 1711.

Chavannes, E. Review of V. Thomsen's ' Inscriptions de l'Orkhon déchiffrées' 1894, I. J. A., 1895, IX, vol. vi, pp. 191–3.

—— Mémoires historiques. Paris, 1895–1905.

—— Dix inscriptions chinoises de l'Asie centrale d'après les estampages de M. Ch.-E. Bonin. Paris, 1902.

—— Documents sur les Tou-Kiue (Turcs) occidentaux. Collection of Documents of the Orkhon Expedition, VI. St. P., 1903.

—— Review of A. von Le Coq's ' Köktürkisches aus Turfan'. T. P., 1908, sér. II, vol. X, p. 717.

—— Review of V. Thomsen's ' Ein Blatt in türkischer Runenschrift aus Turfan'. T. P., 1910, sér. II, vol. XI, p. 303.

—— Les Documents chinois découverts par Aurel Stein dans les sables du Turkestan. Oxford, 1913.

Chavannes, É., and **Pelliot, P.**   Un Traité Manichéen retrouvé en Chine.   J. A., 1911, II.

Chazaud, Bertaud du.   La mission de Lacoste dans la Mongolie septentrionale.   Bull. Soc. anthr. de Paris, 1910, sér. VI, pt. i, pp. 127–33.

Cherkassoff, A.   Journey to the ruins of Otrar.   Proc. Turk. Circle F. Arch., 1902–3, VIII, pp. 70–74. — *Черкасовъ, А.* Поѣздка на развалины Отрара.

Chermak, L.   The Sedentary Kirghis Agriculturists on the R. Chu.   Mem. W. Sib. Sect. I. R. G. S., 1900, XXVII. — *Чермакъ, Л.*   Осѣдлые Киргизы-земледѣльцы на р. Чу.

Chertoff, V. I.   The ancient kurgans in the Katta-Kurgan district. Annual Book of the Samarkand Territory, 1897, V, pp. 247–51. — *Чертовъ, В. И.* Древніе курганы въ Катта-Курганскомъ уѣздѣ.

Chirol, Sir V.   The Far Eastern Question.   London and New York, 1896.

—— The Middle Eastern Question; or some political problems of Indian Defence.   London, 1903.

Chupin, N.   On some ancient roads from European Russia into Siberia.   News-sheet from the Irbit Fair, 1872, pp. 16–25. — *Чупинъ, Н.*   О нѣкоторыхъ древнихъ дорагахъ изъ Европейской Россіи въ Сибирь.

Church, P. W.   Chinese Turkestan, with caravan and rifle. London, 1901.

Cigny, F. de: *see* Levshin, A.

Cohn, L.   Die Ruinen des alten Merw.   Petermann's Mitteilungen, 1894, pp. 68 ff.

Compte-rendu des travaux de la Société Finno-ougrienne du 2/xii 1906 au 2/xii 1907.   J. Soc. Finno-ougr. XXV, pt. v, pp. 35–70.

Cordier: *see* Yule.

Courant, M.   L'Asie centrale aux xviie et xviiie siècles.   An. Univ. Lyon, N.S. 1912, II, pp. 151 ff.

Courteille, P. de, and **Vambéry, A. V.**   Jagataische Sprach-studien.   Leipzig, 1867.

—— Mémoires de Baber.   Paris, 1871.

Cowley, A. Another unknown language from Eastern Turkestan. J. R. A. S., 1911, pp. 159–277.

Croizier. Les monuments du Samarcande de l'époque des Timourides. Paris, 1891.

Cuinet, V. La Turquie d'Asie. Paris, 1890–5.

Cuno, J. G. Forschungen im Gebiete der alten Völkerkunde. I. Theil. Die Skythen. Berlin, 1871.

Curtin, J. The Mongols: a History. London, 1908.

—— A journey in S. Siberia. Boston, 1909.

Curtis, W. C. Turkestan : ' the heart of Asia'. London, 1911.

Curzon, Lord G. N. Russia in Central Asia in 1889 and the Anglo-Russian question. London, 1889.

—— Problems of the Far East. London, 1894.

—— The Pamirs and the source of the Oxus. London, 1898.

Czaplicka, M. A. The influence of environment upon the religious ideas and practices of the aborigines of Northern Asia. Folklore, March, 1914.

—— Aboriginal Siberia. Oxford, 1914.

—— Review of E. H. Minns's ' Scythians and Greeks'. Man, 1917, No. 108.

—— The evolution of the Cossack communities. J. Centr. As. S., 1918, V, pt. 2.

—— The Samoyed. E. R. E.

—— and **Hall, H. U.** ' Report of the Expedition to the Yenisei, 1914–1915.' [To be published shortly.]

D. Review of W. Radloff's ' Proceedings of the Orkhon Expedition. Atlas of the Mongolian Antiquities ', 1892–9. Bull. E. Sib. Sect. I. R. G. S., XXVI, vol. iv, pp. 247–8. — Д. Рец. Радлова В. В. Труды Орхонской Экспедиціи. Атласъ Древностей Монголіи.

Daulbaeff, B. D. Account of the life of the Kirghis of the Nikolaeff district, Turgai territory, from 1830 to 1880. Mem. Oren. Sect. I. R. G. S., 1881, IV, pp. 98–117. — Даулбаевъ, Б. Д. Разсказъ о жизни Киргизовъ Николаевскаго уѣзда Тургайской Области съ 1830–1880.

Davy, Major : *see* Timur.

Davydoff, S. A.   Home industry in Central Asia.   Tashkent, 1890. — *Давыдовъ, С. А.*   Кустарная промышленность въ Средней Азіи.

—— On the ancient monuments and burial remains of the aborigines of the Transbaikal territory, Verkhneudinsk district.   Mem. Sib. Sect. I. R. G. S., II, 1856, pp. 89–101. — О древнихъ памятникахъ и могильныхъ остаткахъ аборигеновъ Забайкальской области, Верхнеудинскаго округа.

Deasy, H. H. P.   In Tibet and Chinese Turkestan.   London, 1901.

Defrémery, C., and **Sanguinetti :** *see* Ibn Batoutah.

Demidoff, E.   After Wild Sheep in the Altai and Mongolia. London, 1900.

Deniker, J.   Notes sur les inscriptions du Yénissei.   T. P., 1891, II, 3, pp. 232 ff.

—— and **Yadrintseff, N. M.**   Discoveries in Mongolia : the travels of Yadrintseff and Radloff, 1889–91.   Bab. Orient. Rec., 1892–3, VI, pp. 43–8.

—— Expédition Radlov.   T. P., 1892, III, pp. 98–100.

—— Articles on ' Tatars ' and ' Turks ' in the Dict. Univ. de Géogr. of Vivien de Saint-Martin and Rousselet, vol. VI, 1894.

—— Les explorations russes en Asie centrale.   Ann. de Géogr., 1897, VI, pp. 408–30.

Desideri, I. : *see* Puini, C.

Desmaisons, Baron.   Abul-Gazy-Bahadur Khan.

Devéria, G.   Inscriptions sibériennes: Comptes-rendus de l'Ac. des Inscript., 1890, XVIII, pp. 448–58.   Paris.

—— Observations sur l'écriture turque-altaïque, la stèle de Gueuk Téghin et l'emplacement de Kara-Korum.   Comptes-rendus de l'Ac. des Inscript., 1891, XIX, pp. 365–8.   Paris.

—— Inscriptions recueillies à Kara-Korum.   Relevé des différents signes figurant dans les copies rapportées par M. Yadrintseff. T. P., 1890, I, pp. 275–6.   Leyden.

—— Transcription, analyse et traduction des fragments chinois du second et du troisième monument. Inscriptions de l'Orkhon, p. xxviii. 1892.

—— La stèle funéraire de Kiuéh Teghin. Notice de Ye-lu-tchou (xɪɪɪᵉ siècle). Extraite de l'ouvrage intitulé Choang-ki-tsoue-intsi. T. P., 1891, II, pt. 3, pp. 229–37.

—— Notes on the Yenisei and Karakorum script. Bab. Orient. Rec., 1891, V, pt. 6, pp. 121–7.

Diez, E. Die Kunst der islamischen Völker.

Divayeff, A. A. Information about the ancient sites in the village of Akjar in the Tashkent district. Proc. Turk. Circle F. Arch., 1895–6, I, pp. 36–8. — *Диваевъ, А.* Сообщеніе о древнихъ урочищахъ въ Акджарской волости Ташкентскаго уѣзда.

—— and **Akhmeroff, P. N.** Inscription in the mosque of Akhmed Asavi. Bull. S. Arch. H. E. I. Univ. Kaz., 1896, XIII, pp. 538–51. — *Диваевъ, А. А., и Ахмеровъ, П. Н.* Надписи мечети Ахмеда Ясави.

—— Note on the grave of St. Khorkhut-At. Mem. E. Sect. I. R. Arch. S., 1897, X, pp. 193–4. — Нѣсколько словъ о могилѣ св. Хорхуть-Ата.

—— Old Kirghis burial customs. Bull. S. Arch. H. E. I. Univ. Kaz., 1897–8, XIV, pp. 181–7. — Древне-Киргизскіе похоронные обычаи.

—— Tradition about the origin of the Asiatic town of Tashkent. Proc. Turk. Circle F. Arch., 1899–1900, V, pp. 145–51. — Преданіе о возникновеніи Азіатскаго города Ташкента.

—— Additional note on the grave of St. Khorkhut-At. Mem. E. Sect. I. R. Arch. S., 1900, XIII, pp. 039–040. — Еще о могилѣ св. Хорхуть-Ата.

—— Concerning the Kirghis cattle-breeding. Dromedary, horse, cow, ram, goat. Tashkent, 1906. — Изъ области Киргизскаго скотоводческаго хозяйства. Верблюдъ, лошадь, корова, баранъ, козелъ.

Djelaleddin, Mustapha. Les Turcs anciens et modernes. Constantinople, 1869.

Dm., N. Asiatic Bibliography. Supplement to Mejoff's Bibliography. Turk. News, 1895, Nos. 15, 16, 18, 26, 28. — *Дт., Н.* Азіатская библіографія. По поводу книги Межова, съ дополненіями къ ней.

Dmitrowski, N. V. Bibliographical index of the Essays on Central Asia printed in Russia and in the Russian language from 1692–1870. Year-book of the Turkestan Country, 1874, pt. III, St. P. — *Дмитровскій, Н. В.* Библіографическій указатель сочиненій о Средней Азіи, напечатанныхъ въ Россіи на русскомъ языкѣ съ 1692 года (по 1870).

Dmitryeff, A. A. Isker on the Irtysh; a town of Kuchum. Bull. S. Arch. H. E. I. Univ. Kaz., 1900, XVI, pp. 257–72. — *Дмитріевъ, А. А.* Кучумовъ Искеръ на Иртышѣ.

Dmitryeff-Kavkaski, L. E. Through Central Asia. Notes of an artist. St. P., 1895. — *Дмитріевъ-Кавказскій, Л. Е.* По Средней Азіи. Записки художника.

Dobrosmuisloff, A. I. Towns of Syr-Daria territory: Kazalinsk, Perovsk, Turkestan, Aulieata, and Chimkient. Tashkent, 1912. — *Добросмуисловъ, А. И.* Города Сыръ-Дарьинской области : Казалинскъ, Перовскъ, Туркестанъ, Ауліеата и Чимкентъ.

Donner, O. Die Felseninschrift bei Suljek. Ofversigt af Finska Vetenskaps-Societetens Förhandlingar, XXXI, pp. 9–13. Helsingfors, 1889.

—— Les Inscriptions en caractères de l'Jénisséi. Système d'écriture. Langue. Inscriptions de l'Orkhon, p. xxxix. Helsingfors, 1892.

—— Wörterverzeichniss zu den ' Inscriptions de l'Jénisséi'. Mém. Soc. Fin.-Ougr., IV, p. 69. Helsingfors, 1892.

—— Sur l'origine de l'alphabet turc du Nord de l'Asie. J. Soc. Fin.-Ougr., 1896, XIV, p. 1.

—— Ueber Ausgrabungen und alttürkische wie uigurische Inschriften aus Turkestan. Verhandlungen des 13. Orientalisten-Kongresses. Hamburg, 1902 (Leiden, 1904), pp. 159–60.

—— Voyage en Turkestan et en Dzonngarie en 1898.   Fennia, 1901, XVIII, No. 4, p. 53.

Dorn, B. Muhammedanische Quellen zur Geschichte der südlichen Küstenländer des Kaspischen Meeres.   Petrograd and Leipzig, 1850–58.

—— Forschungen in der Pehlewy-Münzkunde.   Mélanges Asiatiques tirés du Bull. I. A. S. St. Pétersbourg, IV, pt. 1, pp. 22–4. St. P., 1860.

Drouin, E. La numismatique araméenne sous les Arsacides. J. A., 1889, p. 377.

—— Review of V. Thomsen's 'Inscriptions de l'Orkhon déchiffrées', I, 1894.   J. A., 1894, Sér. IX, vol. iv, pp. 571–5.

—— Review of W. W. Radloff's ' Die alttürkischen Inschriften der Mongolei', Neue Folge, 1897.   J. A., 1898, XII, p. 341.

—— Review of J. Marquart's 'Die Chronologie der alttürk. Inschriften'.   1898.   Revue critique, 1899, IV, pp. 61–3.

—— Sur quelques monnaies turco-chinoises.   Revue numismatique, 1891, IX, pp. 459–73.

—— Les inscriptions sibériennes.   J. A., 1893, Sér. IX, vol. i, pp. 171–7.

Dudin, S. M. : *see* W. W. Radloff's 'Collection of Documents of the Orkhon Expedition, 1892–1903 ', vol. I, pp. 24–7.

—— The ornament and the state of preservation of the mosques of Samarkand. Bull. I. Arch. Commission, 1903,VII, pp. 49–73. St. P. — Дудинъ, С. М.   Орнаментика и современное состояніе старинныхъ Самаркандскихъ мечетей.

Duhousset, Colonel.   Étude sur les populations de la Perse. Paris, 1863.

Dutreuil de Rhins, J. L.   Mission scientifique dans la Haute Asie, 1890–1895, ed. F. Grenard.   Paris, 1897–8.

Dyachkoff, P. A.   Issyk-Kul lake and its northern shore.   Bull. Turk. Sect. I. R. G. S., 1898, I, pp. 1–14. —- Дьячковъ, П. А. Озеро Иссыкъ-Куль и его сѣверный берегъ.

Egnatius (Jo. Baptista).   De origine Turcarum.   Paris, 1539.

Elias, N. Narrative of a Journey through West Mongolia. J.R.G.S., vol. XLII, pp. 184 ff. London.

—— and **Ross, E. D.**   Muhammad Haidar.   The Tarikh i Rashidi. . . . A history of the Moghuls of Central Asia.   An English version, edited, with commentary, notes and map, by N. Elias. . . . The translation by E. D. Ross.   London, 1895. Re-issue 1898.

Eliot, Sir C. N. E.   Turks.   Ency. Brit., 11th ed., XXVII, pp. 468–73.

Ellesmere, Earl of : *see* Major, R. H.

Erckert, E. von. Forschungsreise nach dem Oberlauf des Flusses Orchon zu den Ruinen von Karakorum durch N. M. Jadrinzeff, 1889.   Deutsche Rundschau f. Geogr. u. Stat., 1891, XIII, pt. ii, pp. 516 ff.

Erdmann, F. von. Vollständige Übersicht der ältesten Türkischen, Tartarischen und Mogholischen Völkerstämme nach Rashid-ed-dins Vorgange, bearbeitet von F. von Erdmann.   Kazan, 1841.

—— Temudschin der Unerschütterliche.   Leipzig, 1862.

Erman, A.   Travels in Siberia.   London, 1878.

Erskine, W. (and **Leyden, J.**).   Memoirs of Zehir-ed-Din Muhammed Baber, Emperor of Hindustan, written by himself, in the Jaghatai Turkic, and translated partly by the late John Leyden, partly by William Erskine.   London, 1826.

Etherton, P. T.   Across the Roof of the World.   London, 1911.

Evarnicki, D. I.   Guide to Central Asia from Baku to Tashkent with reference to archaeology and history.   Tashkent, 1893. — Эварницкій, Д. И. Путеводитель по Средней Азіи отъ Баку до Ташкента въ археологическомъ и историческомъ отношеніи.

—— Archaeological Investigation in the Turkestan country (Samarkand).   Bulletins and Notes from the gazette ' Borderland ', 1893, I, p. 29.   Moscow. — Археологическія изалѣдованія въ Туркестанскомъ краѣ (Самаркандѣ).

Expeditions.

Expeditions (1875–88) of Przewalski, N. M.: *see* Morgan, E. D.; *also* Przewalski, N. M.

Expeditions of Roborovsky to Central Asia (1880–95): *see* Roborovsky.

Finnish Expedition to the Orkhon in 1890; *see* Inscriptions; *see also* Heikel, A. O.

Russian Expedition to Orkhon. A. Collection of Documents of the Orkhon Expedition: vol. I, 1892 (*see* Radloff); vol. II, 1895 (*see* Klements, Obrucheff); vol. III, 1897 (*see* Vasilyeff); vol. IV, 1897 (*see* Radloff and Melioranski); vol. V, 1901 (*see* Yadrintseff); vol. VI, 1903 (*see* Chevannes). B. Atlas of Mongolian Antiquities: vol. I, 1892; vol. II, 1893; vol. III, 1896; vol. IV, 1899 (*see* Radloff).

Expedition of Brothers Grzymailo (Grijimailo), (1892–96): *see* Morgan, E. D.; *also* Grum-Grzymailo, G. E.

Expeditions of Obrucheff, V. A. (1892–1906): *see* Obrucheff, V. A.

Expedition to Mongolia (1892–93): *see* Posdnyeff, A. M.

Expedition to Turfan, 1893 (Imp. Acad. of Science, St. Petersburg): *see* Klements, D. A., and Radloff, W. W.; *see also* Turfan.

I. R. G. S. Expedition to Mongolia, 1899–1901: *see* Kozloff, P. K.

Danish Expedition to Pamir: *see* Olufsen, O.

Expedition of Monck and Donner to Chinese Turkestan, 1898: *see* Sénart, E.

German Expeditions to Turkestan: (1) in 1902–3: *see* Grünwedel. (2) in 1904–5: *see* Le Coq. (3) in 1906–7: *see* Grünwedel *and* Le Coq.

Expedition to Mongolia in 1903: *see* Rudnyeff.

Expeditions of Pumpelly, 1903 and 1904: *see* Pumpelly, R.

Notice of Japanese Expedition (Zuicho Tachibana) to Chinese Turkestan and Mongolia. J. R. G. S., Jan. to June, 1910, XXXV, p. 448. London.

Fabricius, M. P. The Sayan Country. Bull. I. R. G. S., 1899, XXXV. — *Фабрициусъ, М. П.* Саянскій край.

Faddeyeff. Collection of antiquities from Afrosyab. Trans. I. Moscow Arch. S., 1894, XV, pt. i, p. 105. — *Фаддѣевъ.* Коллекція древностей изъ Афросіаба.

Farrer, R. The Moslem Problem in China. J. Centr. As. S., 1918, vol. V, pp. 59–71.

Favicki, P. G. The discovery of the ancient ruins near Khojent. Bull. I. R. G. S., 1867, III, pt. ii, No. 7, p. 200. — *Фавицкій, П. Г.* Открытіе древнихъ развалинъ близь Ходжента.

Ferganyets. The Transcaspian Territory with reference to its Archaeology. Turk. News, 1888, Nos. 24 and 25.— *Ферганецъ.* Закаспійская область въ археологическомъ отношеніи.

Finsch, O. Reise nach West-Sibirien im Jahre 1876. Berlin, 1879.

Firdousi (Abu 'l Casim). The Sháh Naméh. Transl. from Persian by J. Atkinson. London, 1886; another ed. 1892. Other transl. by A. S. Werner, 1905; by A. Rogers, 1907.

—— Schahnameh; le livre des rois. Traduit et commenté par Jules Mohl. Paris, 1838–78.

Fischer, J. E. Sibirische Geschichte von der Entdeckung Sibiriens bis auf die Eroberung dieses Landes durch die russischen Waffen. St. P., 1768.

Fischer, H. Ueber Timur's (Tamerlan's) Grabstein aus Nephrit. Archiv für Anthropologie, 1880, XII, pp. 469–74, mit 3 Abbild.

Flinders Petrie, W. M. Review of Tallgren's 'Collection Tovostine des Antiquités préhistoriques de Minoussinsk'. Man, 1917, No. 134.

—— Review of Tallgren's 'Collection Zaoussailov au Musée historique de Finlande à Helsingfors'. Man, 1917, No. 86.

Florinski, V. M. On the stone 'baba' and Siberian inscriptions. Archaeological Museum of Tomsk University. Tomsk, 1888, pp. 166–75. — *Флоринскій, В. М.* Каменныя бабы и Сибирскія письмена.

Fromm, E. Deciphering of Orkhon and Yenisei Inscriptions. Globus, 1894, pt. 66, p. 325.

Foy, K. Die Sprache der türkischen Turfanfragmente in manichäischer Schrift. I. Sitzungsber. d. k. Berl. Akad. d. Wiss. 15, 1904, XII.

—— Türkische Vocalstudien, besonders das Köktürkische und Osmanische betreffend. Mitth. Sem. Orient. Spr. zu Berlin, 1900, III, 2, pp. 180 ff.

Forke, A. Review of E. Chavannes's 'Documents sur les Tou-Kiue (Turcs) occidentaux', 1903. L. Z., 1909, pp. 1128–30.

Forsyth. Report of a mission to Yarkand. Calcutta, 1875.

Franke, O. Beiträge aus chinesischen Quellen zur Kenntniss der Türkvölker und Skythen Zentralasiens. K. P. Ak. Wiss., 1904, Abh. I, pp. 1–111.

—— Eine chinesische Tempelinschrift aus Idikutšahri bei Turfan. K. P. Ak. Wiss., 1907, Abh. I, pp. 92 ff.

Fraser, M. F. A. Translation of N. M. Yadrintseff's 'A journey to the upper waters of the Orkhon and the ruins of Karakorum'. J. China Br. R. A. S. S. N. S., XXVI, pp. 190–207.

Fressl, J. Die Skytho-Saken die Urväter der Germanen. Munich, 1886.

Friederichsen, Max. Review of J. G. Granö's 'Reiseerinnerungen aus Westsibirien und der Mongolei', 1907. Petermann's Mittheilungen 56, II, L, p. 38.

Futterer, K. Durch Asien. Berlin, 1901–1909.

G. Notes on the ancient sites of the Turkestan country. Turk. News, 1879, No. 12. — *Г.* Замѣтка о древнихъ урочищахъ Туркестанскаго края.

G. V. Journey to the basin of Lake Issyk-Kul. (Its antiquities.) Semip. Terr. News, 1890, Nos. 31 and 33. — *Г. В.* Поѣздка въ долину озера Иссыкъ-Куля (о древностяхъ).

G. G. Notes on the antiquities of the Kirghis-Kaizak Steppe. Extract from the 'Review of the Kirghis-Kaizak Steppe'. Siberian News, 1822, XXX, pp. 321–8. — *Г. Г.* Замѣчанія о древностяхъ въ Киргизъ-Кайсацкой степи. Извлеченіе изъ „Обозрѣнія Киргизъ-Кайсацкой степи".

Gabelentz, A. v. d. L'inscription chinoise du premier monument. Inscriptions de l'Orkhon, pp. xxv–vi. Helsingfors, 1892.

Galkin, A. On the subject of the antiquities from Issyk-Kul. Turk. News, 1891, No. 40. — *Галкинъ, А.* Къ вопросу объ Иссыкъ-Кульскихъ древностяхъ.

Galkin, M. N. Ethnographical Materials relating to Central Asia and the Orenburg country. Mem. I. R. G. S., 1867, pt. i, pp. 1–250. — *Галкинъ, М. Н.* Этнографическіе матеріалы по Средней Азіи и Оренбургскому краю.

Gardner, P. Coins of the Greek and Scythic kings of Bactria and India. London, 1886.

Garteveld, V. N. Among the shifting sands and decapitated heads. St. P., 1913. — *Гартевельдъ, В. Н.* Среди сыпучихъ песковъ и отрубленныхъ головъ.

Gaubil, A. Abrégé de l'histoire chinoise de la grande dynastie Tang. Mémoires concernant l'histoire des Chinois, XV–XVI.

—— Histoire de Gentchiscan et de toute la dynastie des Mongols. Paris, 1739.

—— Traité de la chronologie Chinoise, publié par Silvestre de Sacy. Paris, 1814.

Gauthiot, R. Review of E. C. Andreas's ' Zwei sogdische Exkurse zu Wilhelm Thomsen' (1910). J. A., 1910, X, p. 5404.

—— Review of V. Thomsen's ' Ein Blatt in türkischer Runenschrift aus Turfan' (1910). J. A., 1910, XV, pp. 538–54.

—— Note sur la langue et l'écriture inconnues des documents Stein-Cowley. J. R. A. S., 1911, pp. 496–508.

—— De l'Alphabet Sogdien. J. A., XVIII, pp. 81–96. Paris, 1911.

Gedroyć, K. I. : *see* Obrucheff.

Geins, A. K. A sketch of the Kirghis. Military Essays, 1866, XLVII–XLIX, Nos. 1, 6, 7. — *Гейнсъ, А. К.* Киргизскіе Очерки.

Georgi, J. G. Bemerkungen einer Reise im Russischen Reich in den Jahren 1773 und 1774. St. P., 1775.

Gertsulin, M. Y. Kishlak-Tadjik in the Ferghana Territory. 'Niva', 1898, pp. 991, 994, 995. — *Герцулинъ, М. Я.* Кишлакъ-Таджикъ въ Ферганской области.

Geyer, I. I. Account of the ruin of Termez. Proc. Turk. Circle F. Arch., 1896, p. 29. — *Гейеръ, И. И.* Сообщеніе о развалинахъ Термеза.

Giles, H. A. Chung Tzŭ. 1889.

—— China and the Chinese. New York, 1912.

—— Tun Huang Lu. Notes on the district of Tun-Huang. J. R. A. S., 1914.

Gins, G. K. The Taranchi and the Dungan. Sketches from a journey to Semirechie. Historical News, 1911, No. 8, pp. 672–708. — *Гинсъ, Г. К.* Таранчи и Дунгане. Очерки изъ поѣздки въ Семирѣчью.

Gmelin, J. G. Reise durch Sibirien von dem Jahr 1733 bis 1743. Göttingen, 1751–2.

Golovacheff, P. M. Siberia. Moscow, 1914. — *Головачевъ, П. М.* Сибирь.

Golubowski, P. The Pyechenyegi, the Törki, and the Polovtsy until the Tatar invasion. History of Southern Steppes of Russia in IX–XIII cent. Kieff, 1884. — *Голубовскій, П.* Печенѣги, Торки и Половцы до нашествія Татаръ. Исторія Южно-Русскихъ степей IX–XIII в.

Golubyeff, A. Episode from travels in Central Asia in the Trans-Ili country. Mem. I. R. G. S., 1861, No. 3. — *Голубевъ, А.* Отрывокъ изъ путешествія въ Среднюю Азію, Заилійскій край.

Gordlewski, V. A. Note on the 'Turk Darnay' in Constantinople. Eastern Antiquities. Trans. E. Comm. I. Moscow Arch. S., 1913, IV, Moscow. — *Гордлевскій, В. А.* Замѣтка о 'Турецкомъ Собраніи' въ Константинополѣ.

Gorodtsoff, V. A. Description of the collection of Siberian antiquities belonging to O. B. Egerski-Strumillo. Rep. I. R. Hist. Mus., 1915. Petrograd, 1915. — *Городцовъ, В. А.* Описаніе коллекціи сибирскихъ древностей г. О. Б. Эгерскаго-Струмилло.

Gorokhoff. A short ethnographical description of the Kalmuck of Biisk or Altai. J. M. Int., 1840, XXXVIII, pp. 201–28. — *Гороховъ.* Краткое этнографическое описаніе Бійскихъ или Алтайскихъ Калмыковъ.

Goroshchenko, K. I. Burial-masks of gypsum and a special type of trepanation in the Kurgans of the Minusinsk district. Trans. of the Tenth Arch. Congress in Riga, 1896. Repr. 1898. — *Горощенко, К. И.* Гипсовыя погребальныя маски и особый видъ трепанаціи въ курганахъ Минусинскаго округа.

—— Skulls from the Kurgans of the Minusinsk district. Description of the collection in the Minusinsk Museum, II. Minusinsk, 1900. — Курганные черепа Минусинскаго округа.

—— Materials for the anthropology of Siberia. Mem. Krasn. S.W. Sib. Sect. I. R. G. S., 1905, I, pt. ii. — Матеріалы по антропологіи Сибири.

—— and **Ivanowski, A. A.** The Natives of the Yenisei. Russ. Anthrop. Journ., 1907, I, II. — *Горощенко, К. И., и Ивановскій, А. А.* Енисейскіе Инородцы.

Gramienyecki, D. Notes on the ancient sites of the Turkestan country. Proc. Turk. Circle F. Arch., 1897–98, III, pp. 150–57. — *Граменецкій, Д.* Замѣтка о древнихъ урочищахъ Туркестанскаго края.

Granö, J. G. Reiseerinnerungen aus Westsibirien und der Mongolei. Medd. af Ggr. Föreningen i Finland, 1907–9, VIII, pp. 1–104.

—— Archäologische Beobachtungen von meinen Reisen in den nördlichen Grenzgegenden Chinas 1906, 1907. Helsingfors, 1909.

—— Archäologische Beobachtungen von meiner Reise in Südsibirien und der Nordwest-Mongolei im Jahre 1909. Helsingfors, 1910.

—— Ueber die geographische Verbreitung und die Formen der Altertümer in der Nordwest-Mongolei. J. Soc. Fin.-Ougr., 1912, XXVIII. Helsingfors.

—— Matkakertomus. J. Soc. Fin.-Ougr., 1908, XXV, pt. v, pp. 18–19. Helsingfors.

—— Bericht über eine Reise J. G. Granö's nach Uranhai zur Aufnahme alttürkischer Inschriften. J. Soc. Fin.-Ougr., 1907, XXIV, pt. v, pp. 17, 29. Helsingfors.

Grebyenkin, A. D. The Usbegs. Russian Turkestan. Moscow, 1872. — *Гребенкинъ, А. Д.* Узбеки. Русскій Туркестанъ.

Grenard, F. : *see* Dutreuil de Rhins.

Grenman, H. Zur Frage der ostsibirischen Inschriften. Öfvers. Finska Vetenskaps Soc. Förhandl., XXXI, pp. 14–17. Helsingfors.

Grigoryeff, V. V. Description of the Khanate of Khiva and of the road thither from the fortress of Saraychik. Mem. I. R. G. S., 1861, pt. ii, pp. 255–89. — *Григорьевъ, В. В.* Описаніе Хивинскаго ханства и дороги туда изъ Сарайчиковской крѣпости.

—— Eastern or Chinese Turkestan; being Chapter V of Ritter's 'Erdkunde', translated and completed. St. P., 1869. — Восточный или Китайскій Туркестанъ. Переводъ Главы V „Землевѣдѣнія" К. Риттера съ присовокупленіемъ критическихъ примѣчаній и дополненій.

—— The Scythian Nation of Saka. St. P., 1871. — О Скиѳскомъ народѣ Сакахъ.

—— The Karakhanids in Maveraannagr. Trans. E. Sect. I. R. Arch. S., 1874, XVII, pp. 198 ff. — Караханиды въ Маверааннагрѣ.

Grodekoff, N. I. The Kirghis and the Kara-Kirghis of the Syr-Daria Territory. Tashkent, 1889. — *Гродековъ, Н. И.* Киргизы и Кара-Киргизы Сыръ-Дарьинской области.

Grotenfelt, K. Review of W. Radloff's 'Proceedings of the Orkhon Expedition'. Atlas of the Mongolian Antiquities. 1892–99. Valvoja (Helsingfors), 1892, pp. 631–8.

—— Review of V. Thomsen's 'Inscriptions de l'Orkhon déchiffrées', I (1894–6). Valvoja, 1896, pp. 240–48.

—— Review of W. Radloff's 'Die alttürkischen Inschriften der Mongolei' (1894). Valvoja, 1896, pp. 240–48.

Gruleff, M. V. Some geographical-statistical information relating to the Amu-Daria district between Char-Jui and Patta-Gissar. Bull. Turk. Sect. I. R. G. S., 1900, II, pt. i, p. 187. — *Грулевъ, М. В.* Нѣкоторыя географико-статистическія данныя, относящіяся къ участку Аму-Дарьи между Чарджуемъ и Патта Гиссаромъ.

Grum-Grzymailo, G. E., and **Grum-Grzymailo, M. E.**
Description of Travels in Western China. St. P., 1896–9. —
Грумъ-Гржимайло, Г. Е., и Грумъ-Гржимайло, М. Е.
Описаніе путешествія въ Западный Китай, составлено Г. Е.
Грумъ-Гржимайло при участіи М. Е. Грумъ-Гржимайло.

Grum-Grzymailo, G. E.   The historical past of Béy-Shan in
connexion with the history of Central Asia.   St. P., 1898. —
Грумъ-Гржимайло, Г. Е.   Историческое прошлое Бей-Шаня
въ связи съ исторіей Средней Азіи.

—— Materials for the Ethnology of Amdo and the district of
Kuku-Nor.   Bull. I. R. G. S., 1903, XXXIX, pp. 437–80. —
Матеріалы по этнологіи Амдо и области Куку-Нора.

—— Western Mongolia and the Uriankhai country.   St. P., 1914.
— Западная Монголія и Урянхайскій край.

Grünwedel, A.   Bericht über archäologische Arbeiten in Idikut-
schari und Umgebung im Winter 1902–1903.   Abh. K. Ak. d.
Wiss. der philos.-philol, Classe, 1906, Bd. 24, Abt. 1.   Munich.

—— Some critical remarks concerning the archaeological work of
Professor Dr. Albert Grünwedel in Chinese Turkestan.   Bull.
of the Russ. Committee for the Study of Eastern and Central
Asia, 1903, No. 1, pp. 20–29. — *Грюнведель, А.* Нѣсколько
критическихъ замѣчаній относительно археологическихъ работъ
въ Китайскомъ Туркестанѣ проф. Дра Альберта Грюнведеля.

—— Altbuddhistische Kultstätten in Chinesisch-Turkistan. Bericht
über archäologische Arbeiten von 1906 bis 1907 bei Kuia,
Qaraśahr und in der Oase Turfan.   Berlin, 1912.

Guignes, J. de.   Histoire générale des Turcs, des Mongols et des
autres Tartares occidentaux.   Paris, 1756–8.

Gulayeff, S.   Antiquities in course of discovery in the Kirghis
Steppe.   Mess. I. R. G. S., 1853, VII and VIII, pp. 22–5. —
Гуляевъ, С.   Древности открываемыя въ Киргизской степи.

Gutmann, B.   The Smith and his Craft in Animistic Thought.
Z. f. E., 1912, 44, pp. 81 ff.

Gutschmid, A. von.   Die Skythen.   In Kl. Schriften, IV. Leipzig,
1892.

Hakluyt. The Journey of Friar William of Rubruck. Hak. Soc. Publ., Second Series, 1900, No. IV.

—— *see* Yule, H.; Major, R. H.; Herbertstein, S.

Halde, J. B. du. Description géographique, historique, chronologique, politique et physique de l'empire de la Chine et de la Tartarie chinoise. Paris, 1735.

Halévy, J. Review of O. Donner's ' Sur l'origine de l'alphabet turc du Nord de l'Asie ', 1896. Revue Sémitique, 1896, IV, pp. 378–9. Paris.

Hall, H. U., and **Czaplicka, M. A.:** *see* Czaplicka.

Haller, O. Dr. W. Radloff's ' Vorläufiger Bericht über die Resultate der mit Allerhöchster Genehmigung von der K. Akademie der Wissenschaften ausgerüsteten Expedition zur archäologischen Erforschung des Orchon-Beckens '. Aus dem Russischen übersetzt. Bull. I. A. S., N.S. III (XXXV, 1892), pp. 353–98.

Hammer-Purgstall, J. von. Fundgruben des Orients, bearbeitet durch eine Gesellschaft von Liebhabern. Vienna, 1809–10.

—— Geschichte des Osmanischen Reiches. Vienna, 1827–35.

—— Geschichte der Goldenen Horde. Buda-Pest, 1840.

Hartmann, M. Zu der Sprache der Fragmente in Runenschrift. W. Z. K. M., 1910, XXIV, pp. 124–5.

—— Mudammadanism (in China). E. R. E., 1915, VIII, p. 889.

—— Der Islamische Orient. Berlin, 1905.

Hedin, S. A. Through Asia. London, 1898.

—— Central Asia and Tibet. London, 1903.

—— Scientific results of a journey in Central Asia, 1899–1902. Stockholm, 1904–7.

—— Overland to India. London, 1910.

Heger, F. Review of ' Inscriptions de l'Orkhon recueillies par l'Expédition finnoise 1890 . . .' Helsingfors, 1892. Mitth. Anthrop. Ges. Wien, 1892, XXII, pt. 6, p. 224.

Heger, F.   Review of W. Radloff's ' Vorläufiger Bericht über die Resultate der mit Allerhöchster Genehmigung von der K. Akademie der Wissenschaften ausgerüsteten Expedition zur archäologischen Erforschung des Orchon-Beckens '.   Mittheil. Anthrop. Ges. Wien, 1892, XXII, pp. 222–4.

—— Review of W. Radloff's ' Proceedings of the Orkhon Expedition. Atlas of the Mongolian Antiquities', 1892–9. Mittheil. Anthrop. Ges. Wien, 1892, XXII, pt. 6, pp. 222–4.

——Reisen im Kaukasus, in Transkaspien und Russisch-Turkestan. Annalen des K. K. Naturhist. Hofmuseums, Bd. V, Heft IV. Wien, 1890, Notizen, pp. 115–42.

Heikel, A. O.   A notice.   Eastern Review, 1891, pp. 13–14. *Гейкель, А. О.* Замѣтка.

—— Antiquités de la Sibérie occidentale conservées dans les Musées de Tomsk, de Tobolsk, de Tiumien, d'Ékatérinbourg, de Moscou et d'Helsingfors.   Mém. Soc. Fin.-Ougr., VI. Helsingfors, 1892.

—— Les Ouïgours et le troisième monument Kharakorum.   Inscriptions de l'Orkhon, p. xxi.   Helsingfors, 1892.

—— Les Toukioux et les deux premiers monuments.   Inscriptions de l'Orkhon, p. xvii.   Helsingfors, 1892.

—— Antiquités diverses dans la Transbaïkalie.   Inscriptions de l'Orkhon, p. xiii.   Helsingfors, 1892.

—— Les monuments près de l'Orkhon.   Inscriptions de l'Orkhon, p. vii.   Helsingfors, 1892.

—— Voyage jusqu'à l'Orkhon.   Inscriptions de l'Orkhon, pp. i–vi. Helsingfors, 1892.

—— Review of V. Thomsen's ' Inscriptions de l'Orkhon déchiffrées', I, 1894 and 1896.   Hufrudstads bladet, 11th Feb. 1896.

—— Die Grabuntersuchungen und Funde bei Taschebá.   Soc. Finl. d'Archéol., 1912, XXVI.

Hekker, N. A.   Materials for a description of the physical characteristics of the Yakut.   Mem. E. Sib. Sect. I. R. G. S.,

1896. — *Геккеръ, Н. А.* Къ характеристикѣ физическаго типа якутовъ.

Herbelot, B. d'. Bibliothèque Orientale, ou Dictionnaire Universel contenant généralement tout ce qui regarde la connoissance des peuples de l'Orient. Paris, 1867. Another edition with supplement entitled ' Bibliothèque orientale de MM. Visdelou et Galaud, contenant les observations sur ce que les historiens arabes et persiens rapportent de la Chine et de la Tartarie, dans la Bibliothèque Orientale de M. d'Herbelot'. Maestricht, 1776–82.

—— Orientalische Bibliothek. Translated from the French by T. C. F. Schulz. Halle, 1785–90.

Herberstein, Baron von S. Notes upon Russia; being a translation of the earliest account of that country, entitled Rerum Moscoviticarum Commentarii by the Baron Sigismund von Herberstein, translated by R. H. Major. Hakluyt Society. London, 1851–2.

Herrmann, A. Alte Geographie des unteren Oxusgebiets. Abh. Kön. Ges. Wiss., Bd. 15, N.F. Göttingen, 1914.

Herzfeld, E. Zur Islamischen Archaeologie. Berlin, 1907.

Hirth, F. China and the Roman Orient. Leipzig, 1885.

—— Über den Verfasser und Abschreiber der chinesischen Inschrift am Denkmal des Köl-Tägin. T. P., 1896, VII, pp. 151–7.

—— Nachworte zur Inschrift des Tonjukuk. Die alttürk. Inschriften der Mongolei von W. W. Radloff. Zweite Folge. St. P., 1899.

—— Neue Forschungen über das Geschlecht Attila's. Beilage zur Allg. Ztg., 1900, VIII, vol. iv, No. 177.

—— Über Wolga-Hunnen und Hiung-nu. Sitz. der philos.-philol. und hist. Classe der K. B. Ak. d.Wiss., 1900, Bd. II, pp. 245–78. Munich.

—— The Ancient History of China. Leipzig, 1908.

History. Momentous events in Siberian history of the eighteenth cent. St. P., 1882. — Памятники Сибирской исторіи восемнадцатого вѣка.

Historical Records of Seventeenth Century, edited by I. P. Kuznietsoff - Krasnoyarski, 1890. Tomsk. — Историческіе Акты, XVII ст.

Hoernle, A. F. R. The 'Unknown Languages' of Eastern Turkestan. J. R. A. S., 1910, pp. 834–9, 1283–1301 ; 1911, pp. 477–8.

—— A Report on the British Collection of Antiquities from Central Asia. London, 1914.

Houdas, O. : *see* Mohammed-en-Nesavi.

Houtsma, T. Ein türkisch-arabisches Glossar nach der Leidener Handschrift. Leyden, 1894.

—— Review of J. Marquart's 'Die Chronologie der alttürk. Inschriften', 1898. Gelehrte Anzeigen, 1899, No. 5, pp. 384–90.

—— Die Ogusen-Stämme. W. Z. K. M., Bd. II.

—— The Encyclopaedia of Islam. Edited by Th. Houtsma, T. W. Arnold, R. Basset, and H. Bauer (A–H) 1908–14. Leyden and London.

Howorth, Sir H. H. The western drifting of nomades, from the fifth to the nineteenth century. J. A. I., 1872, I, pp. 226–54 ; 1874, II, 452–72.

—— The Avares, or Eastern Huns. J. A. I., 1873, II, pp. 114–27.

—— Introduction to the Translation of the Han Annals. J. A. I., 1874, III, pp. 396–401.

—— History of the Mongols from the ninth to the nineteenth centuries. Part I. The Mongols proper and the Kalmuks (1876). Part II. The so-called Tartars of Russia and Central Asia (1880). Part III. The Mongols of Persia (1888). London.

Huc, E. R. Travels in Tartary and Tibet. London, 1852.

—— The Chinese Empire. 1855.

—— Christianity in China and Tartary and Tibet. London, 1857.

Huntington, E. The pulse of Asia. London, 1907.

—— Problems in Exploration : Central Asia. Geog. Journ., 1910, XXXV.

Hüsing, G. Völkerschichten in Iran. Mitt. Anthr. Ges., 1916, XXXVI. Vienna.

Huth, G. Die Inschrift von Karakorum. Eine Untersuchung über ihre Sprache und die Methode ihrer Entzifferung. Berlin, 1892.

Ibn-Batoutah [Abu Abdullah]. Voyages. Texte et traduction par C. Défrémery et le Dr. Sanguinetti. Paris, 1853–9.

Ibrahimoff, I. Account of the life of the Kirghis. In ' Ancient and Modern Russia ', pt. iii. 1876. — Ибрагимовъ, И. Очерки быта Киргизовъ.

Ignatieff, R. G. Remains of the antiquities of the Kurgan district, Tobolsk Government. Tob. Gov. News, 1873, Nos. 18–22, 24, 25. — Игнатьевъ, Р. Г. Памятники Древностей Курганскагс округа, Тобольской губ.

Ilkin, B. A journey undertaken for the purpose of collecting information about Uljikent. Proc. Turk. Circle F. Arch., 1899–1900, V, pp. 152–6. — Илькинъ. Б. Поѣздка, совершенная съ цѣлью собрать свѣдѣнія объ Ульджикентѣ.

Ilyenko, I. The Transcaspian territory. Moscow, 1902. — Ильенко, И. Закаспійская область.

Infantyeff, P. P. Ethnographical narratives from the life of the Tatars, Kirghis . . .   St. P., 1910. — Инфантьевъ, П. П. Этнографическіе разсказы изъ жизни Татаръ, Киргизовь . . .

Inostrantseff, K. A., and **Smirnoff, Y. I.** : see Smirnoff.

Inscriptions.

Inscriptions de l'Jénisséi recueillies et publiées par la Société Finlandaise d'Archéologie.   Helsingfors, 1889.   *See also* Heikel, A. O.

A marble plate with Arabian inscription found thirty versts from Tashkent.   Rep. I. Arch. Commission, 1890, pp. 113–47. St. P. — Надписи. Блюдо мраморное ся арабской надлисью найденное въ 30 верстахъ отъ Ташкента.

Old Turkish inscriptions in Mongolia.   Nature, LX, p. 262.

Orkhon inscriptions.   Encycl. of Andreevsky, 1st ed., 1897, vol. XLIII, p. 226. — Орхонскія надписи.

Inscriptions de l'Orkhon recueillies par l'Expédition finnoise 1890 et publiées par la Société Finno-Ougrienne. Helsingfors, 1892. *See* Heikel, A. O.

Die Orkhon-Inschriften.   Umschau, III, pp. 775 ff.

The Orkhon inscriptions.   Academy, XLII, p. 242.

Irkibay. Ancient temple situated seven versts from Irkibay, a former fortress of Turkestan.   Bull. I. R. G. S., 1874, X, pt. i, p. 361. — *Иркибай.* Древній храмъ въ 7-ми верстахъ отъ Иркибая, бывшаго укрѣпленія въ Туркестанѣ.

Irtish. Old settlements along the R. Irtish.   Mem. I. A. S., 1877, XXX, No. 2, pp. 9-10. — *Иртышъ.* Городища по рѣкѣ Иртышу.

Iske-toy-tyube. Archaeological discoveries in Iske-toy-tyube. Turk. News, 1875, No. 21. — *Иске-той-тюбе.* Археологическія находки въ Иске-той-тюбе.

Issyk-Kul.

Three stones with Arabic inscriptions found in a temple between the station of Kurumdu and Sazonovka at Lake Issyk-Kul. Archeolog. Bulletins and Notes, 1894, II, p. 409.   St. P. — *Иссыкъ-Куль.* Три камня съ арабскими надписями, въ молельнѣ между ст. Курумду и Сазоновкой на оз. Иссыкъ-Куль.

Archaeological discoveries at Lake Issyk-Kul. Semip. Terr. News, 1890, Nos. 31 and 33. — Археологическія находки у озера Иссыкъ-Куль.

Ruins at the bottom of Lake Issyk-Kul. 'Caucasus', 1891, No. 273. — Развалины на днѣ озера Иссыкъ-Куля.

Ivanin, M. Roads and means of transport in Central Asia. Coll. of Milit. Essays, 1869, No. 8. — *Иванинъ, М.* Пути въ Средней Азіи и перевозочныя средства.

Ivanoff, D. L. Concerning some Turkestan antiquities. Bull. I. R. G. S., 1885, XXI, 162-77. — *Ивановъ, Д. Л.* По поводу нѣкоторыхъ Туркестанскихъ древностей.

Ivanowski, A. A. Memorial stones. Trans. of the Eighth Archaeological Congress in Moscow, 1890, IV, p. 185. — *Ивановскій, А. А.* О намогильныхъ камняхъ.

—— Periodical publications in Siberia and Central Asia. Essays on Ethnography. Bibliographical Notes, 1892, No. 7. — Періодическія изданія Сибири и Средней Азіи. Указатель статей по этнографіи.

—— Anthropological composition of the population of Russia. Bull. Soc. F. S. Anthr. E., 1904, CV. — Объ антропологическомъ составѣ населенія Россіи.

—— Population of the world. Attempt at an anthropological classification. Bull. Soc. F. S. Anthr. E., 1911, CXXI. — Населеніе Земного Шара. Опытъ антропологической классификаціи.

—— *see* Wulfson, E.

—— and **Goroshchenko, K. I.** : *see* Goroshchenko, K. I.

Jankent.
Ruins of Jankent on the left bank of Syr-Daria. Bull. I. R. Arch. S., 1872, VII, pp. 286–90. — *Джанкентъ.* Развалины Джанкента на лѣвомъ берегу Сыръ-Дарьи.

Ruins of Jankent. Year-book of the Turkestan country. III. St. P., 1874. — Развалины Джанкента.

Legends relating to Jankent. Proc. Turk. Circle F. Arch., 1897–8, III, pp. 58–62. — Легенда о Джанкентѣ.

Essays about Jankent. Proc. Turk. Circle F. Arch., 1897–8, III, pp. 62–8. — Статьи о Джанкентѣ.

Jensen, Kr. Sandfeld. Review of V. Thomsen's 'Inscriptions de l'Orkhon déchiffrées', 1894. Nordisk Tidskr. f. Filol. Række 3, IV, 4, 179–83.

Jespersen, O. Tydningen af Orkhon-Indskrifterne. Illustr. Tidende, 1894, XXXV, pp. 387–8.

Jochelson-Brodsky, D. L. Contribution to the anthropology of the women of the North-eastern Siberian tribes. Russ. Anthr. J., 1907, Moscow. — *Іохельсонъ-Бродская, Д. Л.* Къ Антропологіи женщинъ племенъ крайняго сѣверо-востока Сибири.

Jochelson, W.   Kumiss festivals of the Yakut.   Boas Anniversary Volume, New York, 1906.

Johansson, K. F.   Om de fornturkiska inskrifterna från Orkhon och Jenissei samt Prof. Vilh. Thomsens dechiffrering och tolkning därom.   Ymer, 1896, XVI, pp. 151-9.

Joyce, T. A.   On the physical anthropology of the oases of Khotan and Keriya.   J. R. A. I., July, 1903, XXXIII.

Jukowski, S. V.   Relations between Russia, Bokhara, and Khiva for the last 300 years.   Petrograd, 1915. — *Жуковскій, С. В.* Сношенія Россіи съ Бухарой и Хивой за послѣднее 300 лѣтъ.

Jukowski,V. A.   Investigations in the Transcaspian territory.   Rep. I. Arch. Commission, 1890, pp. 79-86, and 1896, pp. 104-5. *Жуковскій, В. А.* Изслѣдованія въ Закаспійской области.

—— Antiquities of the Transcaspian country.   Novoye Vremya, 1891, No. 5301. — О древностяхъ Закаспійскаго края.

—— The antiquities of the Transcaspian country.   Ruins of old Merv.   Materials for the Archaeology of Russia.   I. R. Arch. S., No. 16, St. P., 1894. — Древности Закаспійскаго края. Развалины стараго Мерва.

—— *see* Tisenhausen, Baron.

Julien, S. A.   Documents historiques sur les Toukioue (Turcs). J. A., Série VI, vols. iii-iv.   Paris, 1864.

—— Mémoires sur les Contrées Occidentales, traduits du Sanscrit en Chinois ... par Hiouen-Thsang ... et du Chinois par S. A. Julien.   Voyages des Pèlerins Bouddhistes, Paris, 1853-8.

—— Histoire de la vie de Hiouen-Thsang et de ses voyages dans l'Inde ... par Hoeï-Li et Yen-Thsong, trad. du Chinois par S. A. Julien.   Voyages des Pèlerins Bouddhistes, Paris, 1853-8.

Jung, J.   Die Schriftzeichen von Orkhon.   Sitzb. d. Gel. Estn. Ges., 1898, pp. 34-41.

Junge, R.   Das Problem der Europäisirung orientalischer Wirtschaft dargestellt an den Verhältnissen der Sozialwirtschaft von Russisch-Turkestan.   Arch. f. Wirtsch. im Näheren Orient, 1915.

Juwayni, Ala'u'd-Din 'Ata Malik-i. The Ta'rikh-i Jáhanfusha, edited from seven MSS. by Mirza Muhammad of Qagwin. Vol. I, 1912; vol. II, 1916 (E. W. J. Gibb).

K. D. Review of the book by Y. Y. Trusman, ' The Chud Script '. Mem. E. Sect. I. R. Arch. S., 1899, XI, 1-4, pp. 367-8. — *К. Д.* Рецензія книги Ю. Ю. Трусмана „ Чудскія письмена ".

Kal, E. F. Persian, Arabic and Turkic MSS. in the Turkestan Library. Tashkent, 1889. — *Каль, Е. Ф.* Персидскія, арабскія и тюркскія рукописи Туркестанской Библіотеки.

—— Erections in the Aulieata district of the Syr-Daria territory. Rep. I. Arch. Commission, 1890, pp. 76-7. — Постройки въ Аулieатинскомъ уѣздѣ, Сыръ-Даріинской области.

Kalacheff, A. Excursion to the Telengit of the Altai. L. A. T., 1896, VI, Nos. 3-4, pp. 477-88. — *Калачевъ, А.* Поѣздка къ Теленгитамъ на Алтай.

Kallaur, V. A. Ancient sites in the Aulieata district on the old caravan route from Taras (Talas) to Eastern Turkestan. Proc. Turk. Circle F. Arch., May 5, 1897. — *Каллауръ, В. А.* Древнія мѣстности Аулieатинскаго уѣзда на старомъ караванномъ пути изъ Тараза [Таласа] въ восточ. Туркестанъ.

—— Photograph of a Kirghis grave containing various implements and inscriptions. Proc. Turk. Circle F. Arch., 1899–1900, V, p. 38. — Фотографія киргизскаго надгробія съ изображеніемъ различныхъ инструментовъ и надписью.

—— A stone with old Turkic inscription from the Aulieata district. Mem. E. Sect. I. R. Arch. S., 1899, XI, 1-4, pp. 79-85. — Камень съ древне-тюркской надписью изъ Аулieатинскаго уѣзда.

—— A new archaeological discovery in the Aulieata district. Mem. E. Sect. I. R. Arch. S., 1899, XI, 1-4, pp. 265-71. — Новая археологическая находка въ Аулieатинскомъ уѣздѣ.

—— Ruins of Syrli-Tam in the Perovsk district. Proc. Turk. Circle F. Arch., 1900-1, VI, pp. 14-17. — Развалины „ Сырлы-Тамъ ", въ Перовскомъ уѣздѣ.

Kallaur, V. A. The ruins of ancient towns and villages in the Perovsk district in the valley of Syr-Daria and Yani-Daria. Proc. Turk. Circle F. Arch., 1902–3, VIII, pp. 49–69.—Древніе города и селенія [развалины] въ Перовскомъ уѣздѣ, въ долинѣ р.р. Сыръ-Дарьи и Яны-Дарьи.

—— Mausoleum of Kok-Kesene in the Perovsk district. Proc. Turk. Circle F. Arch., 1900–1, VI, pp. 98-101. — Мавзолей Кокъ-Кесене въ Перовскомъ уѣздѣ.

—— On the traces of the old town of Jend on the lower Syr-Daria. Proc. Turk. Circle F. Arch., 1899–1900, V, pp. 78-89. — О слѣдахъ древняго города „Джендъ", въ низовьяхъ р. Сыръ-Дарьи.

—— Contribution to the history of the town of Aulieata. Proc. Turk. Circle F. Arch., 1902–3, VIII, pp. 11-18. — Къ исторіи гор. Аулiеата.

—— The ancient towns of Saganak (Sunak) Ashnas or Eshnas (Asanas) and others in the Perovsk district destroyed by Jinghis Khan in 1219. Proc. Turk. Circle F. Arch., 1899–1900, V, pp. 6-16. — Древніе города Саганакъ [Сунакъ], Ашнасъ или Эшнасъ [Асанасъ] и другіе въ Перовскомъ уѣздѣ, разрушенные Чингизъ-Ханомъ въ 1219 г.

—— Antiquities from the valley of the R. Talas. Proc. Turk. Circle F. Arch., 1888–9, IV, pp. 73-80. — Древности въ низовьяхъ р. Таласа.

—— Akyr-Tash. Proc. Turk. Circle F. Arch., 1895-6, I, pp. 25-7. Tashkent. — Акыръ-Ташъ.

—— and **Panoff, V. P.** Information about Kara-Khan and mazar of Aulieata, Aysha-bibi. Proc. Turk. Circle F. Arch., May 5, 1897, pp. 6-9. — —— и *Пановъ, В. П.* Сообщеніе о Караханѣ и мазарѣ Аулiета, Айша-биби.

Kamyshta. Remains of ancient fortress between the steppe rivers Kamyshta and Syrali. Sib. Mess., 1886, No. 61. — *Камышта.* Остатки стариннаго укрѣпленія между степными рѣчками Камыштой и Сырали.

Karatanoff, I. Sketches of the home life of the Kachinsk Tatars. Bull. I. R. G. S., 1884, XX. — *Каратановъ, И.* Черты внѣшняго быта Качинскихъ Татаръ.

Karutz, R. Unter Kirgisen und Turkmenen. Leipzig, 1911.

Kasan in the Ferghana territory. Inscriptions on the graves of Jafar, son of Alya Kasan and of Alauddin, khodja of Kasan. Proc. Turk. Circle F. Arch., 1898–9, IV, p. 153. — *Касанъ въ Ферганской обл.* Надписи на могилахъ Джафара, сына Алія Касанскаго и Алауддина ходжи Касанскаго.

Kasem Beg, Mirza A., transl. J. T. Zenker, 'Allgemeine Grammatik der Türkisch-Tatarischen Sprache'. Leipzig, 1848.

Katanoff, N. T. Ethnographical survey of the Turco-Tatar tribes. Kazan, 1879. — *Катановъ, Н. Т.* Этнографическій Обзоръ Турецко-Татарскихъ племенъ.

—— Review of P. M. Melioranski's 'On the Orkhon and Yenisei monuments with inscriptions' (1898). Bull. I. R. Arch. S., XIV, p. 699. — Рецензія П. М. Меліоранскаго, „Объ орхонскихъ и енисейскихъ надгробныхъ памятникахъ и надписяхъ" (1898).

—— Attempt at an investigation of the Uriankhai language. Kazan, 1903. — Опытъ изслѣдованія урянхайскаго языка.

—— Review of P. M. Melioranski's 'Monument in memory of Kiul Tegin'. Bull. S. Arch. H. E. I. Univ. Kaz., XVI, pp. 117 ff. — Рецензія П. М. Меліоранскаго, „Памятникъ въ честь Кюль Тегина ".

—— A journey to the Karagass in 1890. Mem. I. R. G. S., 1891, XVII, pt. ii. — Поѣздка къ Карагассамъ въ 1890 году.

—— Review of W. W. Radloff's 'Die alttürk. Inschriften der Mongolei', 3te Lfr. (1895). Bull. E. Sib. Sect. I. R. G. S., 1896, XXVI, pt. iv, pp. 241 ff. — Рецензія В. В. Радлова, 'Die alttürkischen Inschriften der Mongolei', 3te Lfr. (1895).

—— On burial ceremonies among the Turkic tribes of Central and Eastern Asia. I. Kazan, 1894. — О погребальныхъ обрядахъ у тюркскихъ племенъ Центральной и Восточной Азіи.

Katanoff, N. T. Bibliography. Information about the Turks of the Yeniseisk Government. Eastern Review, 1887, pp. 278–86. — Библіографія. Свѣдѣнія о тюркахъ Енисейской губерніи.

—— Review of J. Marquart's 'Die Chronologie der alttürk. Inschriften' (1892). Bull. I. R. Arch. S., XIV, pp. 698 ff. — Рецензія J. Marquart: 'Die Chronologie der alttürk. Inschriften' (1892).

—— Report on the journey to the Minusinsk district of the Yeniseisk Government in summer of 1896 and 1899. Scientific Bull. of Kazan Univ., 1897 and 1900. — Отчетъ о поѣздкѣ въ Минусинскій уѣздъ Енисейской губерніи лѣтомъ 1896 и 1899.

—— Traditions relating to ancient deeds and people among the tribes living near the Sayan mountains. Anniversary Book of Potanin. Mem. I. R. G. S., 1909, XXXIV, pp. 265–88. — Преданія присаянскихъ племенъ о прежнихъ дѣлахъ и людяхъ.

Kazantseff, I. Description of the Kirghis-Kaizak. St. P., 1867. — Казанцевъ, И. Описаніе Киргизъ-Кайсаковъ.

Keane, A. M. Asia. Vol. I, London, 1906.

Kerki. Submerged towns on the bank of the R. Amu-Daria, near Kerki. Novoye Vremya, 1891, No. 5483. — Керки. Подземные города на берегу рѣки Аму-Дарьи, близь Керки.

Khanikoff, N. de. Samarkand. Bull. de la Société de Géographie, 1896, Vme Série, T. xvii.

Khanykoff, N. Description of the Khanate of Bokhara. St. P., 1843. — Ханыковъ, Н. Описаніе Бухарскаго ханства.

Kharuzin, A. N. The Kirghis of the Bukeyeff Orda. Bull. Soc. F. S. Anthr. E., vols. LXIII, LXIV, and LXXII. Moscow, 1889–91. — Харузинъ, А. Н. Киргизы Букеевской Орды.

—— Bibliography of the ethnographical essays on the Kirghis and the Kara-Kirghis. Ethn. Rev., 1891, vol. IX, No. 2. — Библіографическій указатель статей, касающихся этнографіи Киргизовъ и Кара-Киргизовъ.

—— Concerning the evolution of dwellings found among the nomad and semi-nomad Turkic and Mongolic tribes of Russia.

BIBLIOGRAPHICAL MATERIAL   171

Moscow, 1896. — О развитіи жилища у кочевыхъ и полукоче-
выхъ тюркскихъ и монгольскихъ народностей Россіи.

Khiva. Traces of an ancient commercial route from Astrakhan to
Khiva. Turk. News, 1870, Nos. 7–14. — *Хива.* Слѣды
стариннаго торговаго пути отъ Астрахани къ Хивѣ.

Khojent. Discovery of ancient ruins near Khojent. Bull.
I. R. G. S., 1867, p. 200. — *Ходжентъ.* Открытіе древнихъ
развалинъ близь Ходжента.

—— Antiquities found in Khojent. Bull. I. R. Arch. S., 1872,
VII, p. 475. — Древности найденныя въ Ходжентѣ.

Khondemir. Habib Essher. L'Histoire des Mongols. Trad. par
V. V. Grigorieff. St. P., 1834.

Khoroshkhin, A. P. The nations of Central Asia, Year-book
of the Turkestan Country, 1874, III, pp. 303–30. — *Хорош-
хинъ, А. П.* Народы Средней Азіи.

——- Samarkand. Turk. News, 1872, No. 2. — *Самаркандъ.*

—— Sketches of Semirechie (Taranchi, Dungan, Sibo, Kalmuck).
Turkestan News, 1875, Nos. 4–23. — Очерки Семирѣчья
(Таранчи, Дунгане, Сибо, Калмыки).

—— Collection of essays relating to the Turkestan country.
St. P., 1876. — Сборникъ статей, касающихся Туркестанскаго
края.

—— Itinéraires de l'Asie centrale: recueil d'itinéraires et de
voyages dans l'Asie centrale et l'Extrême-Orient. Paris, 1878.

Khoroshkhin, N. Keneges Usbegs. Turk. News, 1873, No. 13.
— Узбеки Кенегезъ.

Kingsmill, T. W. On the inscriptions of the Upper Jenisei.
Journ. of the China Br. R. Asiat. Soc., 1892–93, N. Series
XXVII, pp. 198–205.

—— Notice in China Review, 1899–1900, XXIV, p. 200.

Kirghis. Kirghis structures over the graves. Bull. S. Arch. H. E.
Univ. Kaz., 1893, XI, p. 389. — *Киргизы.* Киргизскія надгробныя сооруженія.

Kirghis Steppe. Inscriptions found on the walls of Kirghis stone structures called 'astany'. Suppl. to Orenb. Gov. News, 1853, No. 5. — *Киргизская Степь.* Надпись планамъ и фасадамъ имѣющимся въ Киргизъ-Кайсацкой ордѣ „астанамъ" т. е. каменнымъ строеніямъ.

Kittary, M. Y. The Kirghis 'tui'. J. Min. Int., 1849, XXV. — *Киттары, М. Я.* Киргизскій Туй.

—— Headquarters of the Khan of the Middle Orda of the Kirghis-Kaizak. J. Min. Int., 1849, XXVIII. — Ставка хана Внутренней Киргизской Орды.

Klaproth, H. J. von. Abhandlung über die Sprache und Schrift der Uiguren. Berlin, 1812.

—— Traité sur la langue et l'écriture des Ouigours. Paris, 1820.

—— Asia polyglotta. Paris, 1822, 2nd ed., 1829; 3rd ed., 1831.

—— Sur quelques antiquités de la Sibérie. J. A., II, pp. 1–14. Paris, 1823.

—— Mémoires relatifs à l'Asie. Paris, 1824–8.

—— Mémoires sur l'identité des Thoukhiu et des Hioung-nou avec les Turcs. Paris, 1825 and 1871.

—— Tableaux historiques de l'Asie, depuis la monarchie de Cyrus jusqu'à nos jours, accompagnés de recherches histor. et géogr. sur cette partie du monde. Paris, 1826.

—— Rapport sur les ouvrages du Père Bichurin relatifs à l'histoire des Mongols. J. A., 1830.

—— Description du Tibet, traduite partiellement du chinois en russe par le P. Hyacinthe Bitchourin et du russe en français par M. . . . ., accompagnée de notes par M. Klaproth. Paris, 1831.

—— Description de la Chine sous le règne de la dynastie mongole, traduite du persan de Rachid-eddin et accompagnée de notes. Paris, 1833.

—— Uigurisches Wörterverzeichnis. Paris, 1839.

—— Catalogue des livres imprimés, des manuscrits et des ouvrages chinois, tartares et japonais. Paris, 1839.

—— *see* Timkowski.

Klark, P. Viluisk and its district. Mem. Sib. Sect. I. R. G. S., 1864, VII, pt. i, pp. 91–165. — *Кларкъ, П.* Вилюйскъ и его округъ.

Klements, D. A. Antiquities of the Minusinsk Museum. Tomsk, 1886. — *Клеменцъ, Д. А.* Древности Минусинскаго Музея.

—— Archaeological diary of a journey to Central Mongolia in 1891. Collection of documents of the Orkhon Expedition, 1892–1903. Vol. II, 1895. — Археологическій Дневникъ Поѣздки въ Среднюю Монголію въ 1891 году.

—— Short report of a journey of D. A. Klements to Mongolia in 1894. Bull. I. A. S., 1895, III, No. 3. St. P. — Краткій отчетъ о путешествіи Д. А. Клеменца по Монголіи за 1894.

—— Independent journey into Eastern Mongolia. Bull. I. A. S., 1896, IV, No. 1. — Отдѣльная экскурсія въ Восточную Монголію.

—— Preliminary information about the archaeological results of the expedition to Turfan. Mem. E. Sect. I. R. Arch. Soc., 1899, XII, pt. i, pp. 6–13. — Предварительныя свѣдѣнія объ археологическихъ результатахъ Турфанской экспедиціи.

—— Turfan und seine Alterthümer. Nachrichten über die von der K. Akad. der Wiss. zu St. Petersburg im Jahre 1893 ausgerüstete Expedition nach Turfan. Heft I. St. P., 1899.

—— *see* Radloff's Collection of documents of the Orkhon Expedition. 1892–1903, I, pp. 13–23.

—— Voyages de Dmitri Klementz en Mongolie occidentale 1888–1897. Bull. Soc. Géogr., 1899, XX, pp. 308–29. Paris.

—— *see* Veselovski.

Kobeko, D. The knowledge of Merv among the Ancient Russians. Mem. E. Sect. I. R. Arch. S., 1889, III, pp. 115–19. — *Кобеко, Д.* Старо-русское извѣстіе о Мервѣ (1669).

Komaroff, A. V. Antiquities of the Trans-Caspian country. Turk. News, 1888, Nos. 24 and 25. — *Комаровъ, А. В.* О древностяхъ Закаспійскаго края.

Knolles, R. The general historie of the Turkes from the first beginning . . . London, 1603.

Köbke, P. Prof. Vilh. Thomsens tydning af Orkhon-indskrifterne. pp. 756–70. Tilskueren, 1896.

—— Die Orkhon-Inschriften, ein Ereigniss auf dem Gebiete d. Sprachwissenschaft. Nord und Süd, XC, pp. 376–89.

Koch, E. On two stones with Chinese inscriptions. Mem. E. Sect. I. R. Arch. S., 1891, V, pp. 147–56. — *Кохъ, Э.* О двухъ камняхъ съ китайскими надписями.

—— *see* Lemosoff, M. P.

Kohn, F. Preliminary report on the expedition to the Uriankhai country. Bull. E. Sib. Sect. I.R.G.S., 1903, XXXIV.— *Конъ, Ф.* Предварительный отчетъ по экспедиціи въ Урянхайскую землю.

—— Historical sketch of the Minusinsk Local Museum, during the 25 years of its existence. Kazan, 1902. — *Историческій очеркъ Минусинскаго мѣстнаго музея за 25 лѣтъ.*

Kolosovski, V. In the Karatavsk Mountains of the Chimkent district. Archaeological Notes. Proc. Turk. Circle F. Arch., 1900–1, VI, pp. 89–97. — *Колосовскій, В.* Въ Каратавскихъ Горахъ, Чимкентскаго уѣзда.

Kolpakowski, G. A. Concerning the traces of ancient dwelling discovered in the Lake of Issyk-Kul. Bull. I. R. G. S., 1870, pt. vi, No. 3, pp. 101–5. — *Колпаковскій, Г. А.* О древнихъ постройкахъ найденныхъ въ озерѣ Иссыкъ-Кулѣ.

Konshin, N. Memorials of the past in the Semipalatinsk territory. Mem. Semip. S. W. Sib. Sect. I. R. G. S., 1903, pt. i, pp. 1–32. — *Коншинъ, Н.* О памятникахъ старины въ Семипалатинской области.

Kopal. Description of ancient monuments found by Engineer-Lieutenant Nyegotin, near the town of Kopal. Mess. I. R.G. S., 1857, XIX, p. 81. — *Копалъ.* Описаніе памятниковъ древности, найденныхъ близъ гор. Копала инженеръ-поручикомъ Неготинымъ.

Kopyloff. Ancient monuments in the Kirghis Steppe. Mem. Ural S. F. Sc., 1892, XIII, pt. i. — *Копыловъ.* Памятники старины въ Киргизской степи.

Korniloff, I. P. Reminiscences of Eastern Siberia. The town of Achinsk, and the journey to the Bojii Lakes in 1848. Geographical Collection, edited by N. Froloff, III, pp. 605–58. Moscow, 1854. — *Корниловъ, И. П.* Воспоминанія о Восточной Сибири. Г. Ачинскъ и поѣздка въ 1848 г. на Божьи озера.

Korsh, T. E. The most ancient folk-poems of the Turkic tribes. Mem. E. Sect. I. R. Arch. S., 1909, XIX, pp. 139 ff. — *Коршъ, Ѳ. Е.* Древнѣйшій народный стихъ турецкихъ племенъ.

Kosmin, N. N. D. A. Klements and historical and ethnographical research in the Minusinsk country. Bull. E. Sib. Sect. I. R. G. S., XLV. Irkutsk, 1916. — *Козьминъ, Н. Н.* Д. А. Клеменцъ и историко-этнографическія изслѣдованія въ Минусинскомъ краѣ.

—— 'Chern.' Sibirskiya Zapiski, Aug. 1916, No. 3, pp. 95–112. — „Чернь."

—— Historical sketch of the activity of the East Siberian Section of the Imp. Russ. Geog. Soc. Bull. Sib. Sect. I. R. G. S., XXXV, pt. ii, pp. 1–43. — Историческій очеркъ дѣятельности Вост. Сибирск. Отд. И. Р. Геогр. Общ.

Kostyenko, L. Central Asia and its subjection to the Russian state organization. St. P., 1871. — *Костенко, Л.* Средняя Азія и водвореніе въ ней русской гражданственности.

Kostroff, Prince N. A. The Koibal. Mem. Sib. Sect. I. R. G. S., 1863, VI, pp. 109–18. — *Костровъ, кн. Н. А.* Койбалы.

—— The Chulim Natives. Tomsk Gov. News, 1867, Nos. 7–9. — Чулымскіе Инородцы.

—— The Beltir. Mem. Sib. Sect. I. R. G. S., 1857, IV, pt. ii, pp. 4–10. — Бельтиры.

—— The Kachinsk Tatars. Kazan Gov. News, 1852, Nos. 32–40. — Качинскіе Татары.

Kostroff, Prince N. A.   The customary law of the Yakut. Mem. I. R. G. S., 1878. — Юридическіе обычаи Якутовъ.

—— List of stone figures situated in the Minusinsk district of the Yeniseisk Government.   Mem. Sib. Sect. I. R. G. S., 1863, VI, pp. 75–84. Списокъ каменныхъ изваяній находявшихся въ Минусинскомъ округъ, Енисейской Губерніи.

—— The Kamashints. Moskvityanin, 1851, XVIII, pt. v, pp. 100–10. — Камашинцы.

—— The Natives of the Kainsk district.   J. Min. Int., 1858, XXX, No. 5, pp. 9–13. — Каинскіе инородцы.

—— Sketches of the life of the Minusinsk Tatars.   Trans. of the Fourth Archaeological Congress in Kazan, 1877, vol. I. — Очерки быта Минусинскихъ Татаръ.

—— Ethnographical notes on the Kyzyl Tatars.   Mem. Sib. Sect. I. R. G. S., 1865, VIII, pt. ii, pp. 97–121. — Этнографическія замѣтки о Кизильскихъ Татарахъ.

—— The Natives of the Kuznietsk district.   J. Min. Int., 1858, XXX, No. 5, pp. 13–16. — Кузнецкіе инородцы.

Kotwicz, W. L.   Communication on the author's expedition to Mongolia and the discovery, in conjunction with C. Jamtsarano, of a new monument with Orkhon inscriptions.   Mem. E. Sect. I. R. Arch. S., XXII, Proceedings. — *Котвичъ, В. Л.* Сообщеніе о собственной экспедиціи въ Монголію и объ открытіи имъ, совмѣстно съ Ц. Жамцарано новаго памятника съ орхонскими надписями.

—— In Khusho-Tsaidam.   Trans. T.-K. S. Amur Sect. I. R. G. S., XV, pt. i. — Въ Хушо-Цайдамѣ.

Kozloff, P. K.   Mongolia and Kam.   Works of the Imperial Russian Geographical Society's Expedition in 1899–1901, under the leadership of P. K. Kozloff.   Petrograd, 1905–11. Summaries in 'La Géographie', III (1901), pp. 41–6, and V (1902), pp. 273–8. — *Козловъ, П. К.* Монголія и Камъ. Труды экспедиціи И. Р. Г. О., совершенной въ 1899–1901 подъ руководствомъ П. К. Козлова.

Krafft, H. A travers le Turkestan russe. Paris, 1902.

Kraft, I. I. The ancient times of the Kirghis. Orenburg, 1900. — *Крафтъ, И. И.* Изъ Киргизской Старины.

Krasnoff, A. N. Account of the life of the Kirghis of Semirechie. Bull. I. R. G. S., XXIII, 1887, pp. 436–81. — *Красновъ, А. Н.* Очеркъ быта Семирѣченскихъ Киргизъ.

Krasnoyarsk. The twenty years of existence of the Krasnoyarsk town museum, 1889–1914. Krasnoyarsk, 1915. — *Крас- ноярскъ.* Двадцатипятилѣтіе Красноярскаго Городского Музея, 1889–1914.

Krasovski. The territory of the Kirghis-Kaizak. Geographical and statistical materials collected by the officers of the general staff. 3 vols. St. P., 1868. — *Красовскій.* Область Кир- гизскихъ Казаковъ. Матеріалы для географіи и статистики, собранные офицерами Генеральнаго Штаба.

Kriloff, R. N. Journey to the Uriankhai region, 1892. Bull. I. R. G. S., 1893, XXIX, pp. 274–91. — *Криловъ, Р. Н.* Путешествіе въ Урянхайскую страну 1892 г.

Krug, Ph. Inscriptiones Sibiriacae: de antiquis quibusdam sculpturis et inscriptionibus in Sibiria repertis. Scripsit Gregorius Spassky, Petropoli, 1822.

Kulakoff, P. E., and **Kuznietsova, A. A.**: *see* Kuznietsova, A. A.

Kulja. The mosque of the Taranchi. Niva, 1879, No. 50, pp. 1009 ff. — *Кульджа.* Мечеть Таранчей.

Kun, A. A. Plan and description of the ruins found between Kazalinsk and Tashkent. Bull. I. R. Arch. S., 1872, VII, p. 452. — *Кунъ, А. А.* Планъ и описаніе имъ составленные, развалинъ, хаходящихся между Казалинскомъ и Ташкентомъ.

—— Cultural remains in an oasis of the lower Amu-Daria. Year-book of Stat-Mater, relating to the Turkestan country, 1876, IV, pp. 203–59. — Культура оазиса низовьевз Аму-Дарьи.

—— The ruins of Ak-Saray palace of Timur in Shakhrisebz. Mem. I. R. G. S., 1880, IV, pt. i, pp. 224–8. — Остатки бывшаго дворца Тимура Акъ-Сарая въ гор. Шахрисебзѣ.

Kuropatkin, A. Turkomania and the Turkomans. Collection of Military Essays, 1879, vols. I–IX, Nos. 9–10, pp. 128–339. — *Куропаткинъ, А.* Туркменія и Туркмены.

Kushakyevich. Description of the Khodjent district. Turk. News, 1872, No. 4. — *Кушакевичъ.* Очерки Ходжентскаго уѣзда.

Kustanaeff, H. Ethnographical account of the Kirghis of the Perovsk and Kazalinsk districts. Tashkent, 1894. — *Кустанаевъ, X.* Этнографическіе очерки Киргизъ Перовскаго и Казалинскаго уѣздовъ.

Kuun, Graf Géza von. Review of W. Bang's 'Zur Erklärung der köktürkischen Inschriften'. Z. D. M. G., 1899, LIII, pp. 544–9.

—— Kritische Beiträge z. uralaltaischen Philologie. Westöstliche Rundschau, III, pp. 268–85.

—— Review of V. Thomsen's 'Inscriptions de l'Orkhon déchiffrées' (1894). Z. D. M. G., 1897, XXI, p. 339.

—— Review of V. Thomsen's 'Inscriptions de l'Orkhon déchiffrées' (1894). Westöstliche Rundschau, 1897, III, pp. 268–85.

—— Review of W. Radloff's 'Inscriptions de l'Orkhon déchiffrées', I (1894). Westöstliche Rundschau, 1897, III, pp. 268–85.

—— Review of W. Bang's 'Zu den köktürkischen Inschriften'. Z. D. M. G., 1899, pp. 544–9.

—— Gardēzi, Kézirati munkajanak. [Passages from the Zayn-ul-Akhbar of Gardizi (*circ.* A. D. 1051) dealing with the Turks.] Budapest, 1903.

—— Das türkische Sprachmaterial des Codex Comanicus. Budapest, 1880.

Kuznietsoff-Krasnoyarski, I. P. Ancient graves of the Minusinsk district. Tomsk, 1889. — *Кузнецовъ-Красноярскій, И. П.* Древнія могилы Минусинскаго округа.

—— Minusinsk Antiquities, Copper-bronze and transitional periods. Tomsk, 1908. — Минусинскія древности. Мѣдно-бронзовый и переходный періоды.

Kuznietsoff, S. K. Report on the archaeological investigations in the neighbourhood of the town of Tomsk. Bull. of Tomsk Univ., No. 2. Tomsk, 1890. — *Кузнецовъ, С. К.* Отчетъ объ археологическихъ разысканіяхъ въ окрестностяхъ г. Томска.

Kuznietsova, A. A., and **Kulakoff, P. E.** The natives of Minusinsk and Achinsk. Krasnoyarsk, 1898. — *Кузнецова, А. А., и Кулаковъ, П. Е.* Минусинскіе и Ачинскіе инородцы.

Kuznietsoff, P. La Lutte des Civilisations et des Langues dans l'Asie centrale. Paris, 1912.

Kuzu-Kiurpech. Memorial stones of Kuzu-Kiurpech and Bayan-Sulu and legends relating to them. Trans. Fourth Arch. Congress, 1884, I, p. xlvi. — *Кузу-Кюрпечь.* Памятникъ Кузу-Кюрпечь и Баянъ-Сулу и относящаяся къ нему легенда.

Lacoste, de (Commandant **Bouillane**), **E. A. H.** Une lettre adressée de Kobdo le 27 septembre 1909 par le Commandant de Lacoste à Senart. T.P., II, 1908, vol. X, p. 731. Also J. A., vol. X, pt. xiv, p. 552.

—— Exploration en Mongolie septentrionale. La Géographie, 1909, XX, p. 251 ; 1910, XXI, pp. 375–84.

—— Au pays sacré des anciens Turcs et des Mongols. Paris, 1911.

Lacouperie, T. de. Decipherment of the Siberian inscriptions. Bab. Orient. Rec., 1893–4, VII, p. 94.

—— Additional notes on the Yenisei and Karakorum script. Bab. Orient. Rec., 1891, V, 6, pp. 127–31.

Lane-Poole, S. The Mohammadan dynasties. London, 1894.

Langlès, C. Notice de l'Histoire de Djenguyz-Khân, contenue dans le Manuscrit Persan No. 104 de la Bibliothèque Nationale. Notices et Extraits, V, pp. 192–230.

Lansdell, H. Through Siberia. London, 1882.

—— Russian Central Asia. London, 1885.

—— Chinese Central Asia. London, 1893.

Lapin, S. A. Shakh-Zinda and his tombstone. Reference-book of the Samarkand territory, IV, pp. 39–45. — *Лапинъ, С. А.* Шахи-Зинда и его намогильный памятникъ.

Laufer, B.   The Reindeer and its domestication.   Mem. of the Amer. Anthrop. Assoc., April–June 1917, IV, No. 2, pp. 91–147.

Lavrentieff, V.   Short account of the Kurgans in the district of Aulieata.   Proc. Turk. Circle F. Arch., 1899–1900, V, pp. 39–45. — Лаврентьевъ, В. Краткій перечень бугровъ (кургановъ) находящихся въ чертѣ гор. Аулiе-ата.

Le Coq, A. von.   Bericht über Reisen und Arbeiten in Chinesisch-Turkistan.   Z. f. E., 1907, Hefte 4 u. 5.

—— A short account of the origin, journey, and results of the First Royal Prussian (Second German) Expedition to Turfan in Chinese Turkistan.   J. R. A. S., 1909.

—— Ein christliches und ein manichäisches Manuskript-fragment in türkischer Sprache aus Turfan.   Sitz. K. P. Akad. Wiss., 1909, p. 1206 ff.

—— Köktürkisches aus Turfan.   Sitz. K. P. Akad. Wiss., 1909, pp. 1047 ff.

—— Sprichwörter und Lieder aus der Gegend von Turfan, mit einer dort aufgenommenen Wörterliste.   Baessler-Archiv. Beiträge zur Völkerkunde, herausgegeben aus Mitteln des Baessler-Institutes. Unter Mitwirkung der Direktoren der Ethnologischen Abteilung des k. Museums für Völkerkunde in Berlin, redigiert von P. Ehrenreich. Beiheft I.   Leipzig and Berlin, 1911.

—— Türkische Manichaica aus Chotscho I.   Abh. K. P. Akad. Wiss., Berlin, 1911.

—— Chotscho II.   Facsimile-Wiedergaben der wichtigeren Funde der ersten K. P. Expedition nach Turfan in Ost-Turkistan. Ergebnisse der K. P. Turfan-Expeditionen.   Berlin, 1913.

Leclerq, Jules.   Les Monuments de Samarcande. Société Royale Belge de Géographie, Bulletin XIII, 1890, No. 6, pp. 613–32.

Leder, H.   Ueber alte Grabstätten in Sibirien und der Mongolei. Mitth. Anthr. Ges. Wien, 1895, XXV, pp. 9–16.

—— Reise an den oberen Orchon und zu den Ruinen von Karakorum. Mitt. Geogr. Ges. Wien, 1894, XXXVII, pp. 407–36.

—— Eine Sommerreise in der nördlichen Mongolei, 1892. Mitt.
d. K. K. Geog. Ges. in Wien, 1895, XXXVIII, pp. 26–57,
85–118.

Lemosoff, M. P.   Deux pierres avec inscriptions chinoises. T. P.,
II, pp. 113–24.

Lepitre, A.   Review of V. Thomsen's ' Inscriptions de l'Orkhon
déchiffrées' (1894). L'Université Catholique, N.S. 51, pp. 288–
90. Paris.

Lerkh, P. I.   Archaeological journey. Bull. I. R. G. S., 1865, I,
pp. 196–7. — *Лврхъ, П. И.* Археологическое путешествіе.

—— Archaeological researches in Turkestan in 1867. Rep. I.
Arch. Commission, 1867, pp. xxii–xxxi. — Археологическія
изслѣдованія въ Туркестанѣ въ 1876 г.

—— Archaeological investigations of the ruins of the ancient town
of Jankent. Bull. I. R. G. S., 1867, III, pt. i, p. 199 ; 1869,
V, p. ii, pp. 371–3. — Археологическія изслѣдованія въ развалинахъ древняго города Джанкента.

—— Concerning the ruins of Jankent. ' Syn Otyechestva,' 1868,
No. 6. — О развалинахъ Джанкента.

—— Archaeological journey to the Turkestan country in 1867.
St. P., 1870. — Археологическая поѣздка въ Туркестанскій
край въ 1867.

Lessar, P. M.   South-western Turkomania. The Land of the
Saryk and the Salor. Bull. I. R. G. S., 1885, XXI, pp. 1–80.
— *Лессаръ, П. М.* Юго-западная Туркменія. Земли Сарыковъ
и Салоровъ.

Levanewski, M. A.   Account of the Kirghis Steppes of the
Embensk district. Zemlevyedenye, 1894, I, No. 2, pp. 99–
114 ; No. 3, pp. 39–54 ; No. 4, pp. 111–36 ; 1895, No. 2,
pp. 67–100. — *Леваневскій, М. А.* Очерки Киргизскихъ
Степей Эмбенскаго уѣзда.

Lévi, S.   Central Asian Studies. J. R. A. S., 1914, pp. 953–64.

Levin, N. P. : *see* W. W. Radloff. Collection of documents of
the Orkhon Expedition. 1892–1903, vol. I, pp. 41–50.

Levshin, A. Information about the ancient town Saraychik. Northern Archives, 1824, pt. 9, No. 4, pp. 179–90. — Левшинъ, А. Извѣстія о древнемъ городѣ Сарайчикъ.

—— Description of the Ordas and Steppes of the Kirghis-Kaizak. St. P., 1832. — Описаніе Киргизъ-Кайсацкихъ ордъ и степей.

—— Description des hordes et des steppes des Kirghiz-Kazaks. Trad. par Cigny de F. Paris, 1840.

Lidski, S. Materials for the bibliography of Central Asia and the neighbouring countries. Russian Turkestan. Collections of essays, vol. I. Tashkent, 1899. — Лидскій, С. Матеріалы для библіографіи Средней Азіи и сосѣднихъ странъ.

Likoshin, N. S. An account of archeological investigation in the Turkestan country before the foundation of the Turkestan Circle of Friends of Archaeology. Proc. Turk. Circle F. Arch. Supplement, 1895–6. — Лыкошинъ, Н. С. Очеркъ археологическихъ изысканій въ Туркестанскомъ краѣ до учрежденія Туркестанскаго Кружка Любителей Археологіи.

Lüders. Die Sakas und die 'nordarische' Sprache. K. P. Ak. der Wiss., Phil.-Hist. Abhandlung, 1912.

Lutsyenko, E. I. Excursion to the Telengit of the Altai. Preliminary account of a journey to the Altai with an anthropological object. Zemlevyedenye, 1898, I–II, pp. 1–37. — Луценко, Е. И. Поѣздка къ Алтайскимъ Теленгетамъ. Предварительный отчетъ о поѣздкѣ въ Алтай съ антропологическою цѣлью.

Lyall, A. C. Asiatic Studies. London, 1899.

Lloyd, H. E. : *see* Timkowski.

M – off, N. From Samara to Tashkent. Turk. News, 1872. — М – въ, Н. Отъ Самары до Ташкента.

Maak, R. The Vilui district of the Yakutsk territory. St. P., 1887. — Маакъ, Р. Вилюйскій округъ, якутской области.

Macartnay, G. Eastern Turkestan : the Chinese as rulers over an alien race. J. Centr. As. S., 1909.

Major, R. H. History of the two Tartar conquerors of China, including the two journeys into Tartary of Father F. Verbiets

... From the French of Père J. d'Orléans ... To which is added Father Pereira's journey into Tartary. From the Dutch of N. Witsen. Translated and edited by the Earl of Ellesmere : with an introduction by R. H. Major. Hakluyt Society's Publications. London, 1854.

—— *see* Herbertstein.

Makovyetski, P. E.   Materials for the study of the juridical customs of the Kirghis.   St. P., 1890. — *Маковецкій, П. Е.* Матерьялы для изученія юридическихъ обычаевъ Киргизовъ.

—— The Yurta (summer dwelling of the Kirghis).   Mem. W. Sib. Sect. I. R. G. S., 1893, XV, pt. iii, pp. 1–16. — Юрта [лѣтнее жилище Киргиза].

Maksheyeff, A. I.   Description of the valley of the lower Syr-Daria.   Collection of essays on naval subjects, 1856, XXIII, No. 9, pp. 448–527. — *Макшеевъ, А. И.*   Описаніе низовьевъ Сыръ-Дарьи.

—— Additional information on the ruins of Jankent.   Russian Invalid, 1867, No. 87. — Еще нѣсколько словъ о развалинахъ Джанкента.

—— Remains of ancient towns along Syr-Daria.   St. Petersburg News, 1867, Nos. 58, 60. — Остатки стариннаго города на Сыръ-Дарьѣ.

—— Geographical, ethnographical, and statistical materials relating to the Turkestan country.   Mem. I. R. G. S., 1871, II, pp. 1–60. — Географическіе, этнографическіе и статистическіе матеріалы о Туркестанскомъ краѣ.

Maksimoff, A. N.   The Kara-Kalpak.   Encyclopaedic Dictionary, ed. Jeleznoff, XXIII, p. 24. — *Максимовъ, А. Н.*   Каракалпаки.

Malakhoff, E.   Graves of the Semipalatinsk territory.   Bull. Soc. F. S. Anthr. E., 1886, XLIX, pt. iii, pp. 24–7. — *Малаховъ, Е.* Могилы Семипалатинской области.

Mallitski, N.   Fourteenth-century inscriptions on the memorial stones at Khodjo.   Proc. Turk. Circle F. Arch., 1897, Supplement, pp. 10–21. — *Маллицкій, Н.* Ходжокентскія надгробныя надписи XIV столѣтія.

Mallitski, N.   On the connexion between the Turkic 'tamga' and the Orkhon characters.   Proc. Turk. Circle F. Arch., 1897–8, pp. 43–7. — О связи тюркскихъ тамгъ съ орхонскими письменами.

—— Inscription from Rushan (A.D. 1764).   Proc. Turk. Circle F. Arch., 1899, pp. 69–71. — Надпись изъ Рушана (1764 по Р. Х.).

Maloff, C. E.   A few words about Shamanism among the Turkic population of the Kuznietsk district of the Tomsk Government. L. A. T., 1909, Nos. 2–3, pp. 38–41. — *Маловъ, С. Е.* Нѣсколько словъ о шаманствѣ у турецкаго населенія Кузнецкаго уѣзда Томской губерніи.

Maltseff.   Letters about the Soyot, the neighbours of the Yeniseisk Government.   Reference sheet of the Yeniseisk Government, 1890, Nos. 1, 3. — *Мальцевъ.*   Письма о Сойотахъ, сосѣдахъ Енисейской губерніи.

Mangyshlak.   Antiquities of the Peninsula of Mangyshlak.   Mem. I. R. G. S., 1849, pts. i–ii, pp. 333–5. — *Мангышлякъ.* Древности Мангышлакскаго полуострова.

Markoff, A.   Towns of Northern Mongolia.   The Scottish Geog. Mag., Feb. 1896.

Markoff, E.   Russia in Central Asia.   Account of travels in Trans-Caucasia, Turkmania, Bokhara, Samarkand, Tashkent, and Ferghana territories, along the Caspian Sea and the Volga. St. P., 1901. — *Марковъ, Е.* Россія въ Средней Азіи. Очерки путешествія по Закавказію, Туркменіи, Бухарѣ, Самаркандской, Ташкентской и Ферганской областямъ, Каспійскому морю и Волгѣ.

Martianoff, N. M.   The Minusinsk Public Museum.   Tomsk, 1881. — *Мартьяновъ, Н. М.*   Минусинскій Публичный Мѣстный Музей.

Martin, R.   L'âge du bronze au musée de Minoussinsk.   Stockholm, 1893.

—— Sibirische Sammlung (Sibirica).   Stockholm, 1895.

—— Review of J. Campbell's 'Siberian inscriptions'.   Arch. für Anthr., XXII, p. 143.

Marquart, J. Historische Glossen zu den alttürkischen Inschriften. W. Z. K. M., 1898, XII, pp. 157–200.

—— Die Chronologie der alttürkischen Inschriften. Mit einem Vorwort und Anhang von W. Bang. Leipzig, 1898.

—— and **Bang, W.** Osttürkische Dialektstudien. Abh. K. Ges. Wiss. Göttingen, Phil.-Hist. Kl., N.F., 1914, Bd. 13. Göttingen.

Maslovski, S. D. The Galcha: aboriginal population of Turkestan. Russ. Anthr. J., 1901, No. 2. — *Масловскій, С. Д.* Гальча, первобытное населеніе Туркестана.

Matseyevski and **Poyarkoff.** Short ethnographic notes on the natives of the district formerly called Kulja. Omsk, 1883. — *Мацѣевскій и Поярковъ.* Краткія этнографическія замѣтки о туземцахъ бывшаго Кульджинскаго района.

Maulānā, Minhaj-ud-dīn, Abū-'umar-i-'usmān : *see* Raverty.

Mayeff, N. On the investigations of the Samarkand antiquities of architecture. Novosti, 1895. Tr. in 'Beiblatt zur Allgemeinen Zeitung', 1895, No. 231, p. 7. — *Маевъ, Н.* Объ изученіи Самаркандскихъ архитектурныхъ древностей.

—— Sketches on the highland principalities of the Khanate of Bokhara. Turk. News, 1878, Nos. 46–9; 1879, No. 1. — Очерки горныхъ бекствъ Бухарскаго ханства.

—— Tashkent in Asia. Year-book of the Turkestan country, pt. iv, pp. 260–311. St. P., 1876. — Азіятскій Ташкентъ.

Mayendorff, G. de. Voyage à Boukhara. Paris, 1826.

Maynagasheff, S. D. The life beyond the grave as conceived by the Turkic tribes of the Minusinsk country. L. A. T., 1915, XXIV, pp. 277–92. — *Майнагашевъ, С. Д.* Загробная жизнь по представленіямъ турецкихъ племенъ Минусинскаго края.

—— Sacrifice to the sky among the Beltir. Collection of essays of the Anthr. Museum of the Imp. Russ. Academy of Science, vol. III. Petrograd, 1915. — Жертвоприношеніе Небу у Бельтировъ.

Meakin, A. M. B. In Russian Turkestan. London, 1915.

Medvyedski, P.   The Middle Orda of the Kirghis, from an industrial and statistical aspect. J. Min. Prop. State, 1862, LXXX, LXXXI. — *Медвѣдскій, П.* Внутренняя Киргизская Орда въ хозяйственно-статистическомъ отношеніи.

Mejoff, V. I.   Bibliography of Asia. List of books and articles on Asia in Russian and other languages. St. P., 1891. — *Межовъ, В. И.* Библіографія Азіи. Указатель книгъ и статей объ Азіи на русскомъ и иностранныхъ языкахъ.

—— Siberian bibliography. Index to the books and essays on Siberia in the Russian language, and books alone in other languages. St. P., 1891-4. — Сибирская библіографія. Указатель книгъ и статей о Сибири на русскомъ языкѣ, и однѣхъ только книгъ на иностранныхъ языкахъ.

Melioranski, P. M.   Concerning the new archaeological discovery in the Aulieata district. Mem. E. Sect. I. R. Arch. S., 1899, XI, 1-4, pp. 271-3. — *Меліоранскій, П. М.* По поводу новой археологической находки въ Ауліеатинскомъ уѣздѣ.

—— On the Orkhon and Yenisei monuments with inscriptions. J. Min. Educ., June 1898. St. P. — Объ орхонскихъ и енисейскихъ надгробныхъ памятникахъ и надписяхъ.

—— On the Kudatku Bilik of Jinghis Khan. Mem. E. Sect. I. R. Arch. S., 1900, XIII, pt. i, pp. 015-023. — О Кудатку Биликѣ Чингизъ Хана.

—— Monument in memory of Kiul-Tegin. Mem. E. Sect. I. R. Arch. S., 1899, XII, pp. 1-144. — Памятникъ въ честь Кюль-Тегина.

—— Short Orkhon inscription on a silver vessel in the Rumyantseff Museum. Mem. E. Sect. I. R. Arch. S., XV, pp. 034 ff. — Небольшая орхонская надпись на серебряной кринкѣ Румянцевскаго Музея.

—— Two silver vessels with Yenisei inscriptions. Mem. E. Sect. I. R. Arch. S., XIV. — Два серебряныхъ сосуда съ енисейскими надписями.

—— Review of Vambéry's ' Noten zu den alttürkischen Inschriften der Mongolei und Sibiriens' (1899). Mem. E. Sect. I. R.

Arch. S., XII, No. 275. — Рецензія книги Вамбери 'Noten zu den alttürkischen Inschriften der Mongolei und Sibiriens' (1899).

—— and **Radloff, W. W.** Collection of documents of the Orkhon Expedition, vol. IV.

—— *see* Radloff.

Merzbacher, Dr. G. Vorläufiger Bericht über eine in den Jahren 1902 und 1903 ausgeführte Forschungsreise in den zentralen Tian-Schan. Gotha, 1904.

—— Wissenschaftliche Ergebnisse der Reise von G. Merzbacher im zentralen und östlichen Tian-Schan, 1907–8. Abh. d. k. bayer. Akad. d. Wiss., math.-physik. Klasse, Bd. XXVI, Abh. 3–5, 8. München, 1913.

—— Exploration in the Tian-Shan mountains. Geog. Journal, 1909, XXXIII.

Messerschmidt, D. G. Siberian Antiquities. Part I. Materials for the Archaeology of Russia. No. 3. Abstract of a Diary in MS. in the Library of the I. R. Ac. Sc. St. P., 1888. — *Мессершмидтъ, Д. Г.* Сибирскія Древности.

Meyendorf, Baron G. de. Voyage d'Orenbourg à Boukhara fait en 1820. Paris, 1826.

Meyer, L. The Kirghis steppe in the Orenburg territory. St. P., 1865. — *Мейеръ, Л.* Киргизская степь Оренбургскаго вѣдомства.

Middendorff, A. T. von. Reise in den äussersten Norden und Osten Sibiriens während der Jahre 1843–4. St. P., 1847–74.

—— Einblicke in das Ferghana-Thal. Mem. I. R. A. S., 1859, VII série, vol. 29.

—— Die Barabá. Mem. I. R. A. S., 1859, VIIIᵉ série, vol. 14.

Mikhailoff, T. A. The natives of the Transcaspian territory and their life. Askhabad, 1900. — *Михайловъ, Ө. А.* Туземцы Закаспійской области и ихъ жизнь.

Minayeff, I. P. The necessity for the excavation of the Afrosyab ruins, by a person familiar with the archaeology of the country. Mem. I. R. Arch. S., 1886, vol. I, pp. 25 ff. — *Минаевъ, И. П.* О необходимости раскопки Афросіябова городища лицомъ спеці- яльно знакомымъ съ археологіей края.

Minns, E. H. Scythians and Greeks. Cambridge, 1913.

Mohammed-en-Nesavi. Histoire du Sultan Djelaledin, prince du Kharezm. Arab., tr. par O. Houdas. Paris, 1891–5.

Mohl, J. : *see* Firdousi.

Montelius, O. Orienten och Europa. Antiq. Tidskrift, XIII. Stockholm.

Moore, B. B. From Moscow to the Persian Gulf. New York, 1915.

Mordovtseff, D. In the capital of Tamerlan. Picturesque Russia, 1901, I. — *Мордовцевъ, Д.* Въ столицѣ Тамерлана.

Morgan, E. D. Prjevalsky's journeys and discoveries in Central Asia. Proc. R. G. S., April, 1887.

—— Expedition of the Brothers Grijimailo to the Tian-Shan oases and Lob-nor. Translated with notes and introductory remarks. Proc. R. Geog. Soc., 1891, XIII, pp. 208–26.

Moser, H. A travers l'Asie centrale. Paris, 1885.

Moshkoff, V. The Gagauzy. Examples of the folk-literature of the Turkic tribes. Vol. X, ed. by Radloff. St. P., 1904. — *Мошковъ, В.* Гагаузы. Образцы народной литературы тюркскихъ племенъ.

Moule, A. C. Documents relating to the mission of the Minor Friars to China in the thirteenth and fourteenth centuries. J. R. A. S., 1914, II, pp. 533–600.

Mukhin, D. Memorial stones of the Kirghis. Orenburg sheet, 1881, Nos. 34, 35. — *Мухинъ, Д.* Киргизскіе памятники на могилахъ.

Müllenhoff, K. Über die Herkunft und Sprache der Jontischen Skythen und Sarmathen. Deutsche Altertumskunde, III, pp. 101 ff. Berlin, 1870–1900.

Müller, E. Fouilles aux environs de Tachkend. Revue d'Ethnographie, 1887, VI, Nos. 5–6, pp. 516–18.

Müller, F. Unter Tungusen und Jakuten. Leipzig, 1882.

Müller, F. W. K. Sogdische Texte, I. K. P. Akad. der Wiss., 1912.

—— Ein iranisches Sprachdenkmal aus der nördlichen Mongolei. K. P. Akad. der Wiss., 1909.

—— Ein Doppelblatt aus einem Manichäischen Hymnenbuch (Mahrnamag). K. P. Akad. der Wiss., 1912.

—— Handschriften-Reste in Estrangeloschrift aus Turfän, Chinesisch-Turkestan. K. P. Ak. d. Wiss., Phil.-Hist. Kl., Abh. II, 1904, pp. 1–117.

—— Die Sprache der türkischen ' Turfan-Fragmente in manichäischer Schrift'. I. Sitzung d. K. P. Akad. d. Wiss., 1904, LIII.

—— 'Uigurica.' I. K. P. Akad. d. Wiss., Phil.-Hist. Kl., Abh. II, 1908, pp. 1–60. II. K. P. Akad. d. Wiss., Phil.-Hist. Kl., Abh. III, 1910, pp. 1–110.

Murgab. Ruins of ancient towns on the Murgab. Bull. S. Arch. H. E. I. Univ. Kaz., 1893, XI, pp. 295 ff. — *Мургабъ.* Развалины древнихъ городовъ на Мургабѣ.

Murray, H. Discoveries and travels in Asia. Edinburgh, 1820.

Muskjetoff, I. V. Concerning the monolite on Tamerlane's grave in Samarkand. Trans. of the Fifth Archaeological Congress, 1886, pp. 24–6. — *Мушкетовъ, И. В.* О нефритовомъ монолитѣ на гробницѣ Тамерлана въ Самаркандѣ.

—— *see* Obrucheff.

Nadjib Asim. Pek Eski Turk Yazysy. Ed. by Soc. 'Turk Dernayi'. 2nd ed. Stamboul, 1909.

—— Yenisei Turk Yazysy. Constantinople, 1897.

Nalivkin, V. P. History of the Khanate of Kokand. Kazan, 1886. — *Наливкинъ, В. П.* Исторія ханата Коканда.

—— and **Nalivkina, M.** A sketch of the life of the women of the sedentary population of Ferghana. Kazan, 1886. —— *и Наливкина, М.* Очеркъ быта женщины осѣдлаго туземнаго населенія Ферганы.

Nansen, F.   Through Siberia.   London, 1914.

Narshakhy (Abou Bekr Mohammed ibn Jafer).   Description topographique et historique de Boukhara, par Mohammed Nerchakhy, suivie de textes relatifs à la Transoxiane ; texte persan publ. par C. Schéfer.   Paris, 1892.

Nazaroff, F.   Notes on some peoples and lands of Central Asia*   St. P., 1821. — *Назаровъ, Ф.* Записки о нѣкоторыхъ народахъ и земляхъ средней части Азіи.

Nebolsin, P.   The Turkomans.   J. Min. Int., 1852, XXXIX, pp. 50–71. — *Небольсинъ, П.* Туркмены.

Nemeth, J.   Die türkisch-mongolische Hypothese.   Z. D. M. G., 1912, LXVI, pp. 549–76.

Neumann, K.   Die Hellenen im Skythenlande.   Berlin, 1855.

Niazi Mohammed.   Tarihi Shanrohi.   Ed. by Pantusoff, N. N. Kazan, 1885.

Niebuhr, B. G.   A dissertation on the geography of Herodotus, and researches into the history of the Scythians, Getae, and Sarmatians.   Oxford, 1830.

Niegotin : *see* Kopal.

Nikitin, V.   Ancient remains of Karkaralinsk district in the Semipalatinsk territory.   Mem. I. R. Arch. S., 1896, VIII, pt. 1–2, pp. 211–18. — *Никитинъ, В.* Памятники древности Каркаралинскаго уѣзда, Семипалатинской обл.

Nikolski, M. V.   The Nestorian inscriptions on the memorial stones from Pishnek and Tokmak.   'Eastern Antiquities.' Trans. E. Comm. I. Moscow Arch. S., 1896, II, 1, pp. 59–60. — *Никольскій, М. В.* О несторіанскихъ надгробныхъ надписяхъ изъ Пишнека и Токмака.

Nízam-oul-Moulk.   Siasset Namèh.   Traduit en français par C. Schéfer.   Paris, 1893.

Nocentini, L.   Review of W. W. Radloff's 'Die alttürkischen Inschriften der Mongolei', 1899, 2te Folge.   Giorn. della Soc. asiat. ital., 1899, XII, p. 242.

Obrucheff, V. A.   Central Asia, Northern China, and Nian-Shan. Report of the expedition of 1892–4.   Edited by I. V. Mushkietoff.   St. P., 1899–1901. — *Обручевъ, В. А.* Центральная Азія, Сѣверный Китай, и Нань-Шань.   Отчетъ о путешествіи совершенномъ въ 1892–94 подъ редакціей И. В. Мушкетова.

—— List of ancient graves noticed on the way from Kyakhta to Urga and Kalgan.   Extract from letter of V. A. Obrucheff to the Administrator of the East Sib. Sect. Imp. Russ. Geog. Soc. in 1892.   Collection of documents of the Orkhon Expedition, 1902, vol. II.   St. P., 1897. — Списокъ древнихъ могилъ, замѣченныхъ на пути изъ Кяхты въ Ургу и Калганъ.

—— Preliminary report of an expedition to the Barlik and Tarbagatai.   Tomsk, 1907.   Also Petermann's Mitt., 1908, pt. i, pp. 24–39. — Предварительный отчетъ о путешествіи на Барликъ и Тарбагатай.

—— **Byelkin, D. Z. ; Trigoroff, A. V.; Gedroyć, K. I.; and Shiraeff, T. G.**   Systematic index of the publications of the East-Siberian Section of the I. R. G. S., 1851–1911.   Irkutsk, 1912. — ——Бѣлкинъ, Д. З.; Григоровъ, А. В.; Гедройцъ, К. И.; и Шираевъ, Ѳ. Г.   Систематическій указатель изданій Восточно-Сибирскаго Отдѣла И. Р. Г. О., 1851–1911.

Ohsson, Baron M. d'.   Tableau historique de l'Orient.   Paris, 1804.

—— Histoire des Mongols depuis Tchinguiz-Khan jusqu'à Timour Bey ou Tamerlan.   La Haye and Amsterdam, 1834–35, repr. 1852.

Oldenburg, S.: *see* Veselovski.

Olsen, O.   Et primitivt folk de Mongolske Ronnomader.   Christiania, 1915.

Olufsen, O.   The second Danish Pamir Expedition.   Old and new architecture in Khiva, Bokhara, and Turkestan.   Copenhagen, 1904, 26 pp. with 24 pl.

—— Muhamedanske Gravminder in Transcaspien, Khiva, Bokhara, Turkestan og Pamir.   Geograf. Tidskrift, Kjøbenhavn, XVII, pp. 110–20, 146–59.

Orkhon.   Orkhon discoveries.   Collection of essays on Siberia. 1894, V–VI, pp. 55–9. — Орхонъ.   Орхонскія открытія. „Сибирскій Сборникъ."

Orléans, Père J. d'.: *see* Major, R. H.

Ostrovskikh, P. E. Ethnographical notes on the Turks of the Minusinsk country. Report on a journey in 1894. L. A. T., 1895, V, Nos. 3, 4, pp. 297–348 — *Островскихъ, П. Е.* Этнографическія замѣтки о тюркахъ Минусинскаго края. Отчетъ о поѣздкѣ 1894 г.

—— Short report of a journey to the Todjin Khoshun of the Uriankhai country. Bull. I. R. G. S., 1898, XXXIV. — Краткій очеркъ о поѣздкѣ въ Тоджинскій Хошунъ Урянхайской земли.

—— The importance of the Uriankhai region to Southern Siberia. Bull. I. R. G. S., 1899, pp. 321–53. — Значеніе Урянхайской земли для Южной Сибири.

Ostroumoff, N. P. A Tatar-Russian Dictionary. Kazan, 1892. *Остроумовъ, Н. П.* Тата рско-русскій словарь.

—— The Sarts. Tashkent, 1890; 3rd ed., 1908. — Сарты.

Østrup, J. Review of V. Thomsen's 'Inscriptions de l'Orkhon déchiffrées', I (1894), pp. 325–30. Nordisk för Vetenskap, &c. Tidskrift, 1896.

—— Review of V. Thomsen's 'Inscriptions de l'Orkhon déchiffrées', I (1894). Norsk Aftenposten, 18th Feb., 1896.

—— Review of V. Thomsen's 'Inscriptions de l'Orkhon déchiffrées', I (1894). Berlingske Tidende, 1896, No. 35.

Otrar. Remains of ruins of the town of Otrar. Proc. Turk. Circle F. Arch., 1897–8, III, pp. 236–8. — *Отраръ.* Развалины города Отрара.

P — ff, N. Weights and measures in Central Asia. Turk. News, 1874, No. 33; 1875, No. 16. — *П—въ, Н.* Вѣсы и мѣры въ Средней Азіи.

Palladius (Archimandrite). Travelling notes on a journey in Mongolia. With a preface by E. V. Bretschneider. Bull. I. R. G. S., 1892, XX. — *Палладій* [*Архимандритъ*]. Дорожныя замѣтки на пути по Монголіи. Съ введеніемъ Е. В. Бретшнайдера.

Pallas, P. S.   Reise durch verschiedene Provinzen des Russischen Reichs.   St. P., 1771–6.

—— Sammlungen historischer Nachrichten über die mongolischen Völkerschaften.   St. P., 1776.

——Travels through Siberia and Tartary.   Vol. II of 'TheHabitable World described', edited by J. Trusler, 20 vols.   London, 1788.

—— Von einer in Sibirien gefundenen unbekannten Steinschrift. Neue Nordische Beiträge zur physikalischen und geographischen Erd- und Völkerbeschreibung, Naturgeschichte und Oekonomie.   V, pp. 237–45.   St. P., 1793.

Pälsi, S.   Mongolian matkalta.   Helsingissä, 1911.

Pantusoff, N. N.   Ferghana according to the memoirs of Baber. Mem. I R. G. S., 1880, IV, pt. i, pp. 151–99. — Пантусовъ, Н. Н.   Фергана по запискамъ Султана Бабура.

—— The war between the Musulman and the Chinese.   Kazan, 1881. — Война Мусульманъ противъ Китайцевъ.

—— Tomb of Ak-Tash, near Jarkent.   Proc. Turk. Circle F. Arch., 1900–1, VI, pp. 6 ff. — Могила Акъ-Ташъ близь Джаркента.

—— Concerning the ruins of Tash-Rabat.   Proc. Turk. Circle F. Arch., 1901–2, VI, pp. 5 ff. — Сообщеніе о развалинахъ Ташъ-Рабатъ.

—— Tash-Rabat.   Bull. I. Arch. Commission, 1902, pt. iv, pp. 15–23. — Ташъ-Рабатъ.

·—— Antiquities of Central Asia : Memorial Dengek in the Lepsin district.   Memorials Kuzu-Kurpech and Bayan-Salu in the Lepsin district.   Kazan, 1902. — Древности Средней Азіи : Памятникъ Денгекъ въ Лепсинскомъ уѣздѣ.   Памятники Кузу-Курпечъ и Баянъ-Салу въ Лепсинскомъ уѣздѣ.

—— Christian influence traced from the Kirghis memorial stones along the R. Kokshal in Kashgar.   Mem.W. Sib. Sect. I. R.G.S., 1903, XXX, pp. 231–6. — Слѣды христіянства въ надмогильныхъ киргизскихъ памятникахъ по р. Кокшалу въ Кашгаріи.

—— *see* Niazi Mohammed.

Paquet, Dr. A.   Südsibirien und die Nordwest-Mongolei.   Mitt. der Geog. Ges. in Jena, 1909, XXVII, pp. 1–127.

Parker, E. H.　Review of V. Thomsen's 'Déchiffrement des inscriptions de l'Orkhon et de l'Jénisséi'.　Notice préliminaire (1894).　The Academy, 1894, XLVI, No. 1133.

—— Review of W. W. Radloff's 'Die alttürkischen Inschriften der Mongolei', 2te Folge, 1899.　Progress in Old Turkish discoveries.　China Review, 1899, XXIV, pp. 21-38.

—— The origin of the Turks.　Eng. Hist. Review, 1896, pp. 431-45.

—— Review of W. W. Radloff's ' Die alttürkischen Inschriften der Mongolei' (1899), 2te Folge.　Eng. Hist. Review, 1901, XV, pp. 149-52.

—— Inscriptions de l'Orkhon, déchiffrées par Vilh. Thomsen. Journ. China Br. R. A. S., 1896-8, XXXI, pp. 1-38.

—— Progress in Old Turkish discoveries.　China Review, 1899–1900, XXIV, pp. 21-38.

—— The Orkhon inscriptions.　Academy, 1895, XLVIII, pp. 547-51.

—— A Thousand Years of the Tartars.　Shanghai, 1895.

—— History of the Wu-wan or Wu-Woan Tunguses of the first century.　China Review, XX, pp. 71-100.

—— China, Past and Present.　London, 1903.

Patkanoff, S.　Statistical data for the racial composition of the population of Siberia, its language and tribes.　St. P., 1912. — Паткановъ, С.　Статистическія данныя, показывающія племенной составъ населенія Сибири, языкъ и роды инородцевъ.

Pauthier, G. : *see* Polo, Marco.

Paye, de.　Review of 'Inscriptions de l'Jénisséi recueillies et publiées par la Société Finlandaise d'Archéologie' (1889). Bull. Soc. Antiq., 1889, IV, pp. 273 ff.

Pelliot, Paul.　Les Influences iraniennes en Asie central et en Extrême-Orient.　Revue de l'Histoire et de la Littérature religieuses.

—— La Mission Pelliot en Asie centrale.　Ann. de la Soc. de Géog. Commerciale.　*See* Indo-Chinoise Map.　Hanoi, 1909.

—— and **Chavannes, É.** : *see* Chavannes.

Pereira, Father : *see* Major, R. H.

Pétis de la Croix, F. Relation de Douɪy Efendy, ambassadeur de la Porte Othomane auprès du roi de Perse ; traduite du turc et suivie de l'extrait des voyages de F. Pétis de la Croix.

Petri, B. E. Guide to the Peter the Great Museum of Anthropology and Ethnography : Archaeology. Petrograd, 1916. — *Петри, Б. Е.* Путеводитель по музею антропологіи и этнографіи имени Петра Великаго. Археологія.

—— Neolithic finds on the shore of Lake Baikal. Publication of the Museum of Anthropology and Ethnography. I. A. S., vol. III. Petrograd, 1916. — Неолитическія находки на берегу Байкала.

Piassetsky, P. Russian travellers in Mongolia and China. Translated by J. Gordon-Cumming. London, 1884.

Piekarski, E. A Yakut Dictionary. St. P., 1899. — *Пекарскій, Э.* Словарь Якутскаго языка.

—— and **Vasilyeff, P.** The Coat and Drum of the Yakut Shaman. Materials for the Ethnography of Russia, I, pp. 93–116. St. P., 1910. — —— и *Васильевъ, П.* Плащъ и бубенъ якутскаго шамана.

Pietroff-Borzna, D. O. Concerning archaeological documents, collectors of antiquities and excavators in Central Asia. Trans. Fourth Archeol. Congress, 1884, vol. I, pp. lxv–lxvi. — *Петровъ-Борзна, Д. О.* О вещественныхъ доказательствахъ археологіи, а также о собирателяхъ древностей и кладоискателяхъ въ средней Азіи.

Pietrowski, N. T. The Tower of Burana, near Tokmak. Mem. E. Sect. I. R. Arch. S., IX., pp. 145–55. — *Петровскій, Н. Ѳ.* Башня Бурана, близь Токмака.

Polferoff, A. Among the graves of the Kirghis. Turgai Gazette, 1896, Nos. 1, 6, 16. — *Полферовъ, Я.* Среди Киргизскихъ могилъ.

Polo, Marco. Le Livre de Marco Polo, citoyen de Venise (1298), ed. by Pauthier, M. G. Paris, 1865. English, ed. H. Yule. London, 1875.

Popoff, N. I. Concerning the ' pisanitsy ' of the Minusinsk country. Bull. Sib. Sect. I. R. G. S., 1856, III, pp. 223–84 ; V, p. 49. — *Поповъ, Н. И.* О писаницахъ Минусинскаго края.

Popoff, N. I.   On the Runic writing of the Minusinsk country. Bull. Sib. Sect. I. R. G. S., V, No. 2, pp. 1 ff. — О руническихъ письменахъ въ Минусинскомъ краѣ.

———   Short historical review of the various phonetic writings of the people of Northern and Central Asia. Bull. Sib. Sect. I. R. G. S., V, No. 2, pp. 12–28. — Краткій историческій обзоръ различныхъ родовъ фонетическаго письма у народовъ Сѣверной и Средней Азіи.

Popoff, P. S.   Notes concerning a new translation of the inscription on the monument Tsue-Tegin. Bull. I. A. S., 1894, LXXV, pt. i, pp. 1 ff. — Поповъ, П. С. Замѣчанія по поводу новаго перевода надписи на памятникѣ Цюэ-Тэгину.

Posdnyeff, A. M.   Mongolia and the Mongols. Results of the journey to Mongolia in 1892–3. St. P., 1896–8. — Позднѣевъ, А. М. Монголія и Монголы. Результаты поѣздки въ Монголію, исполненной въ 1892–3 гг.

Poslawski, I.   Concerning the ruins of Termez. ‘Sredne-asiatskii Vyestnik’, December, 1896.—Пославскій, И. О развалинахъ Термеза.

Potanin, G. N.   Materials for the history of Siberia. Moscow, 1865. — Потанинъ, Г. Н. Матеріалы къ исторіи Сибири.

———   Winter excursion to Lake Zaysan in 1863–4. Mem. I. R. G. S., 1867, I, pp. 429–61. — Зимняя поѣздка на озеро Зайсанъ зимой 1863–4.

———   Sketches of North-Western Mongolia. The results of the expeditions of 1876–7 and 1879–80. St. P., 1881–5. — Очерки Сѣверо-Западной Монголіи. Результаты путешествія исполненнаго въ 1876–7 и 1879–80.

———   Survey of G. N. Potanin's journey in N. W. Mongolia, 1876–7, and map. Petermann's Mitt., 1881, XXVII, pt. 5.

———   The Tangut-Tibet borderland of China. Travels in 1884–6. St. P., 1892. — Тангутско-Тибетская окраина Китая и Центральная Монголія. Путешествіе 1884–6.

———   Review of W. Radloff's ‘ Die alttürkischen Inschriften der Mongolei ’ (1894). Ethn. Rev., XXI, pp. 189–99.

—— Anniversary book of Potanin; on the occasion of his seventieth birthday. Edited by Rudnyeff, A. D. Mem. I. R. G. S., XXXIII. St. P., 1909. — Сборникъ въ честь семидесятилѣтія Григорія Николаевича Потанина.

Poulsen, F. Der Orient und die frühgriechische Kunst. Leipzig, 1912.

Poyarkoff and **Matseyevski** : *see* Matseyevski.

Prelovski, P. The Karagass of the Nijne-Udinsk district. Mem. and Trans. of the Irkutsk Government Statistical Committee, 1868–9, IV, pp. 1–30. — *Преловскій, П.* Нижне–Удинскіе Карагассы.

Price, M. P. Siberia. London, 1912.

Priklonski, V. A. Materials for the ethnography of the Yakut of the Yakutsk territory. Bull. E. Sib. Sect. I. R. G. S., 1887, XVIII, p. 143. — *Приклонскій, В. А.* Матеріалы для этнографіи Якутовъ Якутской области.

—— Materials for a bibliography of the Yakutsk territory. Eastern Review, 1893, pt. i, p. 183. — Матеріалы для библіографіи Якутской области.

Przewalski, N. M. Mongolia and the country of the Tangut. Three years travels in Eastern High Asia. St. P., 1875–6. — *Пржевальскій, Н. М.* Монголія и страна Тангутовъ. Трехлѣтнее Путешествіе въ Восточной Нагорной Азіи. Translated by E. D. Morgan, with introduction and notes by H. Yule. London, 1876.

—— From Kulja across the Tian-Shan to Lob-Nor. Travels . . . in 1876–7. St. P., 1878. — Отъ Кульджи за Тянь-Шанъ и на Лобъ-Норъ. Путешествіе въ 1876–7. Translated by E. D. Morgan, including notices of the lakes of Central Asia, with introduction by Sir T. D. Forsyth. London, 1879.

—— Third journey to Central Asia. From Zaysan through Hami and Tibet to the sources of the Yellow River. St. P., 1883. — Третье путешествіе въ Центральной Азіи. Изъ Зайсана черезъ Хами въ Тибетъ и на Верховья Желтой Рѣки.

Przewalski, N. M. Fourth journey to Central Asia. From Kiakhta to the sources of the Yellow River; investigation of the northern part of Tibet and of the route through Lob-Nor and Tarim valley. St. P., 1888. — Четвертое Путешествіе въ Центральной Азіи. Отъ Кяхты на истоки Желтой Рѣки; изслѣдованіе сѣверной окраины Тибета и пути черезъ Лобъ-Норъ по бассейну Тарима.

Puini, C. Il Tibet. Secondo la relazione del viaggio del Ippolito Desideri (1715–21). Mem. della Soc. Geogr. Ital., vol. X, 1904.

Pumpelly, R. Explorations in Turkestan, with an account of the basin of Eastern Persia and Sistan. Expedition of 1903, under the direction of R. Pumpelly. Carnegie Institution, No. 26. Washington, 1905.

—— Explorations in Turkestan: expedition of 1904. Prehistoric civilization of Anau. Origins, growth, and influence of environment. Carnegie Institution Publications, No. 73. Washington, 1908.

Pyennina, Z. M. Trans-Caspian country. Collection of the bibliographical data relating to books and essays on the Trans-Caspian country and neighbouring countries. St. P., 1865–85. — Пеннина, З. М. Закаспійскій край. Система-тическій сборникъ библіографическихъ указаній книгъ и статей о Закаспійскомъ краѣ и сопредѣленныхъ странахъ.

Pyevtsoff, M. V. Description of a journey to Mongolia. Omsk, 1883. — Пѣвцовъ, М. В. Очеркъ путешествія по Монголіи.

Radde, G. Reisen im Süden von Ost-Sibirien in den Jahren 1855–9. 2 vols. St. P., 1862–3.

Radloff, W. W. Examples of the folk-literature of the Turkic tribes who inhabit Southern Siberia and Jungarian Steppes. Ed. by Radloff. I, 1866; II, 1868; III, 1870; IV, 1872; V, 1885; VI, 1886; VII, 1896; VIII, 1899; X, 1904. Imp. A. Sc. St. P. — Радловъ, В. В. Образцы народной литера-туры Тюркскихъ племенъ, живущихъ въ Южной Сибири и Дзунгарской степи. Изд. Радловымъ.

—— Itinéraire de la vallée du Moyen Zérafshan. Recueil d'itinéraires et de voyages dans l'Asie centrale, pp. 260–356. Paris,
1878.

—— Ancient architectural remains (medressé, mosques, and gravestones) in Samarkand. Mem. I. R. G. S., 1880, VI, pt. i,
pp. 23–5. — Остатки стариннаго зодчества [медресе, мечети, и
могильные памятники] въ Самаркандѣ.

—— Die alten Gräber in Sibirien. Z. f. E., 1882, XIV, pp. 430 ff.

—— Vergleichende Grammatik der nördlichen Türksprachen, I.
Leipzig, 1882.

—— Aus Sibirien. Lose Blätter aus dem Tagebuche eines reisenden
Linguisten. Leipzig, 1884.

—— Zur Sprache der Komanen. Intern. Zeit. f. allg. Sprachwiss.,
Pt. I, 1884, pp. 377–82 ; pt. II, 1885, pp. 13–42.

—— Bericht über die Ausgabe des Sprachmaterials des Codex
Comanicus. Bull. I. R. A. S., 1866, XXX, pp. 121–4.

—— Ethnographical survey of the Turkic tribes of Southern Siberia
and Jungaria. Translated [from the German] by D. A. Klements.
Tomsk, 1887. — Этнографическій обзоръ Тюркскихъ племенъ
Южной Сибири и Дзунгаріи.

—— Siberian antiquities. Materials for the archaeology of Russia,
ed. by the I. Arch. Commission, Nos. 3, 5, 15, 27. St. Pet.,
1888, 1891, 1894, 1902. — Сибирскія древности. Мат. по арх.
Россіи. Изд. И. Арх. Коммиссіею.

—— The Yarlyks of Tokhtamysh and Temir-Kutlug. Mem. E.
Sect. I. R. Arch. S., 1888, III. St. P. — Ярлыки Токтамыша и
Темиръ-Кутлуга.

—— Attempt at a vocabulary of the Turkic dialects. I, 1888
(1–320); II, 1889 (321–640) ; III, 1889 (641–960); IV, 1890
(961–1280) ; V, 1892 (1281–1600) ; VI, 1893 (1601–1914).
Vowels : VII, 1895 (1–320) ; VIII, 1896 (321–640); IX,
1897 (641–960); X, 1898 (961–1280); XI, 1898 (1281–
1600) ; XII, 1899 (1601–1814). Consonants : XIII, 1900
(1–320); XIV, 1901 (321–640); XV, 1902 (641–960); XVI,

1903 (961–1280); XVII, 1903 (1281–1600); XVIII, 1905
(1601–2204); XIX, 1905 (1–320); XX, 1906 (321–629).
St. P. — Опытъ словаря тюркскихъ нарѣчій.

Radloff, W. W. Über alttürkische Dialekte. Die Geldschuki-
schen Verse im Rebâb-Nâmeh. Bull. I. A. S., 1889, XXIII,
pp. 291–351.

—— Kudatku Bilik. Facsimile der uigurischen Handschrift der
K. K. Hofbibliothek in Wien. Im Auftrage der K. Ak. d.
W. herausgegeben. St. P., 1890.

—— Das Kudatku Bilik des Jusuf Chass-Hadschib aus Bälasagun.
Theil II. Der Text in Transscription herausgegeben. St.P., 1891.

—— Titles and names of the Uigur Khans. Mem. E. Sect.
I. R. Arch. S., 1891, V, pp. 265 ff. — Титулы и имена
уйгурскихъ хановъ.

—— Collection of documents of the Orkhon Expedition. Vol. I.
St. P., 1892. — Сборникъ Трудовъ Орхонской Экспедиціи.

Radloff, W. W. 1–12. Preliminary report of the results of the
archaeological expedition for the investigation of the basin of
the R. Orkhon. — *Радловъ, В. В.* Предварительный отчетъ
о результатахъ снаря женной съ высочайшего соизволенія
И. Акад. Наукъ экспедиціи для археологическаго изслѣдованія
бассейна рѣки Орхона.

Klements, D. A. 13–23. Letter. — *Клеменцъ, Д. А.* Письмо.

Dudin, S. M. 24–27. Preliminary report of a journey from
Erdeni-Tsu to Kyakhta. — *Дудинъ, С. М.* Предварительный
отчетъ поѣздки изъ Эрдени-Цзу въ Кяхту.

Yadrintseff, N. M. 27–40. Preliminary report of the investigations along the Rivers Tola and Orkhon and in Southern
Khangai. — *Ядринцевъ, Н. М.* Предварительный отчетъ объ
изслѣдованіяхъ по р. Толѣ, Орхону и въ Южномъ Хангаѣ.

Levin, N. P. 41–50. Preliminary report. — *Левинъ, Н. П.*
Предварительный отчетъ.

Yadrintseff, N. M. 51–113. Preliminary report of an expedition to the Orkhon undertaken in 1889 by request of the East
Siberian Imp. Geog. Soc. — *Ядринцевъ, Н. М.* Отчетъ
экспедиціи на Орхонъ совершенной въ 1889.

—— Atlas der Alterthümer der Mongolei. Arbeiten der Orchon-Expedition. St. P., Lfg. I, 1892 ; Lfg. II, 1893; Lfg. III, 1896; Lfg. IV, 1899.

—— Eine neue Methode zur Herstellung von Abklatschen von Steininschriften. Translated from Russian. Bull. I. A. S., 1892–4, New Series III (XXXV), pp. 153–66; and Mél. Asiat, 1892, X. 2, pp. 257–70.

—— Über eine neu aufgefundene uigurische Inschrift. Bull. I.A.S., 1892, New Series III (XXXV), pp. 327–9 ; and Mél. Asiat., 1892, X. 2, pp. 387 ff.

—— On the question of the Uigur. From the foreword to the author's edition of 'Kudatku Bilik'. Supplement Bull I. A. S., 1893, LXXII, No. 2. — Къ вопросу объ Уйгурахъ. Изъ предисловія къ изданію Кудатку-Билликъ.

—— Radloff's Untersuchung des Orchon-Beckens. Review of W. Radloff's ' Vorläufiger Bericht ' (1892). Globus, 1893, LXIV. 5, pp. 69–72.

—— Das Denkmal zu Ehren des Prinzen Kül Tegin. Die altürkischen Inschriften der Mongolei, I. St. P., 1894.

—— Die Denkmäler von Koscho-Zaidam. Text, Transscription und Übersetzung. Die alttürkischen Inschriften der Mongolei. 1ste Lieferung. St. P., 1894.

—— Verbesserungen, Zusätze und Bemerkungen zu den Denkmälern von Koscho-Zaidam; die übrigen Denkmäler des Orchon-Beckens und die Denkmäler im Flussgebiete des Yenissei. Die alttürkischen Inschriften der Mongolei. 3te Lfr. St. P., 1895.

—— Die alttürkischen Inschriften der Mongolei. Neue Folge, 1897. See Barthold, V. V.

—— and **Melioranski, P. M.** The old Turkic monuments in Kosho-Tsaidam. Collection of documents of the Orkhon Expedition, vol. IV. St. P., 1897. — и Меліоранскій, П. М. Древнетюркскіе памятники въ Кошо-Цайдамѣ.

—— Eine neu aufgefundene alttürkische Inschrift. Vorläufiger Bericht. Bull. I. A. S., Jan. 1898, VIII, No. 1, pp. 71–6.

Radloff, W. W., and **Melioranski, P. M.**   Zum Kudatku-Bilik.
Z. D. M. G., 1898, LII, pp. 715 ff.

—— Über eine in Kairo aufgefundene zweite Handschrift des
Kudatku-Bilik.   Bull. I. A. S., 1898, 4th ser., IX, pp. 309–19.
St. P.

—— Decipherment of the Old Turkic inscription on a stone found
in the Airtam-Oi in the village of Kenkolsk in the Aulieata
district.   Mem. E. Sect. I. R. Arch. S., 1899, XI. 1–4, pp. 85–6.

— Разборъ древнетюркской надписи на камнѣ найденномъ на
урочищѣ Аиртамъ-Ой въ Кенкольской волости Ауліеатинскаго
уѣзда.

—— Die Inschrift des Tonjukuk.   Die alttürkischen Inschriften der
Mongolei.   Zweite Folge.   St. P., 1899.   *See also* Hirth, F.;
Barthold, V. V.

—— Altuigurische Sprachproben aus Turfan.   Nachrichten über
die von der K. Akad. d. Wissenschaft zu St. Petersburg im
Jahre 1893 ausgerüstete Expedition nach Turfan.   Heft I.
St. P., 1899.

—— Researches of Dr. Hirth on the genealogy of Attila.   Mem.
E. Sect. I. R. Arch. S., 1900, XIII. 1, pp. xx–xxi. — Изслѣдованія дра Гирта о родословной Аттилы.

—— Das Kudatku-Bilik des Jusuf Chass-Hadschib aus Bälasagun.
Theil II.   Text und Übersetzung nach den Handschriften von
Wien und Kairo herausgegeben.   1. Lfg.   St. P., 1900.

—— Zur Geschichte des türkischen Vokalsystems.   Bull. I. A. S.,
1901, 4th series, XIV. 4, pp. 425–62.   St. P.

—— Einleitende Gedanken zur Darstellung der Morphologie der
Türksprachen.   Mem. I. A. S., 1905, 8th ser. 7.

—— Die Jakutische Sprache in ihrem Verhältnisse zu den Türksprachen.   Mem. I. A. S., 1907.

—— Die vorislamitischen Schriftarten der Türken und ihr Verhältniss zu der Sprache derselben.   Bull. I. A. S., 1908.   St. P.

—— Alttürkische Studien.   Bull. I. A. S., 1909, p. 1213.   St. P.

—— Ein Fragment in türkischer Runenschrift.   Bull. I. A. S.,
1910, III, p. 1025.   St. P.

—— Einleitende Gedanken zur Untersuchung der alttürkischen Dialecte. Bull. I. A. S., 1911, IV, p. 305.

—— Die alttürkischen Dialecte. Bull. I. A. S., 1911, V, p. 427. St. P.

—— For the seventieth birthday of Wasily Wasilyevich Radloff, 1907. *See* Salemann. — Ко дню Семидесятилѣтія Василія Васильевича Радлова.

Ramstedt, G. J. Etymology of the word ʻOiratʼ. Anniversary book of Potanin. Mem. I. R. G. S., 1909, XXXIV, pp. 547–58. — *Рамстедтъ, Г. И.* Этимологія имени Ойратъ.

—— Mongolische Briefe aus Idigur-Schähri bei Turfan. Abh. K. P. Akad. der Wiss., 1909.

—— How the ʻSelenginsk Stoneʼ was found. Trans. T.-K. S. Amur Sect. I. R. G. S., 1912, XV, pt. i. — Какъ былъ найденъ „ Селенгинскій Камень “.

—— Translation of the inscription on the Selenginsk Stone. Trans. T.-K. S. Amur Sect. I. R. G. S., 1913, XV, pt. i. — Переводъ надписи на Селенгинскомъ Камнѣ.

—— Zwei uigurische Runeninschriften in der Nord-Mongolei. J. Soc. Fin.-Ougr., 1913.

Rashid al-Dīn Tabīb (Fazl Allah). Introduction à l'Histoire des Mongols de Fadh Allah Rashid ed-Din. Translated by E. Blochet. E. J. W. Gibb Memorial, vol. XII. Leyden and London, 1910.

—— Histoire des Mongols de la Djami el-Tevaikh. Vol. II, contenant l'histoire des Fricasseurs de Schinkkiz Khaghan. 1911. E. J. W. Gibb Memorial.

—— *see* Erdmann, F. von ; Klaproth, H. J. von.

Rasmussen, J. L. Annales islamismi, sive tabulae synchronisto-chronologicae Chaliforum et regum orientis et occidentis. Includes trans. of chaps. 45–53 of Ahmed Ibn Yusuf's Universal History. Copenhagen, 1825.

Raverty, H. G. Tabakāt-i-Nāsirī : A general history of the Muhammadad dynasties of Asia, including Hindūstān, from

A.H. 194 (A.D. 810) to A.H. 658 (A.D. 1260) and the irruption of the Infidel Mughals into Islam. By the Maulānā, Minhaj-ud-dīn, Abū-'umar-i-'usmān. Translated from original Persian manuscripts. Bibliotheca Indica. A collection of Oriental works published by the Asiatic Society of Bengal, vol. 78. (Published in parts, 1873–81.) London, 1881.

Read, Sir C. H. Siberian Bronzes and Chinese Jade. Man, January 1917, No. 1.

Reclus, E. L'Asie russe. Paris, 1881.

Reinach, S. La Représentation du Galop dans l'art ancien et moderne. Rev. Arch., 1901, XXXVIII, pp. 27 ff.

Reinecke, P. Ueber einige Beziehungen der Altertümer China's zu denen des skythisch-sibirischen Völkerkreises. Z. f. E., 1897, XXIX, pp. 140 ff.

—— Aus der russischen archäologischen Litteratur. Mainzer Zeitschrift, 1906, p. 42 f.

Rémusat, H. H. 'Mémoires sur les relations politiques des princes chrétiens et particulièrement des rois de France avec les empereurs mongols.' Mém. de l'Acad. des Inscrip. et Belles-Lettres, Pt. I, vol. vi, pp. 396–469; Pt. II, vol. vii, pp. 335–431.

—— Nouveaux mélanges asiatiques, ou Recueil de morceaux de critique . . . Paris, 1829.

—— Review of 'Inscriptiones Sibiriacae', by Gr. Spassky. Jour. des Savants, Oct. 1822, pp. 595–602.

—— Histoire de la ville de Khotan. Paris, 1820.

—— Recherches sur les langues tartares, ou Mémoires sur différents points de la grammaire et de la littérature des Mandchous, des Mongols, des Ouigours et des Tibétains. Paris, 1820.

Reypolski, A. F. The Middle Orda of the Kirghis. Proc. of the All-Russian Congress of Medical Men in St. Petersburg in 1874–5. — Рейпольскій, А. Ф. Киргизская Внутренняя Орда.

Rialle, G. de. Mémoire sur l'Asie centrale. Paris, 1875.

Rickmers, W. R. The Duab of Turkestan. Cambridge, 1913.

Ritter, C. Die Erdkunde im Verhältniss zur Natur und zur Geschichte des Menschen, oder Allgemeine Vergleichende Geographie. Teil II, Buch ii, Asien; Bd. 1, Der Norden und Nord-Osten von Hoch-Asien. Berlin, 1832. Teil III, Buch ii, Asien; Bd. 2, Der Nord-Osten und der Süden von Hoch-Asien. Berlin, 1833.

Roborovsky, V. I. Results of the expedition to Tibet in 1888–90. St. P., 1891–2. — *Роборовскій, В. И.* Труды Тибетской Экспедиціи 1880–90.

——— Works of the Imperial Russian Geographical Society's Expedition to Central Asia, 1893–5, under the leadership of V. I. Roborovsky. St. P., 1899–1901. — Труды экспедиціи Императорскаго Русскаго Географическаго Общества но Центральной Азіи, совершенной въ 1893–5 гг. подъ Начальствомъ В. И. Роборовскаго.

——— Conclusion of Roborovsky's expedition. Note in Geog. Journ., 1897, vol. IX.

——— The Russian expedition to Central Asia under Colonel Pievtsoff. Translation from letter of V. I. Roborofsky. Proc. of the Royal Geog. Soc., 1890, XII, pp. 19–36, 161–6; 1891, XIII, pp. 99–105.

Rocca, F. de. De l'Alaï à l'Amou-Dariä. Paris, 1896.

Rommel. Review of G. Spassky's 'Inscriptiones Sibiriacae'. Göttingische gelehrte Anzeigen, 1823, No. 205, p. 2047.

Rosen, Baron V. R. Translation of V. Thomsen's 'Déchiffrement des inscriptions de l'Orkhon et de l'Jénisséi', Notice préliminaire, 1894. Bull. E. Sect. I. R. Arch. S., VIII, pp. 327–37.

——— Review of 'Inscriptions de l'Jénisséi recueillies et publiées par la Société Finlandaise d'Archéologie', 1889. Bull. E. Sect. I. R. Arch. S., IV, p. 443. — *Розенъ, Баронъ В. Р.* Рецензія 'Inscriptions de l'Jénisséi recueillies et publiées par la Société Finlandaise d'Archéologie'.

Rosen, Baron V. R. Suum cuique. Concerning the decipherment of Orkhon and Yenisei inscriptions. Bull. E. Sect. I. R. Arch. S., VIII, pp. 323–5. — Suum cuique. По поводу дешифровки орхонскихъ и енисейскихъ надписей.

Ross, Sir E. D., and **Skrine, F. B. H.** : *see* Skrine.

—— et **Gauthiot, R.** L'Alphabet Soghdien d'après un témoignage du xiiie siècle. J. A., 1913.

Rostislavoff, M. Further details concerning the archaeological researches in the Zerafshan district. Turk. News, 1876, XLIII. — *Ростиславовъ, М.* Еще по поводу археологическихъ изысканій въ Зеравшанскомъ округѣ.

—— Concerning archaeological researches in the Zerafshan district. Proc. Turk. Circle F. Arch., 1897–8, III, pp. 144–9. — Объ археологическихъ изысканіяхъ въ Зеравшанскомъ округѣ.

Rubruck, William of : *see* Yule.

Rudanowski, K. A. Concerning the conical dwellings of Ferghana. Proc Turk. Circle F. Arch., 1897–8, III, pp. 233–5. — *Рудановскій, К. А.* О циклопическихъ постройкахъ въ Ферганѣ.

Rudnyeff, A. D. Traces of old towns along the Syr-Daria. Proc. Turk. Circle F. Arch., 1899–1900, V, pp. 57–62. — *Руднев, А. Д.* Слѣды древнихъ городовъ по Сыръ-Дарьѣ.

—— Vilhelm Thomsen. Trans. T.-K. S. Amur Sect. I. R. G. S., XV, pt. i. — Вильгельмъ Томсенъ.

—— Short report of a journey to the extreme north-east of Mongolia in summer 1903. Bull. Russ. Committee, 1904, No. 2, pp. 7–10. — Краткій отчетъ о поѣздкѣ на крайній сѣверо-востокъ Монголіи лѣтомъ 1903 г. Командированнаго Русс. Комитетомъ прив. доц. А. Д. Руднева. Изв. Русс. Комитета, 1904, No. 2, pp. 7–10.

—— The expedition of Dr. G. J. Ramstedt to Mongolia. Russkia Vyedomosti, Dec. 1909, No. 280. — Экспедиція Дра. Г. И. Рамстедта по Монголіи.

—— A new discovery in Mongolia. Ryech, Oct. 7, 1912. No. 2229. — Новое открытіе въ Монголіи.

Selivanoff, A. I.   Antiquities of the valley of Isyk-Kul.   Rep. I.
Arch. Commission, 1895, pp. 47–8. — *Селивановъ, А. И.*
Древности Иссыкъ-Кульской котловины.

Semenoff, A. A.   Ethnographical sketches of the mountains
of Zerafshan, Karategin and Darvaz.   Moscow, 1903. —
Семеновъ, А. А. Этнографическіе очерки Зарафшанскихъ горъ,
Каратегина и Дарваза.

—— A short information concerning the method of making
weapons in Central Asia.   L. A. T., 1909, Nos. 2–3, pp. 153–5.
— Два слова о ковкѣ среднеазіатскаго оружія.

Semenoff, P. P.   Dzungaria and the Celestial Mountains.   Journ.
of R. G. S., 1865, XXXV.

—— Die Gräber bei den Kirgisen.   Mittheil. d. Geog. Gesellschaft
in Wien, 1871, p. 199.

Semenoff, V. P.   Tribes of Western Siberia.   ' Russia,' 1907,
XVI.   St. P. — *Семеновъ, В. П.*   Племена Западной Сибири.

Semirechie.

Stones with Arabic inscriptions in the district of Semirechie.
Trans. E. Comm. I. Moscow Arch. S., 1889, I, pt. i, p. 20.
Семирѣчье. Камни съ арабскими надписями изъ Семирѣченской
области.

Archaeological remains in Semirechie and Kulja district.   Turk.
News, 1879, No. 43. — Археологическіе памятники въ
Семирѣчьи и Кульджинскомъ районѣ.

Sénart, E.   Note sur quelques fragments d'inscriptions du Turfan.
J. A., March–April 1900, pp. 343–60.   *See* Expedition.

Setälä, E. N.   Review of V. Thomsen's ' Déchiffrement des
inscriptions de l'Orkhon et de l'Jénisséi '.   Notice préliminaire,
1894.   Uusi Suometar, 1894, No. 11.

—— Review of V. Thomsen's 'Inscriptions de l'Orkhon déchiffrées'.
I (1894).   Uusi Suometar, 1895, No. 283 ; 1896, No. 50.

—— Review of V. Thomsen's ' Déchiffrement des inscriptions de
l'Orkhon et de l'Jénisséi '.   Notice préliminaire, 1894.   Valvoja (Helsingfors), 1894, No. 2.

Shakhmatoff. Notes on the agriculture of the Kirghis-Kaizak of the Middle Orda. Jour. of Agriculture, 1832, No. 8, pp. 617–24. — *Шахматовъ.* Замѣчаніе о хлѣбопашествіе Киргизъ-Кайсаковъ Средней Орды.

Shaw, R. B. Visits to High Tartary, Yarkand, and Kashghar. London, 1871.

—— A sketch on the Turki language as spoken in Eastern Turkistan. Calcutta, 1880.

Shchegloff, I. V. Chronological enumeration of the most important events in the history of Siberia, 1032–1882. Bull. E. Sib. Sect. I. R. G. S. Irkutsk, 1883. — *Щегловъ, И. В.* Хронологическая перечень важнѣйшихъ данныхъ изъ исторіи Сибири 1032–1882.

Shcherbina-Kramarenko, N. Among the Mussulman shrines of Central Asia. 'Reference Book of the Samarkand Territory', pt. iv, pp. 45–61. — *Щербина-Крамаренко, Н.* По мусульманскихъ святыняхъ Средней Азіи.

Shchukin, N. S. Nations speaking Turkic languages in Southern Siberia. J. Min. Int., 1847, XVIII, pp. 255–84. — Народы турскаго языка, обитающіе въ Южной Сибири.

—— The Yakut. J. Min. Int., 1854, VII, No. 7, pt. iii, pp. 1–46. — Якуты.

—— Letter to P. S. Savyelyeff about a stone with Runic inscriptions found by Castrén near the village of Oznachennoye. Bull. I. R. Arch. S., 1859, I, p. 30. — Письмо П. С. Савельеву о камнѣ съ руническими письменами близь села Означеннаго, найденномъ Кастреномъ и впослѣдствіи скопированномъ Титовымъ.

—— Materials for the bibliography of Siberia. Annual book of the Irkutsk government, 1865. — *Щукинъ, Н. С.* Матеріалы для Сибирской библіографіи.

Sherr, N. B. Journey to the Kumandints in 1898. Altayski Sbornik, 1903, V, pp. 81–114. — *Шерръ, Н. Б.* Изъ поѣздки къ Кумандинцамъ въ 1898 г.

Shetikhin. Ruins of ancient towns in Central Asia. Mesht-Dovran; Tash-Arvat-Kola. 1876, St. P., I. — *Шетихинъ*, Развалины древнихъ городовъ въ Средней Азіи. Месть-Доврани. Ташъ-Арвать-Кола.

Shiraeff, T. G. : *see* Obrucheff.

Shiratori, K. Die chinesische Inschrift auf dem Gedenkstein des K'üe-t'e-k'in am Orkhon. Tokio, August 1899.

Shishmareff, Y. P. Information about the Darkhat-Uriankhi of the districts of the Khutukta of Urga. Bull. Sib. Sect. I. R. G. S., 1871, II, pp. 38-43. — *Шишмаревъ, Я. П.* Свѣдѣнія о Дархатахъ-Урянхахъ вѣдомства Ургинскаго Хутукты.

Shishoff, A. The Sarts. Ethnographical and anthropological investigation. Tashkent, 1905. — *Шишовъ, А.* Сарты. Этнографическое и антропологическое изслѣдованіе.

Shkapski, O. A. Kirghis peasants. Bull. I. R. G. S., 1905, XLI, pp. 765-78. — *Шкапскій, О. А.* Киргизы крестьяне.

Shvetsoff, S. P. Primitive agriculture in the Altai. Mem. W. Sib. Sect. I. R. G. S., 1900, XXVII, p. 128. — *Швецовъ, С. П.* Примитивное земледѣліе на Алтаѣ.

Shvetsova, M. The Altai Kalmuck. Mem. W. Sib. Sect. I. R. G. S., 1898, XXIII, p. 134. — *Швецова, М.* Алтайскіе Калмыки.

Sibirische Entdeckungen, I, II, III. Die Nation, 1888, VI, 5, pp. 70-71 ; 6, pp. 83-5 ; 7, pp. 103-5.

Siehe. Primitive Kultur des Türkenvolks. Berlin.

Sieroszewski, W. The Yakut. St. P., 1896. — *Сърошевскій, В.* Якуты.

Silinich, I. P. On the question of the physical type of the population of North-West Siberia. Russ. Anthr. J., 1916, Nos. 3, 4. — *Силиничъ, И. П.* Къ вопросу объ антропологическомъ типѣ населенія Сѣверо-Западной Сибири.

Simonyi, Zs. Esemèny az uràlaltoji nyelvészet terén : Nyelvtud. Közlem, 1895, XXIV, pp. 1-5.

Simonyi, Zs. Review of V. Thomsen's 'Déchiffrement des inscriptions de l'Orkhon et de l'Jénisséi'. Notice préliminaire, 1894. Ungarische Revue, 1894, XIV, pp. 230–1.

—— Review of V. Thomsen's ' Déchiffrement des inscriptions de l'Orkhon et de l'Jénisséi '. Notice préliminaire, 1894. Pesti Napló, 1894, No. 37.

Sirelius, U. T. Die Handarbeiten der Ostjaken und Wogulen. J. Soc. Fin.-Ougr., XXII.

Sitnyakowski, N. T. Concerning some antiquities near Bokhara and along the Zerafshan. Proc. Turk. Circle F. Arch., 1897–8, III, pp. 89–94. — Ситняковскій, Н. Ѳ. О нѣкоторыхъ древностяхъ близь Бухары и по Зеравшану.

—— Information about some antiquities in the neighbourhood of Samarkand and Bokhara. Proc. Turk. Circle F. Arch., 1899–1900, V, pp. 35–6. — Сообщеніе о нѣкоторыхъ древностяхъ въ окрестностяхъ Самарканда и Бухары.

—— The temples of Bokhara (Bagauddin Mazar). Proc. Turk. Circle F. Arch., 1899–1900, V, pp. 49–56. — Бухарскія святыни (Мазаръ Вагауддина).

—— Note on the Bokhara side of the Zerafshan valley. Bull. Turk. Sect. I. R. G. S., 1899, I, pp. 121–78. — Замѣтки о Бухарской части долины Зеравшана.

Skrine, F. H. B., and Ross, E. D. The heart of Asia. A history of Russian Turkestan and the Central Asian Khanates from the earliest times. London, 1899.

Skwarski, P. S. A few words about the antiquities of Shakhristan. Proc. Turk. Circle F. Arch., 1895–6, pp. 41–5. — Скварскій, П. С. Нѣсколько словъ о древностяхъ Шахристана.

Slovtsoff, I. Y. Materials for the distribution of the kurgans and the old sites in the Tobolsk government. Tomsk, 1890. — Словцовъ, И. Я. Матеріялы о распредиленіи кургановъ игородищъ въ Тобольской губ.

Slutski, S. S. The Nestorian inscriptions in Semirechie. 'Eastern Antiquities.' Trans. E. Comm. I. Moscow Arch. S., 1889, I, No. 1, pp. 1–66. — *Слуцкій, С. С.* Семирѣченскія Несторіанскія надписи.

—— About a Turkic inscription on a stone figure ('baba'). 'Eastern Antiquities.' Trans. E. Comm. I. Moscow Arch. S., 1896, II, 1, No. 18, pp. 68–9. — О тюркской надписи на каменной бабѣ.

Smirnoff, E. T. Antiquities in the neighbourhood of Tashkent. Collection of essays, 'Central Asia'. St. P., 1896. — *Смирновъ, Е. Т.* Древности въ окрестностяхъ г. Ташкента.

—— Antiquities on the middle and lower course of the R. Syr-Daria. Proc. Turk. Circle F. Arch., 1897, Supplement, pp. 1–14. — Древности на среднемъ и нижнемъ теченіи р. Сыръ-Даріи.

Smirnoff, V. D. Manuscrits turcs de l'Institut des Langues Orientales du Ministère des Affaires Étrangères. St. P., 1897.

Smirnoff, Y. I. Review of V. Thomsen's 'Inscriptions de l'Orkhon déchiffrées' (1894). Bull. I. R. Arch. S., XII, pp. 71–4. — *Смирновъ, Я. И.* Рецензія В. Томсена.

—— and **Inostrantseff, K. A.** Materials for the bibliography of the Mussulman archaeology. Mem. E. Sect. I. R. Arch. S., 1906, XVI, pt. iv. — *и Иностранцевъ, К. А.* Матеріалы для библіографіи мусульманской археологіи.

—— Eastern silver: album of ancient silver and gold vessels of Eastern origin. Bull. Imp. Arch. Comm. St. P., 1909. — Восточное серебро : атласъ древней серебряной и золотой посуды восточнаго происхожденія.

Sokoloff, D. On the 'tamga' of the Bashkir. Proc. of the Orenburg Archaeological Commission, XIII, p. 84. — *Соколовъ, Д.* О башкирскихъ тамгахъ.

Solunoff. Ancient ruins of towns found in the Kurgan district. 'Otyechestvennya Zapiski', 1824, No. 54, pp. 127–30. — *Солуновъ.* Старинныя городища, существующія въ Курганскомъ уѣздѣ.

Sontsoff, D. P. What can we expect from the excavation of our kurgans? Bull. Soc. F. S. Anthrop. E., I, pts. 1, 2. Moscow, 1867. — *Сонцовъ, Д. П.* Что мы можемъ ожидать отъ раскопки нашихъ кургановъ.

Soret, F. Lettre à M. le capitaine aux gardes impériales, de Kossikowsky, sur un essai de classification des monnaies djoudjides (of P. S. Savel'ev). Revue de la Numismatique Belge, 3ᵉ Série, Tome IV. Brussels, 1860.

Sorokin, N. V. The grave of the Khan Tokhtamysh. Tob. Gov. News, 1869, XXIII. — *Сорокинъ, Н. В.* Могила хана Тохтамыша.

—— The country and the people of Central Asia. Historical News, 1887, No. X; 1888, No. VII; 1889, Nos. VI and VII. — Природа и человѣкъ въ Средней Азіи.

Sosnovski, Miroshnishenko, Matussovski, and **Morozof.** Recent Russian explorations in Western Mongolia. Geog. Magazine, 1875, II, pp. 196–200, map; Proc. R. G. S., 1875–6, XX, p. 421.

Spasski, G. I. Notes on the antiquities of Siberia. Siberian Messenger, 1818. St. P. — *Спасскій, Г. И.* Записки о Сибирскихъ древностяхъ.

—— *see* Krug, Ph.

—— Siberian chronicle containing information about the conquest of Siberian lands by the Russians at the time of Tsar Ivan Vasilyevich the Terrible; with a short exposition of the history previous to this event. St. P., 1821. — Лѣтопись Сибирская, содержащая повѣствованіе о взятіи Сибирскихъ земли Русскими, при Царѣ Іоаннѣ Васильевичѣ Грозномъ; съ краткимъ изложеніемъ предшествовавшихъ оному событій.

—— Account of Mongolia. Siberian Messenger, 1913, pt. ii. St. P. — Обозрѣніе Монголіи.

—— Eastern Bibliography. Translation of the article by Abel Remusat on 'Inscriptiones Sibiriacae', with the translator's comments. Asiatic Messenger, pt. iv, pp. 285–303. St. P.,

1825. — Восточная Библіографія. Переводъ статьи Абель Ремюза объ ‘ Inscriptiones Sibiriacae ’, съ примѣчаніями переводчика.

—— Prominent monuments among the Siberian antiquities. Mem. I. R. Arch. Soc., 1857, pt. xii. — Достопримѣчательные памятники Сибирскихъ древностей.

Specht, E. Étude sur l'Asie centrale. Paris, 1890.

Spiridonoff, P. Journey to the ruins of Jankent. Proc. Turk. Circle F. Arch., 1897–8, pt. iii, pp. 68–72. — *Спиридоновъ, П.* Поѣздка на развалины Джанкента.

Spitsyne, A. A. Monuments of Latin culture in Russia. Bull. I. Arch. Comm., 1904, XII. — *Спицынъ, А. А.* Памятники Латенской культуры въ Россіи.

—— Communal graves along the Upper Yenisei and the Chulim. Mem. I. R. Arch. S., 1899, XI, pp. 1–2. — Коллективныя могилы въ Верховьяхъ Енисея и Чулыма.

Ssanung Ssetsen Chungtaidschi. Geschichte der Ost-Mongolen und ihres Fürstenhauses, übersetzt und mit dem Originaltexte herausg. von I. J. Schmidt. St. P., 1829.

Staël-Holstein, Baron A. von. Siuan-Dzian, and some results of modern archaeological investigations. St. P., 1910 — *Сталь-Гольстейнъ, баронъ А. фонъ.* Сюань-Дзанъ, и результаты современныхъ археологическихъ изслѣдованій.

Stassof, V. V. The throne of the khans of Khiva. ‘ Vyestnik Izyashchikh Isskustv,’ 1886, IV, pp. 405–17. — *Стасовъ, В. В.* Тронъ хивинскихъ хановъ.

Stebnicki, I. I. Report of a journey to the Trans-Caspian country in 1873. Bull. Cauc. Sect. I. R. G. S., 1873–4, II, No. 1, pt. ii. — *Стебницкій, И. И.* Отчетъ о путешествіи въ Закаспійскомъ краѣ въ 1873.

Stein, Sir M. A.: *see* V. Thomsen, J. R. A. S., 1912, I, pp. 181–227.

—— Preliminary report on a journey of archaeological and topographical exploration in Chinese Turkestan. London, 1901.

Stein, Sir M. A. Sand-buried ruins of Khotan. Personal narrative of a journey of archaeological and geographical exploration in Chinese Turkestan. London, 1903.

—— Ancient Khotan. Detailed report of archaeological explorations in Chinese Turkestan carried out and described under the orders of H. M. Indian Government. Oxford, 1907.

—— Explorations in Central Asia, 1906–8. Geogr. Journ., July–September, 1909.

—— Ruins of desert Cathay: personal narrative of explorations in Central Asia and Westernmost China. London, 1912.

Stephens, G. The inscriptions of Yenissei. Academy, Nov. 30, 1889, XXXVI, pp. 359–60.

Stewart, C. : *see* Timur.

Strahlenberg, P. J. Der nördliche und östliche Theil von Europa und Asien. Stockholm, 1730.

Stremoukhoff, N. In Central Asia: Samarkand, Tashkent . . . ' Niva', 1879, pp. 442–83. — *Стремоухов, Н.* Въ средней Азіи: Самаркандъ, Ташкентъ . . .

Struwe, H. Analyse verschiedener antiker Bronzen und Eisen aus den Abakan- und Jenissej-Steppen. Bull. I. A. S., X. St. P., 1866.

Stubendorff, U. T. The Karagass. Mem. E. Sib. Sect. I.R.G.S., 1854, XII, pt. ii, pp. 229–46. — *Штубендорфъ, Ю. Ѳ.* О Карагассахъ.

St. Martin, V. de. Mémoire. Les Huns Blancs, ou Ephthalites des historiens byzantins. Paris, 1849.

Strzygowski, J. Zentralasien als Forschungsgebiet. Österr. Monatss. f. d. Orient, 1914, XL.

—— Ornamentet hos de altaiska och iranska folken. Konsthistoriska sällskapets publikation. Stockholm, 1916.

—— Altai-Iran und Völkerwanderung. Leipzig, 1917.

Sunak. Information about the town of Sunak. Proc. Turk. Circle F. Arch., 1899–1900. — *Сунакъ.* Свѣдѣнія о гор. Сунакѣ.

Swayne, H. G. C. Through the highlands of Siberia. London, 1904.

Sykes, Sir M. The Caliph's Last Heritage. London, 1915.

Sykes, Sir P. M. A history of Persia. London, 1915.

Takacs, S. Chinesische Kunst bei den Hunnen. Ost-As. Z., 1915, II ; 1916, V.

Talbot, F. G. Memoirs of Baber, Emperor of India, first of the great Moghuls, being an abridgement with an introduction, supplementary notes, and some account of his successors. London, 1909.

Tallgren, A. M. Die Kupfer- und Bronzezeit in Nord- und Ostrussland. Journ. de la Soc. Finl. d'Archéol., 1911, XXV, pt. i.

—— Minusinskin arohaudat. Suomen Museo, 1915.

—— Collection Zaoussaïlov au Musée Historique de Finlande, I. Helsingfors, 1916.

—— Collection Tovostine des antiquités préhistoriques de Minoussinsk conservées chez le Dr. Karl Hedman à Vasa. Chapitres d'Archéologie Sibérienne. Soc. Finlandaise d'Archéologie. Helsingfors, 1917.

Talko-Hryncewicz, J. Ancient monuments of Western Transbaikalia. Proc. of Twelfth Archaeological Congress in Kharkhoff, vol. I.

—— Materyały do Etnologji i Antropologji Ludòw Azji Środkowej. Bull. Acad. of Science, Cracow, 1910.

Tallqvist, K. L. Professor Vilhelm Thomsens Tydning af de Sibiriska Inskrifterna. Finsk. Tidskrift, 1897, XLII, pp. 173–83, 336.

Tashkent. Archaeological discovery near Tashkent. Turk. News, 1886, No. 17. — Ташкентъ. Археологическая находка близь Ташкента.

Tchihacheff, P. de. Voyage scientifique dans l'Altaï oriental et les parties adjacentes de la frontière de Chine, fait par ordre de S. M. l'Empereur de Russie par P. de Tchihacheff. Paris, 1845.

Tarnowski, G. Badkhys and Pende. Turk. News, 1893, Nos. 7, 18, 20, 22. — Тарновскій, Г. Бадхызъ и Пенде.

Tekin-Alp. ' The Turkish and Pan-Turkish Ideal.' Engl. tr. London, 1916.

Tereshchenko, A. I.   Traces of Dasht-Kipchak and the Middle Orda of the Kaizak-Kirghis.   Moskvityanin, 1853, VI, No. 22. — *Терещенко, А. И.*   Слѣды Дештъ-Кипчака и Внутренняя Киргизъ-Кайсацкая Орда.

Thomas, E.   Early Sassanian inscriptions, seals, and coins. London, 1868.

Thomsen, V.   Une lettre méconnue des inscriptions de l'Jénisséi. J. Soc. Fin.-Ougr., 1913, XXX, 4.   Helsingfors.

—— Dr. M. A. Stein's MSS. in Turkish ' Runic ' script from Miran and Tun-Huang.   J. R. A. S., 1912, I, pp. 181–227.

—— Ein Blatt in türkischer Runenschrift aus Turfan.   Sitzungsber. d. K. P. Akad. d. Wiss., 1910, pp. 296, 306.

—— Review of V. Thomsen's 'Inscriptions de l'Orkhon déchiffrées'. I (1894).   Beil. Allg. Ztg., LXXXIII, p. 7.

—— Inscriptions de l'Orkhon déchiffrées.   I, 1894.   Mém. Soc. Fin.-Ougr., 1894, V, p. 54 ; 1896, I, p. 224.

—— Sur le système des consonnes dans la langue ouïgoure.   K.S., 1901, No. 4, p. 241.   Budapest.

—— Déchiffrement des inscriptions de l'Orkhon et de l'Jénisséi. Notice préliminaire.   Copenhagen, 1894.   Bull. de l'Académie R. des Sciences et des Lettres de Danemark, 1893, pp. 285–99. Reprinted 1894.

Thonnelier, J.   Dictionnaire géographique de l'Asie centrale. Paris, 1869.

Timkowski, G.   Voyage à Pékin à travers la Mongolie en 1820 et 1821.   Trad. du russe par M. N., publ. par J. Klaproth.   Paris, 1827.   Engl. trans. by H. E. Lloyd.   London, 1827.

Timur.   Memoirs of Timur.   Transl. from Jagatai into Persian by Abu Halib Hussein.   Trans. into English by Major Davy (Oxford, 1783), and by Charles Stewart (London, 1830).

Tisenhausen, Baron V. G.   Review of Jukowski's ' The Antiquities of the Trans-Caspian Country'.   Mem. E. Sect. I. R. Arch. S., 1899, XXI, pp. 327–33. — *Тизенгаузенъ, баронъ В. Г.* Отзывъ о книгѣ Жуковскаго „Древности Закаспійскаго Края".

Tomaschek, W. Zentralasiatische Studien: Sogdiana. Sitzungsb. der phil.-hist. Classe der k. Akad. d. Wiss., LXXXVII. Vienna, 1877.

—— Zentralasiatische Studien. I. Die Pamir-Dialekte. Vienna, 1880.

—— Kritik der ältesten Nachrichten über den skythischen Norden. Sitz. d. K. K. Ak. Vienna, 1888, CXVI, pp. 715-80; CXVII, pp. 1-70.

Tötterman, A. Studien über die Suljekfelsen-Inschriften. Helsingfors, 1889.

—— Entzifferungsversuch einiger Inschriften auf einer Felsenwand bei Suljek. Helsing'ors, 1889.

—— Das Suljekalphabet. Finska Vetensk. S. Förh., XXXI, pp. 136-63.

—— Entzifferungsversuch einiger Inschriften auf einer Felswand im Kreise Minusinsk. Öpfers Finska Vetensk. S. Förh., XXXI, pp. 1-8.

—— Fünf Suljekinschriften, nach ihrem Text festgestellt. Helsingfors, 1891, p. 35.

Tovostine, I. P. Catalogue of Chud antiquities. Remains of the metal ages. Minusinsk, 1913. — Товостинъ, И. П. Каталогъ чутскихъ древностей. Памятники металлическихъ эпохъ.

Toynbee, A. J. Islam in Russia since the Revolution. J.Centr. As. S., 1918, vol. V, pp. 73 ff.

Transactions of the Commission for making chemical and technical analyses of ancient bronze. St. P., 1882. — Труды. Комиссіи по производству химико-техническихъ анализовъ древнихъ бронзъ.

Treidler, H. The Scythians. Arch. f. Anthr., N.F., 1915, pp. 41 ff.

Transcaspian Territory, with regard to its archaeology. Caucasus, 1888, Nos. 66 and 69. — Закаспійская Область, въ археологическомъ отношеніи.

Trigoroff, A. V. : see Obrucheff.

Tripolitova, Z. M. Trans-Caspian country in 1865–1885. A bibliographical index, systematically arranged, of books and essays relating to the Trans-Caspian country and neighbouring lands. St. P., 1888. — *Триполитова, З. М.* Закаспійскій край —1865–1885. Систематическій сборникъ библіографическихъ указаній книгъ и статей о Закаспійскомъ краѣ и сопредѣльныхъ странахъ.

Troll. Individual-Aufnahmen central-asiatischer Eingeborener. Z. f. E., 1890, pt. iii.

Tronoff, V. D. Materials for the anthropology and ethnology of the Kirghis. Mem. I. R. G. S., 1890, XVII, pt. ii. — *Троновъ, В. Д.* Матеріалы по антропологіи и этнологіи Киргизъ.

Troshchanski, V. F. The evolution of the 'Black Faith' ot the Yakut. Kazan, 1902. — *Трощанскій, В. Ф.* Эволюція „Черной Вѣры" у Якутовъ.

—— The Yakut in their domestic life. L. A. T., 1908, XVII, No. 3, pt. i, pp. 332–46. — Якуты въ ихъ домашней обстановкѣ.

Trusman, Y. Y. The Chud Script. Revel, 1896. — *Трусманъ, Ю. Ю.* Чудскія письмена. *See* K., D.

Tschepe, A. Histoire du Royaume de Ou, 1122–473 av. J.-C. Sinolog. Var., 1896, XVII, 2, pp. 175 ff.

—— Histoire du Royaume de Tch' Ou, 1122–223 av. J.-C. Sinolog. Var., 1903, 2, pp. 402 ff.

—— Das Eingleiten der westlichen Nomaden. Ostasiat Stud. Berlin Univ., vol. XIX.

Turfan. Report of the organizing committee of the Turfan and Kuchu Expedition. Bull. Russ. Committee, 1904, No. 4, pp. 4–15. — *Турфанъ.* Докладъ Коммиссіи по снаряженію экспедиціи въ Турфанъ и Кучу.

Turkestan. The Turkestan country and its antiquities. 'Pravitielstvennyi Vyestnik', 1872, No. 126. — *Туркестанъ.* Туркестанскій край и его древности.

—— Note on the study of the Turkestan country with regard to its archaeology. Turk. News, 1875, No. 22. — Замѣтка объ изученіи Туркестанскаго края, въ археологическомъ отношеніи.

Turkomania. Discovery of the ruins of ancient towns of Meshed and Mesteryan in Turkomania. Turk. News, 1876, No. 8. — *Туркменія.* Открытіе развалинъ древнихъ городовъ Мешедъ и Местеріянъ въ Туркменіи.

Turkomans. The Turkomans of the Yomud tribe. Military Essays, LXXXIII, 1872. — *Туркмены.* Туркмены Іомудскаго племени.

Turner, T. Hudson. Unpublished notices of the times of Edward I and of his relations with the Moghul Sovereign of Persia. Arch. Journ., VIII. London, 1851.

Turtkul. Ruins of the Turtkul fortress in the district of Tokmak. Trans. of the Fourth Arch. Congress, 1884, I, p. lxiv. — *Туртку́лъ.* Развалины крѣпости Турткуль въ Токмакскомъ уѣздѣ.

T. W. Review of V. Thomsen's 'Inscriptions de l'Orkhon déchiffrées', I (1894). J. R. A. S., 1896, pp. 632–5.

Tychsen, O. G.: *see* Pallas, P. S. Neue nordische Beiträge, V. St. P., 1793.

Ujfalvy-Bourdon, Mme de. De Paris à Samarkande, le Ferghanah, le Kouldja, et la Sibérie Occidentale. Paris, 1880.

Ujfalvy de Mezö-Kövesd, C. E. Expédition Scientifique Française en Russie, en Sibérie et dans le Turkestan. Vol. I, Le Kohistan, le Ferghanah et Kouldja, avec un appendice sur la Kachgharie. Paris, 1878.

—— E. S. F. en R., en S. et dans le T. Vol. II, Le Syr-Daria, le Zérafchane, le pays des Sept-Rivières et la Sibérie Occidentale. Vol. IV, Atlas anthropologique des peuples du Ferghanah. Paris, 1879.

—— E. S. F. en R., en S. et dans le T. Vol. V, Atlas des étoffes etc. de l'Asie centrale. Vol. VI, Atlas archéologique des antiquités finno-ougriennes. Paris, 1880.

Ujfalvy de Mezö-Kövesd,ˊ C. E. E. S. F. en R., en S. et dans le T. Vol. III, Les Bachkirs, les Vêpses et les antiquités finno-ougriennes et altaiques, précédés des résultats anthropologiques d'un voyage en Asie centrale. Paris, 1880.

—— Aus dem Westlichen Himalaya. Leipzig, 1884.

—— Les Aryens au nord et au sud de l'Hindou-Kouch. Paris, 1896.

—— Essai d'une carte ethnographique de l'Asie centrale. Paris.

Vambéry, A. V. Travels and adventures in Central Asia. London, 1864.

—— Sketches of Central Asia. London, 1867.

—— Uigurische Sprachmonumente und das Kudatku Bilik. Innsbruck, 1870.

—— Geschichte Bocharas oder Transoxaniens. Stuttgart, 1872.

—— History of Bokhara. London, 1873.

—— Ursprung der Magyaren. Leipzig, 1882.

—— Das Türkenvolk in seinen ethnologischen und ethnographischen Beziehungen. 1885.

—— Noten zu den alttürkischen Inschriften der Mongolei und Sibiriens. Mém. Soc. Fin-Ougr., 1899, XII, p. 119.

—— Nyugot Kulturája Keleten. Budapest, 1906.

—— An approach between Moslems and Buddhists. The Nineteenth Century, April, 1912.

—— Muhammadanism in Asiatic Turkey. E. R. E., 1915, pp. 885–8.

—— Die primitive Cultur des Turko-Tatarischen Volkes. Leipzig.

—— and **Courteille, P. de :** see Courteille.

Valikhanoff, C. C. Essays of Chokan Chingisovich Valikhanoff. Mem. I. R. G. S., 1904, XXIX. — Валихановъ, Ч. Ч. Сочиненія Чокана Чингисовича Валиханова.

Vasilyeff, N. The Nomads of Turkestan. An attempt at an economic survey. Samarkand, 1890. — *Васильевъ, Н.* Кочевники Туркестана. Опытъ экономическаго овзора.

Vasilyeff, V. N. A short description of the life of the Karagass. Ethn. Rev., 1910, LXXXIV–LXXXV, Nos. 1–2, pp. 46–76. — *Василевъ, В. Н.* Краткій очеркъ быта Карагассовъ.

Vasilyeff, V. P. Die Denkmäler von Koscho-Zaidam. Glossar, Index und die chinesischen Inschriften. In W. W. Radloff's 'Die alttürkischen Inschriften der Mongolei', 2te Lfr., 1894.

—— The Chinese Inscriptions on the Orkhon monuments in Kosho-Tsaidam and Kara-Balgasun. Collection of documents of the Orkhon Expedition, vol. III. St. P., 1897. — *Василь-евъ, В. П.* Китайскія надписи на орхонскихъ памятникахъ въ Кошо-Цайдамѣ и Кара-Балгасунѣ.

Vattier, P. Portrait du Grand Tamerlan avec la suite de son histoire. Trad. de l'arabe d'Ahmed Arabshah. Paris, 1658.

Velyaminoff-Zernoff, V. V. Historical information about the Khanate of Kokand from the time of Muhammad Ali to Khudayar Khan. Trans. E. Sect. I. R. Arch. S., 1856, XVIII, 2. — *Вельяминовъ-Зерновъ, В. В.* Историческія Извѣстія о Коканскомъ ханствѣ отъ Мухаммеда Али до Худаяра-хана.

—— St. Khorkhut's grave along Syr-Daria. Trans. E. Sect. I. R. Arch. S., 1859, IV, pp. 283–4. — О гробницѣ св. Хорхута на Сыръ-Дарьѣ.

—— The emperors and princes of the line of Kasim. St. P., 1860. — Цари и Царевичи Касимовскіе.

—— Untersuchung über die Kasimofschen Zaren und Zarewitche, aus dem Russischen übersetzt von Dr. J. T. Zenker. Berlin, 1867.

Venyukoff, V. A sketch of the Ili and the Chu country. Mem. I. R. G. S., 1861, No. 4, pp. 79–116. — *Венюковъ, В.* Очерки Заилійскаго края и Причуйской страны.

Vereshchagin, V. Concerning the reception by the Academy of Art of fragments from the grave of Timur in Samarkand. St. Petersburg News, 1872, No. 74. — *Верещагинъ, В.* По поводу присылки въ Академію Художествъ обломковъ изъ гробницы Тимуровой въ Самаркандѣ.

—— Jankent. St. Petersburg News, 1886, No. 2. Джанкентъ.

—— Samarkand in 1868. In 'Russkaya Starina', 1888, pt. 9, pp. 617–46. — Самаркандъ въ 1868 году.

Veselkin. The Uriankhi and geographical information about the southern frontier of the Minusinsk country. Bull. I. R. G. S., 1871, VII, pp. 113–18. — *Веселкинъ.* Урянхи и географическія свѣдѣнія о южной границѣ Минусинскаго округа.

Veselowski, N. I. History of Khiva. St. P., 1877. — *Веселовскій, Н. И.* Исторія Хивы.

—— Archeological researches of N. I. Veselowski in the Turkestan country in 1885. Rep. I. Arch. Commission, 1882–8, pp. lxi–lxxx. — Археологическія изслѣдованія его въ 1885 г. въ Туркестанскомъ краѣ.

—— The excavations carried out by N. I. Veselowski in the ruins of Afrosyab near Samarkand. Mem. I. R. Arch. S., 1887, II, pp. xcii–civ. — О раскопкахъ произведенныхъ имъ въ 1885 г. въ городищѣ Афросьябѣ близь Самарканда.

—— A note concerning the kurgans of the Turkestan country. Mem. E. Sect. I. R. Arch. S., 1888, II, pts. iii–iv, pp. 221–6. — Замѣтка о курганахъ Тукестанскаго края.

—— Dagbid, tomb of Mahdumïaazem, near Samarkand. Mem. E. Sect. I. R. G. S., 1889, III, pp. 85–95. — Дагбидъ, гробница Махдумиаазема, близь Самарканда.

—— Tombstone of Timur in Samarkand. Trans. Seventh Arch. Congress, 1891, II, pp. 67–72. — Надгробный памятникѣ Тимура въ Самаркандѣ.

—— The Orkhon discoveries. J. Min. Educ., April 1894, vol. 292. — Орхонскія открытія.

—— **Klements, D. A.,** and **Oldenburg, S.** Note concerning a scheme for an archaeological expedition to the Tarim basin. Mem. E. Sect. I. R. Arch. S., 1900, vol. XIII, pt. i, pp. ix–xviii. —— —— *Клеменцъ, Д. А., и Ольденбургъ, С.* Записка о снаряженіи экспедиціи съ археологическою цѣлью въ бассейнъ Тарима.

—— Particulars of the death of the Usbeg Khan Muhammed Sheibani. His tombstone and mazar. Trans. Eighth Arch. Congress in Moscow, vol. III, pp. 290-9. — Подробности смерти узбецкаго хана Мухаммеда Шейбани. Его надгробіе и мазаръ.

—— Monument of Khodji Ahrar in Samarkand. In 'Vostochnya Zamyetki', pp. 321–36. — Памятникъ Ходжи Ахрара въ Самаркандѣ.

Virski, M. Ancient kurgans from Samarkand territory. Reference book of the Samarkand territory. Samarkand, 1897. — *Вирскій, М.* Древніе курганы въ Самаркандской области.

Visdelou, C. Notice d'un livre chinois nommé Y-king, ou livre canonique des changemens, avec des notes p. 399 de Chouking par Confucius. Paris, 1770. *See* Herbelot.

Vladimirtsoff, B. V. A visit to the Derbets of Kobdo. Bull. I. R. G. S., 1910, XLVI. — *Владимирцовъ, Б. В.* Поѣздка къ Дербетамъ на оз. Кобдо.

Volodin, A. A. The Trukhmen Steppe and the Trukhmen. Collection of the materials for the description of the Caucasus. XXXVIII, pt. i, pp. 1–98. St. P., 1908. — *Володинъ. А. А.* Трухменская степь и Трухмены.

Voronin and **Nifantyeff.** An account of the Kirghis called Diko-Kamiennyie. Mem. I. R. G. S., 1851, p. 104. — *Воронинъ и Нифантьевъ.* Свѣдѣнія о Дико-Каменныхъ Киргизахъ.

Voronyets, N. S. Rock pictures found on the frontier of Turgai and Syr-Daria territories along the river Lack-Pay. Russ. Anthrop. Journ., 1916, Nos. 3 and 4, pp. 57–61. — *Воронецъ, Н. С.* Изображенія на скалахъ, найденныя на границахъ Тургайской и Сыръ-Дарынской областей, на рѣкѣ Лакъ-Пай.

Voytyekhowski. The Kirghis of the Kustanai district of the Turgai territory. Bull. S. Arch. H. E. I. Univ. Kaz., 1910, XXVI. — *Войтеховскій.* Киргизы Кустанайскаго уѣзда Тургайской области.

Vyatkin, V. L. A contribution towards the historical geography of the Tashkent district. Proc. Turk. Circle F. Arch., 1899–1900, V, pp. 156–9. — *Вяткинъ, В. Л.* Къ исторической географіи Ташкентскаго района.

―――― The past of Samarkand and its neighbourhood, according to the memoirs of Sultan Baber Mirza. Reference book of the Samarkand territory, 1896, vol. IV. — Самаркандъ и его окрестности въ прошломъ по описанію Султана Бабура Мирзы.

―――― Materials for the historical geography of the Samarkand vilayet. Reference book of the Samarkand territory, 1902, pt. vii, pp. 1–83. — Матеріялы къ исторической географіи Самаркандскаго виллайета.

Vyerbitski, V. I. The natives of the Altai. Moscow, 1893. — *Вербицкій, В. И.* — Алтайскіе инородцы.

―――― Dictionary of the Altai and Aladansk dialects of the Turkic language. St. P., 1892. — Словарь алтайскаго и аладанскаго нарѣчій тюркскаго языка.

Viernyi district. Ancient monuments preserved in the Viernyi district of the Semirechie territory. Trans. Fourth Arch. Congress, 1884, I, cviii–ix. — *Вѣрненскій уѣздъ.* Древніе памятники, сохранившіеся въ Вѣрненскомъ уѣздѣ, Семирѣченской обл.

Wachsberger, A. Stilkritische Studien zur Wandmalerei Chinesisch-Turkestaṇs. Berlin, 1916.

Wilser, L. Skythen und Perser in Asien. Berlin, 1902.

Winkler, H. Review of J. Marquart's 'Die Chronologie der altürk. Inschriften', 1898. Litt. Centralblatt, XIX, p. 662.

―――― Review of W. Radloff's 'Die alttürkischen Inschriften der Mongolei', Neue Folge, 1897. Litt. Centralblatt, 1898, pp. 159–61.

—— Review of V. Thomsen's 'Déchiffrement des Inscriptions de l'Orkhon et de l'Jénisséi'. Notice préliminaire, 1894. Litt. Centralblatt, 1894, V, p. 153.

Wirth, A. Geschichte Sibiriens und der Mandschurei. Bonn, 1899.

—— Die Turanier Vorderasiens und Europas. Beil. z. Allg. Z., 1904, No. 287. Munich.

Witsen, N. Noord en Oost Tartarije. Amsterdam, 1905. *See* Major, R. H.

Woeikof, A. Le Turkestan russe. Paris, 1914.

Wolff. Geschichte der Mongolen. Breslau, 1872.

Wolff, J. (Rev.). Narrative of a mission to Bokhara in the years 1843–1845. London, 1845.

Wood. A journey to the source of the river Oxus. 2nd ed., London, 1872.

Worsaae, J. A. A. Ruslands og det Skandinaviske Nordens bebyggelse og ældste kulturforhold. Aarbøger for nordisk Oldkyndighed. Copenhagen, 1872.

Wrangell, Baron F. P. Journey to the north coast of Siberia and to the Arctic Sea, 1820–24. St. P., 1841. — *Врангель, баронъ Ф. П.* Путешествіе по сѣвернымъ берегамъ Сибири и по Ледовитому Морю, совершенное въ 1820–24.

Wright, G. F. Asiatic Russia. New York, 1903.

Wulfson, E. S. How the Sarts live. Moscow, 1908. — *Вульфсонъ, Э. С.* Какъ живутъ Сарты.

—— The Kirghis. In 'The Country and People of Russia'. Edited by A. A. Ivanowski. Moscow, 1901. — Киргизы. Въ изд. „Природа и люди Россіи". Подъ ред. А. А. Ивановскаго.

Wylie, A. The Nestorian Monument: an ancient record of Christianity in China, with special reference to the expedition of Frits V. Holm . . . Ed. by Dr. Paul Carus. Containing: Mr. Holm's account of how the replica was procured, the original Chinese text of the inscription, A. Wylie's English translation, and historical notes on the Nestorians. Chicago, 1909.

Wylie, A. Notes on the Western Regions (Wu-Sun, Hiung-Nu, &c.). Trans. from the Tsin-Han-Shu, bk. 96, pt. 2. J. A. I., 1881–2, p. 83.

—— History of the Heung-noo in their relations with China. Trans. from the Tseen-Han-Shoo. J. A. I., 1874, III, pp. 401–52.

Yadrintseff, N. M. Beginning of sedentary life. Inquiry into the history of the culture of the Ural-Altaic people. Literary essays of the 'Eastern Review'. St. P., 1885. — Ядринцевъ, Н. М. Начало осѣдлости. Изслѣдованіе по исторіи культуры урало-алтайскихъ племенъ.

—— Stone graves and stone figures in Mongolia and Siberia. Trans. of the Eighth Archaeological Congress, Moscow, 1890, IV, p. 158. — Каменныя могилы и каменныя бабы въ Монголіи и Сибири.

—— The Siberian Aborigines : their mode of life and present condition. St. P., 1891. — Сибирскіе инородцы, ихъ бытъ и современное положеніе.

—— *see* Radloff, W. W. Collection of documents of the Orkhon Expedition, 1892, I, pp. 27–40 and 51–113.

—— Investigation of the rune-like inscriptions in Siberia and Central Asia. Eastern Review, 1894, p. 91. — Разгадка руноподобныхъ надписей Сибири и Центральной Азіи.

—— Report and diary of a journey to Orkhon and Southern Khangai in 1891. Collection of documents of the Orkhon Expedition, V. St. P., 1901. — Отчетъ и дневникъ о путеше ствіи по Орхону и въ Южный Хангай въ 1891 году.

—— Preliminary report of a journey for archaeological and ethno-graphical investigation in Northern Mongolia and the Upper Orkhon. Bull. E. Sib. Sect. I. R. G. S., XX, 4, pp. 1–13. — Предварительный отчетъ о поѣздкѣ съ археологическою и этно-графическою цѣлію въ сѣверную Монголію и вершины Орхона.

—— On the Altaians and the Chern Tatars. Bull. I. R. G. S., 1881, XVII, pp. 228–54. — Объ Алтайцахъ и Черневыхъ Татарахъ.

—— Journey along the Upper Orkhon to the ruins of Kara-Korum. Bull. I. R. G. S., XXVI, 4, pp. 257–72. *See* translation of Fraser, M. F. A. — Путешествіе на верховья Орхона, къ развалинамъ Каракорума.

—— and **Deniker, J.** Discoveries in Mongolia : the travels of Yadrintseff and Radloff, 1889–91. Bab. Orient. Rec., 1892–3, pp. 43–8.

—— Report of a journey to the Upper Altai, the Teletsk Lake, and the Upper Katun in 1880. Mem. of the W. Sib. Sect. I. R. G. S., 1882, IV, p. 146. — Отчетъ о поѣздкѣ въ 1880 г. въ горный Алтай, къ Телецкому озеру и въ вершины Катуни.

—— Ancient monuments and inscriptions in Siberia. Literary collection of the 'Eastern Review ', pp. 456–76. St. P., 1885. — Древніе памятники и письма въ Сибири.

—— Résultats de son exploration archéologique dans la Mongolie occidentale au sud du lac Baical et aux sources de l'Orkhon. Bull. Soc. Ant., 1890, III, pp. 255 ff.

—— Archaeological album of M. S. Znamyenski. Eastern Review, 1884, XXV. — Археологическій альбомъ М. С. Знаменскаго.

—— An ancient town of the Usuni on the shore of Lake Issyk-Kul. Eastern Review, 1885, III. — Древній усуньскій городъ на берегу оз. Иссыкъ-Куля.

—— Archaeological researches and discoveries of Dr. Poyarkoff near Tokmak. Mem. I. A. S., 1886, LII, pp. 152–64. — Археологическія изысканія и открытія д-ра Пояркова близь Токмака.

—— The ancient capital of the Siberian empire. Archaeological discoveries of M. S. Znamyenski. Eastern Review, 1884, XXII. — Древняя столица Сибирскаго царства. Археологическія находки М. С. Знаменскаго.

Yakovleff, E. K. Ethnographical survey of the native population of the valley of Southern Yenisei. Description of the Minusinsk Museum, IV. Minusinsk, 1900. — Этнографическій обзоръ инородческаго населенія долины Южнаго Енисея. Описаніе Минусинскаго Музея, IV.

Yariloff, A. A.   The past and the present of the Siberian natives. Pt. ii : the natives of Myelyetsk.   Pt. iii : the Kyzyl and their farms.   Yuryeff, 1899. — *Ярилов, А. А.*   Былое и настоящее Сибирскихъ Инородцевъ.   Ч. ii : Мелецкіе Инородцы.   Ч. iii : Кызыльцы и ихъ хозяйство.

—— In defence of learning and of those condemned to death. [Reply to the book by Kuznietsova and Kulakoff ' The Natives of Minusinsk and Achinsk '.] Yurieff, 1900. — Въ Защиту Науки и приговоренныхъ къ смерти.

Yastreboff, M.   The Shamans of the Kirghis.   Moskvityanin, 1851, pt. ii. — *Ястребов, М.*   Киргизскіе Шаманы.

Yaworski, I. L.   An anthropological sketch of the Turkomans. Trans. of the Anthropological Society of the Imp. Military Medical Academy, 1897, II, pp. 145–206.   St. P. — *Яворскій, И. Л.*   Антропологическій очеркъ Туркменъ.

Yefimenko, P.   Legal symbols.   J. Min. Educ., 1874, X, XI, XII. — *Ефименко, П.*   Юридическіе Знаки.

Yermolayeff, A.   Description of the collection of the Krasnoyarsk Museum.   Archaeological Section I.   Krasnoyarsk, 1914. — *Ермолаев, А.*   Описаніе коллекціи Красноярскаго Музея.

Yevreinoff, A.   The Middle or Bukeyeff Orda of the Kirghis-Kaizak.   Sovremyennik, 1851, Nos. 9, 10. — *Евреинов, А.* Внутренняя или Букеевская Киргизъ-Кайсацкая Орда.

Younghusband, Col. F. C.   The heart of a Continent : a narrative of travels in Manchuria, across the Gobi Desert, through the Himalayas, the Pamirs, and Hunza, 1884–94.   London, 1896.

Yudin, P. A.   The Kirghis : an ethnographical sketch.   Oren. Gov. News, 1890, Nos. 50–2; 1891, Nos. 1–5. — *Юдин, П. А.* Киргизы.   Этнографическій очеркъ.

Yuferoff, V. de.   Étude sur les inscriptions sibériennes.   Mém. de la Soc. des Étud. Jap.-Chin., July 1884, No. 3.   Paris.

Yule, Col. Sir Henry.   Travels of Marco Polo.   Edited by Cordier.   London, 1903.

—— Cathay and the Way Thither, being a collection of mediaeval notices of China, translated and edited by H. Y.   Hakl. Soc. Pub., 1866, XXXVI, XXXVII.

Yurenski.   The cave and the ancient inscriptions on the banks of the river Mangut (in South-East Siberia).   Mem. Sib. Sect. I. R. G. S., 1856, II, pp. 80–7. — *Юренскій.*   Пещера и древнія письмена на берегахъ рѣчки Мангута (въ Юго-Вост. Сибири).

Yushkoff, I.   Siberian Tatars.   Tobolsk, 1861. — *Юшковъ, И.* Сибирскіе Татары.

Zagrajski, A. G.   The Kara-Kirghis.   Turk. News, 1874, Nos. 41–5. — *Загряжскій, А. Г.*   Кара-Киргизы.

—— The condition of the Nomad population of the valleys of Chu and Syr-Daria.   Turk. News, 1874, Nos. 25–32. — Быть кочевого населенія долинъ Чу и Сыръ-Дарьи.

Zaleski, B.   Descriptions, récits et contes.   La vie des steppes Kirghises.   Paris, 1865.

Zeland, N.   The Kirghis.   Mem. W. Sib. Sect. I. R. G. S., 1885, VII, pt. ii, pp. 1–78. — *Зеландъ, Н.*   Киргизы.

—— From the shore of Issyk-Kul.   Turk. News, 1891, XXXV, XXXVI. — Съ береговъ Иссыкъ-Куля.

—— Kashgaria and the Passes of Tian-Shan.   Mem. W. Sib. Sect. I. R. G. S., IX, pp. 22–5.   Omsk, 1888. — Кашгарія и перевалы Тянь-Шаня.

Zelenin, D. K.   Bibliographical index of the Russian ethnographical literature, 1700–1910.   Mem. I. R. G. S., 1913, XL, p. 1. — *Зеленинъ, Д. К.*   Библіографическій указатель Русской этнографической литературы, 1700–1900.

—— Among the Orenburg Kaizak.   Ethn. Rev., 1905, LXVII, No. 4. — У оренбургскихъ Казаковъ.

Zenker, J. T.: *see* Velyaminoff-Zernoff, V. V.

—— Bibliotheca Orientalis.   Leipzig, 1848–61.

—— *see* Kasem Beg.

Zichy, E., Comte de. Voyages au Caucase et en Asie centrale. La Migration de la Race Hongroise (Zichy, E., Comte de). La Description des Collections (Jankó, J., et Pósta, B. de). Budapest, 1897.

Znamyenski, M. S. Iskier. Tobolsk, 1891. — *Знаменскій, М. С.* Искеръ.

—— Cape Chuvash. An archaeological and historical sketch. Tobolsk, 1891. — Чувашкій мысъ. Изъ археолого-историческихъ набросковъ.

INDEX

242 THE TURKS OF CENTRAL ASIA